Inside England

Jonathan Northcroft
and Rob Draper

Inside England

Behind the Scenes of the Three Lions' World Cup Dream

bl!nk

First published in the UK in 2026 by Blink Publishing
An imprint of Bonnier Books UK
5th Floor, HYLO, 105 Bunhill Row,
London, EC1Y 8LZ

A CIP catalogue record for this book is available from the British Library.

Hardback ISBN: 978-1-785122-51-4
Paperback ISBN: 978-1-785122-54-5

Also available as an ebook and an audiobook

1 3 5 7 9 10 8 6 4 2

Design and Typeset by Envy Design Ltd
Printed and bound in Great Britain by CPI (UK) Ltd, Croydon CR0 4YY

FSC www.fsc.org MIX Paper | Supporting responsible forestry FSC® C013604

At Bonnier Books UK, we are committed to publishing sustainably. Find out more here:
bonnierbooks.co.uk/sustainability

The authorised representative in the EEA is
Bonnier Books UK (Ireland) Limited.
Registered office address:
Block B, The Crescent Building
Northwood, Santry
Dublin 9, D09 C6X8
Ireland
compliance@bonnierbooks.ie

www.bonnierbooks.co.uk

To Dad, dear Englishman.

Jonathan Northcroft

To Helen, Oliver and Anna. For everything.

To Chris. For Euro 96.

Rob Draper

CONTENTS

PREFACE

The pristine Wembley turf kept catching Thomas Tuchel's eye as he spoke. Open the window and you would have been able to smell the freshly cut grass, feel the warm glow of the March sunshine and breathe in the unmistakable air of springtime optimism. 'I feel quite excited,' said the German entrusted with England's seemingly unobtainable dream. 'I felt it today coming to Wembley. It gives you a kind of edge.'

His eyes darted around the press conference, his smile natural and broad. Tuchel looked completely in his element. This was not the tense, confrontational character fighting battles at the end of his tenures at Borussia Dortmund, Chelsea or Bayern Munich. This was Tuchel at his best: authoritative, and willing to take risks. He had just explained why he was announcing a squad of 35, allowing eleven of his favourite players to have the week off before joining up, replacing those who would be sent home on the Saturday night after the first game against Uruguay. What seemed bizarre initially, soon had journalists nodding at his wisdom once the Tuchel charm and explanation had got to work. True to character, Tuchel had torn up convention and come up with an elegant solution to the problem of holding an international camp while everyone's minds remain focused on club matters.

The Germans probably have a word for that sense of premature enthusiasm and enlightenment the English feel in the run-up to a World Cup. It was almost palpable that spring morning in 2026. When Sir Alf Ramsey and Bobby Moore left for Mexico in 1970, there was a feeling that a great England side would bring the cup home once more, despite the fact that Brazil also seemed to have a decent team. That year, and every year since, they have been disappointed, returning home with stories of what might have been, often citing refereeing conspiracies. Usually, springtime optimism turns into mid-summer madness, with one unfortunate member invariably scapegoated for the entire debacle. From Peter Bonetti to David Beckham, the story has remained largely unchanged over the years.

And yet (there's always an 'and yet',) England set off to the Americas once again amidst genuine expectation. This is the story of how, ten years ago, Gareth Southgate began the rebuild of a nation's football culture and turned one of the worst-performing teams, per capita and per head of population, into a serious contender, albeit one that still invariably fell short. It is a tale of how he became caught up in culture war amidst one of the most turbulent periods of modern British history, hailed as a visionary leader yet, at the end of it all, was showered with stale lager.

One man was required to complete the job and it seemed unlikely that an intense Bavarian with a modest playing career in the lower leagues of German football would be that figure. And yet, here was Thomas Tuchel at Wembley, exuding confidence as he contemplated assembling a group of players that most fair-minded people would agree are some of the world's finest footballers. Only history stands against them. Were it not for the burden of repeated failures, it would be clear that England are among the three or four nations most likely to contest a World Cup final in New Jersey this summer. Their past remains inescapable, but their future remains tantalising.

On that bright March day, the German with the broad smile and assured strut seemed genuinely intent on putting a second star on the England shirt, a proposition that will now be tested in the heat of World Cup competition. An American dream awaits.

Rob Draper, Jonathan Northcroft, March 2026

CHAPTER 1

MUD MARINES

The Royal Marines talk about a dislocation of expectation. How does a person cope when conditions change, crisis comes and their comfort zone is suddenly very, very far away?

And so, shattered, unslept, muddy and wet, Harry Kane, Raheem Sterling, John Stones and Kyle Walker came to a clearing in a forest in Devon, with a little shore and a bowtie-shaped stretch of freezing, brown water. Five metres long. Filthy. With a nickname that nodded to its inhumanity – 'the sheep dip'.

In the sheep dip you cannot see, you cannot breathe and you only have one option, which is to plunge down and through, arms forward, fully submerged, body straight and no twisting round or turning back.

The sheep dip is about fear, about mind-over-matter composure, and most of all about trust. You plunge in, pushed by one instructor with another waiting at the end of the tunnel of water ready to pull you out and you surrender other instincts, trusting that these guys are going to do their jobs and keep you safe. Trusting the process.

Not everyone wanted to carry on. Jermain Defoe was petrified and among several players fighting fears about water. The group were warned of the Marine who once got it wrong in the sheep dip and got stuck, almost dying before the tunnel was drained and he was freed.

So, Gareth Southgate took the lead: 'I'll go first. I'll go in.' And down he plunged, into the cold, brackish tank, emerging eyes closed and mouth clamped shut as a commando grabbed him by the shoulders and hauled him from the depths.

'That was part of the theme of the camp. How will we be adaptable in moments of difficulty?' Southgate recalled. 'There were some team objectives around pushing themselves beyond where they thought they could go and knowing you don't want to let any of your teammates down.

'We wanted to expose the guys to an elite environment with one of the elite forces in the world. We wanted them to see that there's another world out there.'

This was Woodbury Common, the Royal Marines' Commando Training Centre (CTCRM), near Lympstone on the River Exe, on Saturday 3 June 2017. On the same weekend 21 years previously, Southgate was part of an England squad who were flying home in disgrace from a tour in the Far East after the alcohol-fuelled debauchery of Paul Gascoigne in the infamous 'dentist's chair' in a Hong Kong nightclub. That was the team's 'preparation' for Euro 96 but now as England manager, Southgate had a different strategy for team-bonding in mind.

It was his second camp after getting the job on a permanent basis and he was thinking not just about upcoming games versus Scotland and France but already ahead to the World Cup in Russia the following summer, and he wanted something that would make a statement to his players about togetherness, about being different, about pushing to extremes. Woodbury was his choice: the wet, the cold, the fear, the 'trust the man next to you'. The mud.

The trip was suggested by Dave Reddin, the FA's head of team strategy and performance. In 2013, a year into his role as technical director, Dan Ashworth was looking for someone to drive changes in culture, planning and preparation he wanted in all England teams, men's and women's, from seniors to the youngest junior levels. He identified Reddin, a former non-League footballer with Boston United who was a key part (as national fitness coach) of Sir Clive Woodward's staff when England won the Rugby Union World Cup in 2003, and helped mastermind Team GB's success at the 2012 London Olympics as their head of performance services.

Spiky and exacting, Reddin's willingness to challenge is not for everyone – 'sometimes I was peacemaker, sometimes I was fire-starter,' he wrote in a personal essay reflecting on his stint with the FA. But his success is not in doubt and when he met Ashworth he said, 'I need to be convinced you're really up for it, as we're going to have to smash this up and really go for it.' Ashworth, whose understated-ness belies his boldness, replied, 'Absolutely.'

On arriving at St George's Park, Reddin was deeply unimpressed. 'At that point the England team had no clear purpose, vision, targets or principles to work with,' he wrote – and in an interview with Henry Winter in *The Times* reflected on values surrounding the senior men's side that he found particularly anachronistic. 'If there was something in the walls, it was probably rooted in white working-class culture, it was a bit Stuart Pearce, "Come on," blood on the shirt, but that's not England today. They are still valuable qualities, the fight, the hard work, but that's not representative of this generation. Our country looks really different,' Reddin said.

For his first two years, Reddin largely worked with England women and the coach of their senior women's team, Mark Sampson, helping to deliver Sampson's side a surprise third place at the 2015 World Cup in Canada. Only when Southgate succeeded Sam Allardyce – initially on an interim basis – in September 2016 was Reddin brought inside the tent, when it came to the senior men's team. '[Southgate] recognised my strengths in strategy and planning complemented his strengths in other areas.'

Reddin's view is that coaching is a 'creative art' where the power of the story is key, and once Southgate had been given the England job permanently the pair started planning for a shift in narrative, the markers for which would be laid down immediately. At Southgate's first camp as permanent boss, in March 2017, players were brought into a meeting room at St George's Park and presented with a detailed strategy for the way forward, under the banner of 'Time for Change'.

Among the materials they were shown was an image where England's objective was spelled out in a headline: 'TO BE RECOGNISED AS THE NUMBER 1 TEAM IN THE WORLD' and below this were four pie charts, red for playing principles, blue for physical/medical, yellow for identity/culture, green for media/family/fans ('Dave *loves* colour coding' chuckled an FA department head and veteran of many a Reddin meeting). The players were shown a film, a Southgate-Reddin co-production designed to 'emotionalise' the message.

But to cement things, Reddin suggested that something even more visceral was needed – an 'iconic event' that would leave staff and players absolutely certain that a 'new England' was nigh. He had witnessed Woodward take England's rugby players to Woodbury Common to train with the Marines in the run-up to their 1999 World Cup and although England only reached the quarter-finals of that tournament, a 'Marines culture' took hold in the group, leading to their 2003 triumph. How about taking Harry Kane and co. to Woodbury? Reddin suggested. It was bold. Southgate loved it. And Ashworth was delighted – understanding that this was exactly the kind of cultural cage rattling that he had recruited Reddin for. 'It was a brilliant concept for getting people together,' Ashworth said.

The trip was kept secret from all but a very small number of FA staff. 'That was a brave decision by Gareth,' Reddin told Winter. 'Someone turns an ankle, Gareth would get it completely in the neck. We couldn't tell the clubs! If we did, the answer would have been "absolutely no".'

So on Friday 2 June, players reported to St George's Park and were told to go straight to the Billy Wright dressing room. They were midway through a presentation when the door burst open and through it stepped a Royal Marine. Leave everything, even phones, he said, and don't tell anyone where you are going. The players were allowed one text – to loved ones, to say they would not be contactable for the next 48 hours.

They boarded a bus with Southgate, his number two Steve Holland and goalkeeping coach, Martyn Margetson, plus some of the key personnel who support the England team like Greg Demetriou and Andy Walker, from the communications department, and head of security Tony Conniford. Staff would be going too; a theme of the next two days would be 'all in this together'. The road journey from Staffordshire to Lympstone would take five hours and Reddin had wanted the 'dislocation of expectation' for the shocked travelling party to be even more dramatic. 'The original plan was three Lynx helicopters to take them away but the bastards cancelled the helicopters!' he said.

Arriving at CTCRM, Southgate, players and staff changed in a gym into camouflage 'rig' and were issued with 21-litre backpacks, sleeping mats and boots. They boarded three trucks and went out to Woodbury Common. They smeared mud on their faces and struck out into woodland, setting up camp among the trees. No luxuries – the 'toilet' was in a hole in the forest – and not even proper tents:

the players were put in pairs and had to set up their own shelter under fly sheets.

Ryan Bertrand and Jake Livermore's set-up was 'the most Gucci tent you've ever seen. Absolutely incredible. They had hangers up on the trees, it was Pukka. Others were an absolute shambles, stuff all over the place, disaster!' Reddin recalled. For sustenance, everyone was issued a cannister of standard Marines rations including a freeze-dried dinner, eaten straight from the bag.

Walker and Kieran Trippier were so excited they cooked everything in their backpacks. Stones could not stop yakking, Alex Oxlade-Chamberlain was in his element and Sterling loved it – despite his initial expectations. 'To be fair, at first I was not interested,' he said. 'I was thinking: "Oh my goodness gracious me!" In my head, I was: "No! No!" Because you just know what the Marines is! I've gone off to play football, come to camp with no knowledge [of what lay ahead] and all of a sudden you're getting this Marines thing and you're thinking: "Nah, not today."

'At first I wasn't with it. Then you got there, and they made everything fun but at the same time there was structure, teamwork and you kind of understood throughout the sessions what we were doing there. It was like: "That's my brother next to me, that's my other brother next to me". We'd have good fun and laugh when we were camping or chilling on the down time. And then when it was go time, there was teamwork and you understood how that associates with football.

'In football, a lot of players have our own agendas and that was a massive part in making everyone understand we're all in this together first and foremost – and the reason is to come away with a World Cup or a major trophy. I felt like it was another stepping stone that brought everyone closer together.'

At 2 a.m. players were still running around excitedly, not wanting to go to bed. With no phones, no music players, no screens, people just *talked*.

'In the dark of the night I had the privilege to be there within the woods and listen to those players talk about their experiences so far, laughing and joking as well as reminiscing. One member of the support team spoke with me and said he had never ever seen an England squad behave like this,' said Ben Williams, one of the Marines instructors. Ashworth said, 'There was the [argument of] "the players won't like it, they're not going to do without their phones, they're not going to sleep under a bivvy," but they loved it. There's the dangerous assumption about footballers that really annoys me: they're multimillionaires, they won't like sleeping in a sleeping bag and they won't like traipsing through the woods and won't like not having their phone. Nonsense. They're young people. It was like being a kid again. Going camping! Of course some did like it more than others but in the main it was really well received.'

Despite their late night, players were up at 5.30 the next morning, packing up camp, downing their breakfast of porridge and getting ready to go. The Marines were impressed. As they were with how their supposedly pampered guests navigated the day that lay ahead of them. It was challenging, beginning with a three-mile yomp carrying equipment on their backs. There were exercises in a field, and an assault course where players lugged heavy items over a tower, working as units, and other obstacles so tough that non-athletes were almost sick.

Players fired soft pellet weapons and performed a mock attack on a fake house, which they had to imagine was held by the enemy, using paintball guns, during which Jamie Vardy took a well-aimed shot to the middle of the forehead. Then there was a traditional commando 'thrashing' – akin to circuit training, where the exercises are based on activities a Marine might perform on manoeuvres. Players waded waist-deep through a river, holding a rope and submerging themselves every time a whistle blew and staying submerged until another whistle – if anyone raised even a small part of their head above water too early, the whole group had to do it again. They clambered up mud heaps and crawled on their bellies right down the middle of a stream. In the middle of it all came the dreaded sheep dip – and at the end, just when they thought it was all over, came another yomp back to the training centre. Perhaps the most strenuous challenge involved splitting into partners then performing a 'drop and drag' along a mud trail, where one person fell to the ground pretending to be unconscious and the other had to haul their dead weight along the course. Trippier – who had never been called up by England before – turned to Demetriou. 'Is it always like this?' he asked.

'We had to follow the Marines. Whenever they shouted "Down", we had to crawl in the mud, through stone, and a tunnel full of sheep dip. [By the end] we were all soaking wet with sand and mud everywhere, and thought we were going to get in a car and go back to camp. Until they told us we were walking back, which was another hour on the road,' remembered Kane.

'That was probably the hardest part; it was mentally tough. Then we got back to the place where we were staying and I was looking forward to a nice, hot shower . . . and it was just a bit of water dripping out. That was brutal.'

Said Sterling, 'There was one you had to dive down a tunnel, swim underneath it, with your friends and team-mates waiting the other side. Basically, you had weight on your back, the same as the Marines would carry. They put those backpacks on your back and we had to do races, go over loads of different obstacles, things they would do.

'It was physical output and pushed you mentally and physically. There were bits that were fun, and bits that when you finished, and while you were doing it, you could understand what it was for.

'But everyone bought into it. At first you definitely had people saying: "Oh my God! What's this?" But at the end of it, when you get back to the Marine camp and you broke down the day, and everyone was going through it, it was such a lovely thing – because they [the Marines] have such a strong bond.

'What we don't realise, as footballers, is that we're playing a match and then we go home. Where with The Marines, you can see that if one is not helping the other, how that could go – it's life and death for them. But at the same time, in our field you have to be all on the same point too because these small details [are the difference why] you win something or don't win something. You could see how it correlated.'

The afters were just as important. The Marines staged a regimental dinner in the officers' mess. The Champions League final was on – Juventus v Real Madrid at the Millennium Stadium, Cardiff – and Southgate and Reddin were worried that players would duck out of the meal early to watch it. 'Look, we're guests here, we'll record the game,' they told the squad. The dinner started with a speech about leadership from the regimental commander followed by a brilliant speech from Southgate in reply. Round the table sat player, Marine, player, Marine, everyone mixing together. There were games of Spoof and a story from the sergeant major about the history of the dagger represented in the Marines' badge.

The Marines presented each of their visitors with a little medal. The evening ended with drinks and everyone watching the Champions League final together. 'A real memorable moment was looking around the bar, and I didn't see a cluster of players. I saw an England player with three Marines around him, having a ball, a real laugh,'

Reddin said. 'Some of the backgrounds of these kids are not entirely different and there's a connection in hard work, sacrifice and huge respect for each other.'

* * *

Pulling Southgate out of the sheep dip water was Major Scotty Mills, a soldier with an arresting story. The highest-ranking commissioned black officer in Royal Marines history, he was an accidental recruit – a South London lad who one day was walking down his local high street after going roller-skating and bolted into the nearest shop when it started raining, not wanting to get his skates wet. It was a recruiting office. 'You look fit; can you do a few pull-ups?' said the sergeant on duty. With his skates still over his shoulder, Mills did them effortlessly and three decades later, after fighting in four war zones including Iraq, found himself head of sport at CTCRM and in charge of hosting England. He and Southgate – in profound ways – hit it off.

Mills, like the other Marines, was immediately impressed by how Southgate took the lead at Woodbury Common – making sure he did every challenge first and thereby adhering to an old commando wisdom that a superior should never ask his troops to do something he would not do himself. He was also struck by Southgate's communication skills – something Southgate also appreciated in Mills. 'He has a fantastic way of talking to you that really hits into the inner drive and his values and the pride in wearing the beret and achieving the beret and how that aligned to the pride of wearing the Three Lions,' Southgate said.

They maintained a bond beyond England's visit to Lympstone with Southgate inviting Mills to his side's match at Hampden the following weekend, and Mills sending a message on behalf of the Marines to the Three Lions at the Russia World Cup. Southgate drew inspiration from his new friend. 'We've had some very personal conversations about experiences and I don't mind saying we've hugged a couple of times and shed a tear and there aren't many people I'd open up to in that way for sure,' Southgate told the Forces Network after presenting Mills with an award in December 2018.

'But they were very deep moments that helped with my leadership, helped with my understanding of what elite leadership in his world would be and the respect I have for him is enormous. We've developed a very strong bond through those discussions.'

Mills was not the first Marine to shape the England manager. His maternal grandfather, Arthur Toll, served in the Corps during the Second World War. The other grandchildren called him 'Grumpy' but little Gareth found him a delight, and when the Southgates visited Arthur in Watford, he played football with his grandad. Arthur never lost his military ways. Waking at 5.30 or 6 a.m., he would go down to the kitchen to shave and polish his shoes. Hearing him about, Gareth would often get up and join him, watching his daily rituals with fascination.

Arthur was a man of impeccable manners and always Brylcreemed his hair, then put on a shirt, tie and waistcoat for his morning walk into the centre of Watford. The waistcoat Southgate would wear in Russia was a nod to Grumpy and when 'God Save the King' plays, Southgate always sings it loudly – struck by the thought that from somewhere up above, Grandad might be looking down.

Standards and setting examples come from his parents too. Barbara, his mum, was a teacher, his dad Clive a manager at IBM, who coached Southgate's boys' team, never lost his temper and felt it important, win or lose, to compete with dignity. Perhaps this heritage was why Southgate captained all three of the clubs he played for beginning with Crystal Palace, where he took the armband aged just

23. Those leadership qualities were what first made an impression on Adrian Bevington, who would later prove instrumental – twice – in bringing Southgate to the FA.

'Gareth, for me, was always someone who potentially had a future with the FA – and I don't mean from the end of his career but when he was still a player. My first thinking was when Peter Taylor took the Italy game,' Bevington said. He referred to a November 2000 friendly in Turin when Taylor, then England Under-21 manager, took the senior team in a caretaker capacity. Taylor named a symbolically young squad where every outfield player was under 30 except for one. 'He cut some big players out but still picked Gareth. The captaincy went to David Beckham but he wanted Gareth there as a big brother to the other players. Peter's thinking showed me something,' said Bevington.

Bevington, a senior FA press officer then, would rise via a long stint as media chief to become managing director of Club England from 2010 to 2014. He bonded with Southgate during the 2002 World Cup in Japan, by which time Southgate played for Middlesbrough – the club Bevington supports – and was an unused member of Sven-Göran Eriksson's squad, wryly observing the circus around Beckham and a little different to the other players: accessible and ready to shoot the breeze with everyone, including ordinary staff.

* * *

In January 2011, the FA published its 'Young Players Development Review' and announced it would soon appoint a head of elite development, who would be tasked with working across younger age groups and helping director of football Sir Trevor Brooking drive through changes advocated by the review – notably the move to small-sided games in children's football. Brooking had been talking to Bevington about who he wanted and kept circling back to Southgate, who had been working as an ITV pundit having since been dismissed as Middlesbrough manager in late 2009. Backed by Bevington, Alex Horne and Danielle Every, the FA head of coach education, Brooking recruited his man.

'Gareth came in and was excellent to deal with. Warm, unegotistical, flexible with the staff. Not many people with Gareth's career would be happy going up to Crewe town hall on a Thursday night to sell small-sided football, but it showed his willingness and openness. You can join an organisation and just be the lead coach or you can immerse yourself and all the legwork he did undoubtedly made him better when he got the big job because he had a different level of understanding,' said Bevington.

With Brooking wary that clubs were planning a land grab over youth development, it was Southgate who the FA chose to represent them in meetings with the Premier League during the formulation of EPPP (Elite Player Performance Plan). And when, in November 2011, the FA booked a fact-finding trip to Brazil to inspect facilities and hotels with the 2014 World Cup in mind, who did it ask to step in and take the technical lead? Good old Gareth again.

'I know it sounds glamorous, you're going to Brazil for a week, but you're not sitting round the pool. You're on and off budget flights, you're staying in a whole range of hotels, you're in traffic jams in different vehicles. It's not glamour and I've seen other managers on similar trips have the hump after 24 hours,' said Bevington.

'But Gareth did not behave in the manner of somebody with 50 caps for England. He was one of the team, up at the crack of dawn and getting fully stuck in. Everyone was blown away by him and I remember Oliver Ballhatchet, from the Foreign Office, who accompanied us, saying, "He is amazing." I thought I knew Gareth beforehand, but after that trip I thought, "This guy is for us. Culturally, this guy is where I want us to be."'

In February 2012, Capello quit. Harry Redknapp was favourite with the media and bookmakers to succeed him, but the FA chose Roy Hodgson – and their four-person recruitment panel of Bevington, Horne, Brooking and chairman David Bernstein was supported by an unofficial fifth member – Southgate – who did not sit in on interviews and every meeting but was regularly invited to offer his counsel.

However, having been unenthusiastic when the idea of becoming Hodgson's assistant was mooted – the role went to Gary Neville – Southgate stunned the FA by quitting his post and pulling out of the running to fill a new post of technical director, shortly after Euro 2012. The manner of his leaving was abrupt and out of character – an email sent to Brooking overnight. It seemed he still nursed ambitions to get back into management, but after a wilderness year, during which he failed to find another club role, he was interested when the England Under-21 job came up.

Stuart Pearce – Southgate's friend, who once took him to a Sex Pistols concert when they were players – had been sacked following a disappointing performance at the European Under-21 Championship. Ashworth was now at the FA as assistant technical director and, with Brooking and Bevington, interviewed ten candidates at a hotel in Crewe. The choice came down to a final two 'and the opinion in the room was such that we could have appointed either. But from my own point of view it had to be Gareth and I was resolute on that,' said Bevington. 'I thought he'd be fantastic for the organisation and buy into the long-term vision.'

Bevington swayed the vote and over the next 18 months watched Southgate bring change. One of his first big decisions, made in late 2013, was to take England back into the Toulon tournament.

They would return from the 2014 edition, having been absent since 2005. 'It was a really important moment, a tournament where [ultimately, in 2016] we learned how to win. It came about because the guys at Pitch International had acquired the broadcast rights and I knew them well, as did [ex-FA commercial director] Stuart Turner. We took Gareth to lunch with them and they explained the attractions: Brazil are there, you can play players of different ages, it's by invitation, it's about development.

'Gareth got it – and the following summer I went out to Toulon for a few days. His camp was an absolute breath of fresh air. Openness, cooperation. He'd invited John McDermott from Tottenham, Neil Dewsnip from Everton, Bryan Klug from Ipswich and they were totally included in the set-up. The acorns were there for what he was going to do in his senior England camps – and we'd talked about all that stuff at the breakfast table at the World Cup in 2002. You know, Gareth has a really dry sense of humour. He used to laugh about previous England camps, how ridiculously claustrophobic it got, like how Sol Campbell couldn't go out for an ice cream in 2001,' said Bevington.

One of Bevington's last matches as Club England MD was in Vinkovci, a small Croatian town near the Serbian border, where Southgate's youngsters completed a 4-2 aggregate victory in a play-off to reach the 2015 European Under-21 Championship. England's performance was dominant, with Kane assisting one of their goals.

Bevington: 'The night before I flew in on Ryanair. We were invited for a meal with Gareth and his staff. That was another big moment, another which pointed to the future of what he was going to do. We went in, sat at the coaches' table, all the staff were there and everyone was at ease with each other, the players were popping round, and we sat talking for hours. Some of those staff – like Steve Holland – stayed with Gareth all the way through.

'At the game I had Davor Šuker sitting on one side of me and Niko Kovač on the other. They were saying, "We've never seen England play like this before." It was the early days of FATV and Gareth allowed cameras into the dressing room. Celebrations. Capture the moment.

'At the airport I was sitting with Gareth and Steve, waiting for the flight. Over walks Jack Butland and Ben Gibson. "Hi boss, are you all right? The lads are just wondering, would it be possible to have a beer to celebrate?" Gareth is, "Yeah, of course, no problem, get yourselves a beer." What I loved was how the conversation was so relaxed but at the same time respectful.

'But then the lads went away and brought a drink back for every member of staff before they had one themselves. They weren't asked to do it, they just did it. And I'm sitting there thinking, "This feels good. This doesn't feel like the England I've known." I don't want to belittle anyone that went before but this was different, it just felt right.'

* * *

Kirchweidach, deepest Bavaria, on old village inn. A Sunday morning where, as church bells peel across sleepy cobbled streets, the locals are having beer for breakfast and singing, to the tune of 'Jingle Bells', 'Harry Kane, Harry Kane, Harry all the way. Oh what fun it is to see, Harry scores again!'

Kane himself steps out of a 4x4 to the parping of an oompah band and enters the function hall to a heavy metal anthem about his conquest of the Bundesliga. Over the next three hours, with unfailing geniality, he will take part in all manner of Germanic high jinks – beer-mug curling, a soup-salting ceremony, an ancient pub game that involves hammering a nail into a tree trunk. There are long speeches, an even longer Q&A, and endless selfies to pose for and autographs to sign. He is presented with a wooden object that looks alarmingly like the Arsenal cannon but is reassured that it is actually a play on the Bundesliga Golden Shoe trophy (also a cannon) and that it is a *schnupftabakmaschine*.

A what? Yeah, you know, a *schnupftabakmaschine* – a 'snuff cannon' designed to shoot tobacco up your nose. The guy handing it over turned out to be the former president around here and he made this machine, for Harry, lovingly, using a base of old mousetraps. While the flesh-and-bone Kane performs his increasingly surreal duties, a cardboard cut-out Kane stands near him on the stage. It is him as James Bond. The England captain: sent to Germany on His Majesty's Service and licensed to score.

This was January 2024, and a visit Kane made to a Bayern Munich fan club at the peak of his extraordinary first season in the Bundesliga, following his £100 million transfer from Tottenham to Bayern in the summer of 2023. The biggest takeaway from accompanying him on his trip was the underestimated power of his straightforward personality. The charisma of common decency he projects. He is not exactly like Southgate but there are similar dynamics in the sense that these are leaders not in the 'Stuart Pearce blood on the shirt' mode that Dave Reddin identified as the England of the past, but ones reliant on calmer, softer, more understated skills.

Kane may not have grabbed the mic and shouted any battle cries to the supporters during his three hours in Kirchweidach, preferring to smile and play along as they brought the noise, but he had them swooning like he was the Walthamstow Elvis. 'One of the best days of my life,' gushed Martin Pichler, vice president of the fan club and by day a sober marketing executive. The supporters agreed Kane was much better than a previous star visitor they had – a surly, uninterested former Germany captain.

In 2024, Kane was a grown man of 30, father of four, and role model of some depth, campaigning to support a hospice in Woodford and promoting Children's Mental Health Week as part of his foundation. Through video interviews and digital animations he has produced materials to encourage resilience in young people – a cause he feels especially passionate about. In reality, he is a far cry from the caricature reinforced by the award-winning *Dear England* play. The play portrays Kane as the archetypal affable but simple-minded footballer who, upon being given the England armband, says in a team address, 'My goals . . . apart from scoring goals . . .'

If that is all there was to Kane, it is unlikely he would have lasted seven years in the role and be set, at Euro 2024, to surpass Southgate's hero, Bryan Robson, on the list of most games as England skipper. Only the uber-greats, Bobby Moore and Billy Wright, will lie beyond him.

He has scored well over twice as many goals while Three Lions captain as any other player in history, leading with a style described thus by Jordan Pickford: 'Harry is very open. When he is around new lads who come into the squad for the first time, he talks to them and fulfils that leadership role. On the training pitch, with the standards he sets for himself, [he] shows what it takes to be captain of England.'

Not one iota of this has surprised Scotty Mills and colleagues. At the end of England's two days with the Corps, Southgate quietly asked the Marines who, among his players, had the best leadership qualities. The answer was emphatic. Kane – and by a distance.

A moment, captured in a video of the FA group being put through their paces on Woodbury Common, summed Kane up. The challenge was to scramble up a mud heap. An FA staffer slipped in a puddle and landed face-first against the bank. Behind him, Kane and

Tom Heaton dissolved in hysterics but then Kane – while still laughing and being one of the lads – quickly ran to assist, putting his head under the guy's shoulder and helping him to the top. 'I think Gareth did use that trip to see who stood out in terms of leadership and maybe it was the way I got on with the Marines and handled certain situations,' Kane said.

'I know he asked some of the Marines who they thought were natural leaders, who were approachable, and who other players were leaning towards to talk to, and that might have helped me becoming captain.'

Southgate had tried out different captains since dropping Wayne Rooney and upon returning from Woodbury Common told Kane that the following weekend – when England played Scotland in a World Cup qualifier at Hampden – he would get a shot at the role. It seemed a bold choice. Kane was 23, and had struggled in his biggest international challenge – Euro 2016 – and had not scored for England in more than a year. Hampden would be hostile and Kane had never led a team before.

Three minutes into stoppage time, in Glasgow, Southgate's pick felt no more convincing. England trailed after two late Leigh Griffiths' free kicks and the Tartan Army were baying for the final whistle when Kane ghosted on to a Raheem Sterling cross and, leaping, struck a sweet volley past Craig Gordon to rescue England a draw. 'Captain Kane' was born in that instant; a pattern was set. England, at points of need, so often able to rely on their skipper. 'Sometimes you look back at moments that, at the time, you don't realise how big and important they were,' Kane said. 'As a captain, losing to Scotland in your first game is not something you want on your résumé at all. Who knows, things might have been a little different if I hadn't scored that goal.'

Some players shrink with responsibility. Kane is one of the ones whose shoulders broaden and whose chest swells. Being chosen to lead his country (he was confirmed as permanent captain just before the 2018 World Cup) 'gave me loads of confidence. It was the start of a journey, where none of us knew how it was going to go.

'It gave me the belief that the manager trusted me as a number nine. I was pretty young and pretty new into my career, so just to have that faith from Gareth was important – and I think I've been able to repay him.'

Woodbury, believes Kane, brought everyone involved in Southgate's England 'closer together' and in an article with Forces Network he suggested the trip had a direct bearing on England's late comeback and his 93rd-minute equaliser at Hampden. 'When we went away with the Marines, we spoke about being ready for any situation. If things do take a turn for the worse, then always be ready for that. Never drop your heads.'

* * *

When Robert Sullivan thinks of Kane at the 2018 World Cup, what he thinks of first are not the goals that made the striker England's first winner of the tournament's Golden Boot since Gary Lineker, but of what Kane did at the ForRestMix Club hotel every day at breakfast time.

In England's modest base at Repino, openness was prized. Everybody sat with everybody, players, coaches and staff alike. And each morning the skipper helped set the tone. 'I'll never forget Harry,' said Sullivan. 'He would come into breakfast every morning and go round shaking hands with everybody, or giving them a fist bump. I always thought, "Huge respect: you take your leadership seriously."'

Sullivan considered Woodbury Common to be a pivotal experience

– and not just for those on the football side of the England operation but those from the support departments such as his own one. 'It was the starting pistol on "this is going to be different when we go to Russia." The great thing was that everyone was equal. You had Tony Conniford, Greg and Andy (who worked under Sullivan as England's head of communications and senior communications manager) and all those guys were treated exactly the same as the players and that was an important message. As for the players, who liked having people like those three in their midst, it was important that those barriers came down too.

'Though when everyone was away I do remember sitting back at the office, knowing they were all in the middle of Woodbury with no phones, thinking, "If anything happens, it's all on me."'

After Hampden, however, England went to Paris for a friendly against a stellar French team featuring Kylian Mbappé, N'Golo Kanté, Paul Pogba and Ousmane Dembélé. The 3-2 scoreline in France's favour flattered England who were outplayed, even throughout the final 43 minutes when their hosts were down to ten men. Southgate appeared shaken, as if suddenly realising the gulf that still lay between his side and those of the very best nations. France were sixth in the world while England were 13th, equal with Wales and just ahead of Peru. 'It's the only time I looked at him in a post-match press conference and thought, "You're not sure here" – though I might have misread him,' Sullivan said.

In the dressing room, without raising his voice, Southgate gave his players a frank assessment of where they were still falling short on the pitch. 'Our game without the ball has got to improve,' he said, and admitted in his press conference there was 'no magic wand' that could fix shortcomings, merely work. He was not the only one having doubts. Newspapers sneered about the Woodbury Common trip in the wake of the near-disaster against Scotland, a headline in *The Independent* declaring, 'Jumping in puddles counts for zero when Hampden roars.' In the article beneath it, Kevin Garside described Southgate's attempt at team bonding as 'naff'.

Martin Samuel, in the *Daily Mail*, wrote, 'Southgate has won many admirers since taking charge of England, but the idea that his squad could build grand mental strength over two days playing soldiers with the Royal Marines is intellectually shallow.' The negative coverage intensified following defeat in Paris. The *Mirror*'s Andy Dunn felt Southgate 'looked like a man who had just realised he will, in a year's time, have to go into battle with a balloon on a stick.' Writing for the *Liverpool Echo*, the former England striker Robbie Fowler questioned whether England would even qualify for the World Cup.

The bright spot in Paris had been Kane, who scored twice, and he followed up with four goals in England's final four qualifiers to render Fowler's take a little foolish. Southgate's team topped their group, unbeaten with 26 points, before finishing the year with creditable draws at Wembley against Germany and Brazil. A little momentum was building and England took it into the New Year, beating the Netherlands away and drawing with Italy in March 2018.

By then exactly a year had passed since 'Time for Change' was presented to the players. A year on from that, England were in a completely different place – World Cup wonders and heading towards another summer tournament, the Nations League finals. The change in Southgate's status was reflected by him being given a tribute night by the Football Writers' Association. At the event, at The Savoy hotel in January 2019, among those making speeches was Ben Williams – the Marines instructor who had lain awake on Woodbury Common, listening to England players sharing their stories and noting the camaraderie.

Before talking about England's visit to CTCRM, Williams told a story. It was about being on duty in Afghanistan in 2011 when his patrol were tasked with going into a Taliban village to push out the enemy to allow local people to return to their homes. As the Marines entered the village, the Taliban detonated a large IED (improvised explosive device). He and his fellow commandos lay on the ground in shock and pain, mindful of a principle of their training – when an IED goes off, Marines should get down, stay still, let the dust settle and observe what had occurred, the reason being that the Taliban tended to place bombs in clusters and movement could set off further devices or be the trigger for an ambush.

Following the training was very hard, he said, when you saw comrades lying hurt. The impulse was to rush and help them. And on that day, sticking to principles proved impossible. Looking down the track behind him, after the first IED exploded, Williams could see six Marines stretched out, injured, including his commander, Paul Vice, who looked in serious trouble. 'Vicey', as he was known to his men, was a leader who time and again had saved them in fatal situations.

'Within seconds of realising he was severely injured, Marines ignored their own safety and sprinted to his aid,' said Williams. 'The Taliban was circling and there was little doubt there were many more devices beneath us. But Marines didn't hesitate in risking their own lives to help the one person who repeatedly saved theirs.

'Vicey was our leader. A man whom we unflinchingly trusted . . . His inspiring leadership created followers who would do anything for him out of devotion, not necessity.'

Williams left the military to become a motivational speaker and author of a book, *Commando Mindset*. Having told the story of 'Vicey', he turned to the top table, where the England manager sat. 'When people ask me to describe leadership I reply it is simply to create followership within the group you lead,' Williams said.

'I've met many inspiring leaders over my career but few have I met away from our elite organisation who reflect such incredible leadership qualities as Gareth Southgate.'

It was a moment 'Grumpy' might have thought his grandson had done rather well.

CHAPTER 2

OLD ENGLAND

The ball came sweetly off Frank Lampard's boot and arced through the thin, dry air of the Highveld, over Manuel Neuer, and off the underside of the bar, dropping to earth two clear feet over the line.

Goal.

Wasn't it?

Seeing there was no signal from Jorge Larrionda, the Uruguayan referee, Neuer grabbed the ball and got it away before the official changed his mind. A third German goal would follow, then a fourth, both finished by Thomas Müller on lightning counter-attacks as their young starlets streaked past half-fit, half-paced, ageing English stars.

The second round of the 2010 World Cup, Free State Stadium, Bloemfontein: Germany 4 England 1. Back home in London, Robert Sullivan's BlackBerry pinged with notifications as the last two German goals went in. Sullivan, the Football Association's head of corporate affairs, had a series of meetings for planning England's homecoming celebration in his diary – and each time Müller rammed the ball into David James's net, those appointments were being cancelled. No, Sullivan would not need to see Greater London Authority to discuss policing costs for a trophy parade. No, scrap the procurement meeting about open-top bus hire.

Lampard's goal was a seminal moment for football. It prompted Sepp Blatter, the FIFA president, who had watched from the VIP section of Free State Stadium, to drop his opposition to the use of video technology in refereeing, setting the game on the path that led to the introduction of VAR. But for England, Bloemfontein was business as usual. They had simply done what they always did at tournaments: flickered briefly, before finding another novel way to crash out. To embarrass themselves.

* * *

World Cup 2010, hosted by South Africa, was supposed to be different. The FA secured a manager from the highest end of the market, Fabio Capello, a stern Italian who commanded one of the top wages in world football – £6.5 million per year. The chief executive who hired him, Brian Barwick, trumpeted Capello as 'a winner with a capital W', but what he delivered was a masterclass in how not to do things, a car crash nonpareil of hubristic England failure.

He did leave behind some happy memories, like a brilliant 5-1 victory over Croatia at Wembley, and the fun journalists had getting him, with his mangled English, to say the name of Phil Jagielka. But 2010 would prove his legacy. Wrong priorities, a fractured squad, a terrible camp, a broken culture, wars with the press, disconnect with supporters, poor preparation, bad communication, fear on the pitch, a team too much centred on stars. All the hallmarks of England tournament farce – bar a penalty shoot-out – were bound up in his South Africa campaign.

The nonsense started the day before the announcement of England's provisional squad. The press were invited to a briefing from Capello at the London Stock Exchange. What, an FA initiative? A new contract? No, the England manager was launching his own commercial enterprise called the 'Capello Index', a system for rating players' performances backed by an online gaming company which would be debuted in South Africa. 'That was fucking weird,' said a senior FA figure, looking back on Capello's regime, 'and the nearer it got to the World Cup, the weirder it all looked.'

Under pressure from the FA, Capello agreed to shelve the 'Capello Index' until after the tournament but then embarked on a skittish and unnecessarily fraught build-up to the finals. It involved two separate, grinding, week-long boot camps at altitude in the Austrian Alps. 'In the middle of nowhere, you sat in your bedroom every night, with an oxygen mask strapped to your face. It was so boring,' Rooney would later recall in a *Sunday Times* column. 'We went home, the standby lads left the squad, and then we went . . . back to Austria. That was torture. We thought, "Jesus Christ!"'

On the eve of England's final warm-up game, a fluky victory after a dismal performance against Japan, Capello pulled a stunt by telling a press conference he felt suddenly insecure about whether his employers wanted him following the resignation of Lord Triesman as FA chairman. Panicked by the rush of 'England crisis' headlines, the FA hurriedly improved Capello's contract by removing a break clause that allowed for his dismissal if the World Cup did not go well.

Speaking of panic, spooked by listless displays in training and the warm-up matches, Capello lost confidence in the group he had selected and began ringing round older players whose England careers were in the past to see if they would accept call-ups. These included Paul Scholes, who retired from internationals six years previously, Phil Neville, who had just undergone a knee operation, and Owen Hargreaves who, because of injuries, had played one minute of competitive football in the previous 20 months.

Capello even considered Sol Campbell and Gary Neville – who

last played for England in 2007 – before finding two elder pros to come in and try and add the mentality he suddenly felt his squad lacked: Jamie Carragher, three years retired from internationals, and Ledley King, who had imagined his England days were long done because of a knee condition.

Capello seemed to have two staffs. The entourage of trusted Italians the FA agreed to employ as part of his package and those who predated his reign, like head England physio Gary Lewin whose advice he ignored when he sent his squad out for a full-bore training session on their first day in South Africa. Rio Ferdinand, England's captain, got injured in a collision with Emile Heskey and was out of the finals. While England's training pitches and media centre at the Royal Bafokeng Sports Complex were top end, no-expense-spared stuff, the location was alienating – an outpost near the forlornly off-season resort of Sun City, far from the vibe and bustle of the host country's main cities. Players stayed in a purpose-built hotel at their training complex and felt there was little to do.

The FA installed an entertainment room with TVs, darts and computer games, but staff took a liking to it and began hanging out there, leading the players to stay away. When the fact that players felt they needed more amusement began filtering into the press, Capello seemed nonplussed. Used to the Italian practice of *ritiro* – monastic training camps where football and only football is serviced – Capello said with a haughty shrug, 'They can play ping-pong,' when reporters suggested his squad were bored.

Asked by press to describe how players spent their days, Rooney was memorably pithy. 'Breakfast, train, lunch, bed, dinner, bed,' he said. In an attempt to while away time, a group of players even watched Rooney's wedding video. All of it, from start to finish.

Communication was minimal. Capello's habit was to keep his

squad guessing and name his starting eleven via a big reveal where, 90 minutes before kick-off, he turned a flip chart over with the names on it. This led to the absurd scenario of players texting journalists to try and find out if they were playing. The goalkeepers did not know which one of them would start England's opening game against the US until the flip chart flipped over and Rob Green, who got the nod, made a humiliating error when he fumbled a Clint Dempsey shot into his net. The game ended 1-1.

'There was never a nudge from the manager (about who was number one) and it played on your mind. You didn't know how to prepare,' Green would reflect. Capello only spoke to him once more at the finals: 12 hours before England's next match, to say he was dropped. This was typical. When Capello talked to players it was usually brief and to point out something they were doing wrong, like a mistake in training captured on video, or that the daily weigh-in he insisted on had revealed they were a little 'fat'.

There were no takers when the FA tried to arrange a tour for players of Robben Island and the few players who accepted the invitation of a safari were photographed looking miserable on their bus. England were criticised for being bad tourists and contrasts were drawn with Germany, whose squad of young, bright-eyed, empathetic players praised South Africa's culture and won the affections of locals near their base in Pretoria.

England did not even bond with their own fans. At their final group game, a laboured 1-0 win over Slovenia in Port Elizabeth, an English banner in the crowd said '6,000 miles for what?' The previous game, a stalemate with Algeria in Cape Town, ranked among the most turgid 90 minutes the Three Lions had ever played. England supporters started jeering after ten minutes and Rooney caused a major incident when, walking off at full-time, he shouted into a television camera, 'Nice to see your own fans booing you, you football "supporters".'

Press relations remained a headache, despite the best efforts of a team working under Adrian Bevington, newly promoted from director of communications to managing director of Club England, the FA department overseeing the Three Lions. After Green's howler against the US, around 30 photographers camped outside the keeper's parents' house. Press conferences and interviews were often adversarial and players were so fearful of negative coverage that some were afraid to even smile during training, in case the cameras caught them doing so and they were pilloried on the back pages for not taking national duty seriously enough.

Capello made clumsy, belated attempts to lighten the mood, suddenly lifting his ban on butter and ketchup at the players' meal table and allowing the squad to have a drink in the aftermath of the Cape Town debacle. As they sat around sipping beers, Joe Cole, with a certain gallows humour, piped up, 'F***ing hell, I'm not going to be playing anyway,' and got the waiter over and ordered a sex on the beach cocktail.

If the non-granting of Lampard's 'goal' in Bloemfontein was unlucky – England were in the ascendancy and would have made it 2-2 – there was no real argument that the better team overall went through. Germany seemed everything England were not. They had the third youngest squad at the tournament whereas Capello's was the second oldest and were a collection of expressive kids from diverse backgrounds: Müller, Mesut Özil, Sami Khedira, Neuer, Jérôme Boateng, Lukas Podolski, Toni Kroos.

They spoke of a rebirth of their country's football and how it was benefiting from a pipeline of new talent, with four of their starting eleven plucked from an Under-21 side that destroyed England in the final of the previous summer's European Championship. Behind their rebirth lay a push on development by their intelligent FA. They had a home-grown, empathetic manager in Joachim Löw.

Bevington had been with the FA for 13 years and had experienced tournament disappointment before, but World Cup 2010 was a gut punch. When would these England disasters ever end? From the team bus, as it pulled away from Free State Stadium, he texted a friend, the former manager of the club he worked for and supported, Middlesbrough. 'That's me done, mate,' he wrote. The message came back: 'Don't do anything hasty that you might regret.'

The sender – Gareth Southgate – still believed. In England. In the power of change. In there being a better way. Working at the tournament as a pundit for ITV, he said sadly, 'We look frightened,' as he offered his analysis during the nil-nil with Algeria. He was privy, after the game, to a visit made by Prince William and Prince Harry to the England dressing room.

The young royals entered braced for a downbeat scene, but were still shocked by the desolation they found. Players were sitting with their heads bowed, utterly mute, and Green – still nursing the pain of being dropped – was alone and detached from the rest. William and Harry took it upon themselves to go from player to player, attempting to raise spirits, but with limited success, and swiftly left. In Southgate's mind one problem was crystal clear: the vacuum of true leadership in the group. Two young royals had shown more of it in five minutes than an overblown England manager and squad demonstrated during the entire finals.

* * *

The pratfall of World Cup 2010 nagged at the psyche of English football like the buzzing of vuvuzelas. Surely it was time to end its addiction to star power. Big players, big manager, no team, no connection – for a decade this had been the story, starting with the Keegan era, continuing with that of Sven-Göran Eriksson and peaking with Capello.

The former international Chris Waddle spoke for a disillusioned nation when he accused the FA of 'sitting on their backsides doing nothing, tournament after tournament' and it did not raise optimism when the FA decided on a root and branch review. There had been these before – in fact, at the time of the South Africa finals, the governing body was still trying to implement recommendations from a review instigated after England's failure to reach Euro 2008. It had involved announcing a four-year 'strategic vision' to reach the 2010 World Cup or Euro 2012 semi-finals, a cap on foreign players in the Premier League and the opening of a national football centre by 2010.

There seemed little prospect of a foreign player cap. The political skill and heft of the Premier League's chief executive, Richard Scudamore, was fabled and Scudamore was at the peak of his powers, defending the interests of his clubs ruthlessly. A 330-acre site near Burton upon Trent in Staffordshire had been purchased for the national football centre but it was almost nine years since Howard Wilkinson announced plans to build one and the site remained a half-finished mess of mud and bulldozers. Even the very best football writers in the country were sceptical – like *The Independent*'s Sam Wallace, who termed it a 'grandiose scheme that belongs to a bygone era when the organisation thought it had money to burn'.

Such cynicism was understandable. The FA's other recent big infrastructure project, the 2003–07 rebuilding of Wembley, had spiralled over budget and left the association in significant debt – but that had not curbed the self-importance behind making

£130,000-per-week Capello the most expensive international manager in history. Having mothballed the idea for several years and only resurrected it after the 2008 review, the FA could not even agree internally on a national football centre's value.

The 2009 collapse of its broadcasting partner, Setanta, had increased the FA's financial crisis and FA executives and councillors worried about a national football centre's costs. There was a 'will they, won't they' meeting where some pushed for the project to be shelved for good and it only turned after Jack Pearce, representing Bognor Regis Town, stood up and said, 'This is insane. We've got to do this. England needs this.'

St George's Park – saved by the man from Bognor.

The 2010 'root and branch' would prove different to other reviews. It would actually look at the roots and branches, instead of focusing on headline-friendly big-ticket ideas that the newspapers would like. The prowess of Germany (who reached the semi-finals) and Spain (who won it) at World Cup 2010 made England's need to change something fundamental with its football obvious. Both countries had pipelines gushing talent, making them successful through the age groups, and distinctive ways of playing which seemed aligned with the best club teams in the Champions League.

One systemic issue was glaring. In 2008, UEFA published data showing England had just 2,769 UEFA (Pro, A or B) licensed coaches whereas Germany had 34,970 and Spain 23,995. Both went to the World Cup under home-grown managers who had spent years coming through their own systems. And on the pitch, English football's inability to cultivate its own future was becoming glaring.

Seven of England's starting eleven in Bloemfontein had been 29 or older. There one green shoot. In May 2010, England won the European Under-17 Championship for the first time with a team containing some promising talents in the shape of Ross Barkley, Connor Wickham and Josh McEachran.

Left in charge of the FA following the 2010 World Cup was Alex Horne, a bespectacled accountant promoted from chief operating officer to chief executive a month before the tournament when the previous CEO, Ian Watmore, quit after falling out with the Premier League. Horne could not dispense with Capello without enormous cost, following the change in Capello's contract, but he could look beyond the senior team.

And that is what he did.

To get to those roots and understand the branches, Horne decided to convene a giant brainstorming session. It was held late in 2010 at the Staverton Park Hotel, a golf resort in Daventry, and featured a wide-ranging cast: FA suits, coach educators, development experts, prominent English managers like Sam Allardyce and Tony Mowbray, the FA head of grassroots coaching, Les Howie, and representatives from the PFA (Professional Footballers' Association) and the LMA (League Managers Association).

There were breakout groups, ideas pinned on walls and collective exercises, such as one on age banding where delegates were asked to line up according to their birthdays. Everything was up for grabs, from the schools' football calendar to fast-tracking elite English players into management. It was stimulating. Almost fun.

It led to a document: 'The Young Players Development Review'. This was a 25-point plan to revamp the English game from ground level up and included a graphic that Horne had initially sketched out himself. Shaped like a rocket sitting on its side, it had a wide base and narrow tip and sections shaded in different colours. The base represented the entry point of children into the organised game, how they learned, the matches they played, the coaching they would receive.

The next portion denoted club academies. What training would the best kids receive? What rules and standards would be applied? What styles, tactics and skills would be taught? What standards of education and sports science would apply?

Then came a part relating to coach education. How could the FA better fulfil one of its core missions – to develop the country's coaches? Could building that national centre give the FA a 'university of coaching' through which to bond coaches and promulgate ideas like the Italians had at Coverciano and the Germans at the Hennes-Weisweiler-Akademie in Cologne?

The final sections, as the rocket narrowed to a tip, involved international football, from the development teams to the senior Three Lions. Could pathways be improved? What would these look like?

Sullivan was one of Horne's closest lieutenants and an understated but razor-sharp operator with a background in communications and politics. Eight years later, he sat in a hotel mezzanine in Russia with a coffee and a smile on his face.

Behind him were journalists playing darts and pool with England footballers, somewhere in a side room was an England manager giving a wry and intelligent briefing to an audience lapping up his words. Outside the sun shone, and to look forward to was the remainder of an exhilarating campaign that would sweep England to within a few minutes of a World Cup final. This was Repino, Russia, 2018.

Sullivan had been thinking about something. He grabbed a napkin, borrowed a pen and began to sketch out a shape. A rocket, lying on its side. 'There's only one person who could have done this,' he said. 'Only one is fundamental to all of these parts working.'

He explained how this individual had been key to implementing more enlightened thinking at grassroots level, spending six months slogging round town halls and working men's clubs from Hartlepool to Truro to Crewe to sell new ideas on small-sided football to difficult audiences of blazers and bruisers from local FAs.

Then, he had been the FA's representative, sitting round the table with the Premier League to help thrash out its brilliant 2012 blueprint for academies, EPPP. After that, he was both coach of England Under-21s and head of coaching for all development teams. Now he had the top job and was drawing on his own, almost unique experience as an England player – 57 caps and four tournaments, the first as a young starter, the last as a senior pro who didn't play a single minute. Oh, and a certain penalty shoot-out.

Who was he, England's rocket man, this engineer-turned-pilot who at last had everything pointing to the sky?

Sullivan put down the pen and glanced over his shoulder towards the press conference room.

'Gareth,' he smiled.

* * *

In the rooftop bar of the elegant Côte d'Azur hotel it was the small hours of the morning, but the midsummer breeze off the Mediterranean retained the warmth of the day, before it had all gone so horribly wrong. Beers had been bought, grown men chatted; the setting was idyllic, the mood funereal as Gary Neville turned to Wayne Rooney, Roy Hodgson and Ray Lewington.

There were no answers that night. This wasn't really an inquest. No one, least of all the four men at the table, could quite believe what they had just witnessed. Rooney, the England team captain, was sitting alongside coach Neville, England manager Hodgson and his assistant Lewington. All three coaches had just resigned after the latest biggest humiliation in English football since the last one. They knew there was no coming back from this in terms of their England careers. It now seems significant that Rooney, still just 30, was already sitting at the coaches' table, an unconscious uncoupling in progress.

The beachside hotel in Nice city centre was by the swish Promenade des Anglais and in the streets below, in those early hours, the quartet could hear the wild celebrations of the Iceland fans. This was the night of their nadir, Iceland 2 England 1. England hadn't just lost the Euro 2016 knockout game, they had fallen apart. To compound the humiliation, Iceland's second goal came from a long throw routine ironically borrowed directly from the English football playbook. For the three coaches and for Rooney, their captain, who had been onside with the changes they had been making and who himself wanted to push for more, there was the bitter, visceral disappointment that encouraging performances earlier that season had ended like this.

Rooney was undeniably England's generational talent, but in this monstrous carbuncle of a game, he was spraying misplaced passes and shooting wildly from distance as the national team laboured to overcome a nation with a population of 370,000 people, the size of Coventry. Yet only the previous month, Rooney had excelled in midfield to drag his club Manchester United over the line to win the FA Cup. Blame could not be pinned on any one player anyway. It had been like witnessing a collective psychological breakdown.

'I never thought we'd lose the game,' said Rooney. '[But] with about 30 minutes to go we panicked, we changed how we played and gambled too early. We lost our shape, lost our discipline and once we did that against a very stubborn, hard-to-beat team, there was no way we were ever going to get back in it. It's almost that we were actually trying too hard. Everything you've worked on goes out of the window.'

Defeats like these go beyond the senior team. The entire reputation of English football was a laughing stock: richest league in the world, poorest national team was the line delivered around Europe with relish. Dan Ashworth, the FA's director of development, had been at the game. 'It was horrible,' he said. 'We went 1-0 up. "Great, this will settle the nerves . . ."' One of his most profound memories though is going home to St George's Park, England's training centre, to speak to FA coach educators and sensing the heavy gloom in the room. 'I said: "Listen, it's been a really disappointing tournament, everyone is going to come home feeling down." The coaches are delivering courses and it's "What do you know? You can't even beat Iceland?" You lose credibility, whether that's in coach education or the men's senior national team.'

In the hotel lobby, as the enormous kitbags were packed for loading, Harry Kane, then just 22, sought out one of the FA suits, chief executive Martin Glenn. 'Look,' said Kane. 'We all want to do better. It's not just about being unlucky, we have to figure out how to make this better.'

Glenn recalls pressing Hodgson to meet the press, an expected duty for a departing England manager. 'Roy wasn't going to come. I said, "Roy, you're still on the payroll. You might have resigned, but you kind of owe us this one." It was really uncomfortable because everyone was pissed off.'

Kane himself had come into the tournament with high hopes, the Premier League's top goalscorer and new golden boy of the team. He had ousted Rooney from the centre-forward role, forcing the captain to play in midfield. But Rooney himself saw a player falling into familiar failings, as he himself had when he too had once been a talismanic young leader at the 2006 World Cup, where he was infamously sent off after stamping on Cristiano Ronaldo. 'I could see in 2016 that Harry's head was in the same place as mine in 2006, when you have all this expectation and start thinking: "Am I going to score here?" You start making the wrong decisions. Harry was shooting from 40 yards instead of laying it out wide. You could see exactly what was happening in his head.'

England had a psychiatrist under Hodgson, Steve Peters, at the time a cause célèbre, as author of the best-selling *The Chimp Paradox* book and hailed as the mental support brains behind Team Sky's cycling dominance, led by Bradley Wiggins and Chris Froome in the days before we knew about the mystery testosterone deliveries to Team Sky.

'Steve Peters has been great; he's equally disappointed,' said Glenn in Chantilly. 'Fair play to Roy Hodgson for getting him in. It was a bit of a leap in the dark. I think there is an open question as to whether we could use people like Steve or his organisation or others in a more structured way, in a way that we do with the development teams. I would want the next England manager to be open to that idea. Given the scrutiny our players are under, it's about mental resilience.'

It's fair to say that not everyone was wild about Peters. Hodgson and Steven Gerrard liked him. Some fellow professionals saw the model Hodgson had set up as flawed, mindset being seen as something you addressed if you had a problem rather than being an integral part of the structure. You could argue that Peters was trying to change that. But his introduction as a peripheral figure had perpetuated the idea that the psychiatrist was there for the weak players having a meltdown rather than something normal for everyone.

Rooney was supportive of the idea of extra help and has used psychologists, but he never gelled with Peters. 'Roy brought Steve in before the 2014 World Cup,' said Rooney. 'He had worked with Steven [Gerrard] and Liverpool. Stevie pushed for him to come in and I was fine with him being there. The issue I had was that it was going up on the team noticeboard that "you have to speak to Steve Peters at this time". I questioned it and said, if the players want to speak to him individually, let them, and if Steve Peters wants to speak to us as a team, that's fine. But as an individual, the player has to be the one to go to him. You can't make people do it; you could mess their heads up.'

Peters hadn't helped England in 2016 nor in 2014, where they were eliminated after just two games, their worst ever World Cup. 'He had a bad couple of weeks in 2014,' said Rooney. 'Liverpool lost the title. Ronnie O'Sullivan lost in the [world snooker] final and then we went out in the group stages. I don't think he had the best of months.' That reflection is straight out of a dressing-room culture honed by relentless piss-taking. Getting inside the heads of these young men might well prove the impossible job.

Yet two weeks before the Iceland debacle, at a rather lesser football tournament, the Toulon Under-21 championships, an England team was actually winning something. To qualify this triumph, Toulon is a relatively minor competition which has a degree of extra gravitas only in that South American, African and Asian teams often play there, so it becomes like a (very) mini World Cup. The games were only 80 minutes long, a rule only changed in 2019. It's not the pinnacle of elite international football but Paul Gascoigne, Cristiano Ronaldo and Zinedine Zidane have won the award for the tournament's best player over the years while Alan Shearer and Thierry Henry have headed the goalscoring lists. For identifying future talent, it was once a must-attend event and scouts loved it.

And it was important to Gareth Southgate. He might have felt he was in the last chance saloon in 2016. Certainly another failure would have been hard to recover professionally. Perhaps that explained his uncharacteristic behaviour the night England did win. It was well past midnight, the hotel pool was definitely closed for the evening and some still doubted Southgate, the staid Captain Sensible, would really go through with the dare. But a sense of mischief had overwhelmed him. He took a running jump and then plunged himself fully clothed into the hotel swimming pool.

It couldn't really classify as a dive, though he was head first and he did emerge at the deep end, soaked and ecstatic in his team kit. The cheers of teenagers and young men filled the midnight air at Toulon in France. This was more akin to the behaviour of rowdy English holidaymakers, yet here was Southgate, 45, leading the way. A chant went up. 'Jonny! Jonny!' yelled the young men. Nathan Redmond, then a callow 20-year-old youth at Norwich, led the pack hunting its next prey, Jonny Zneimer, the team's psychologist. Zneimer was dragged from the bar area of the Ibis Styles into the pool area and also threw himself into the pool in an ugly dive and embraced a soaked Southgate.

All around them the England Under-21 team were cheering. Jordan Pickford was there, Jack Grealish too, as were Ruben Loftus-Cheek and James Ward-Prowse. 'It was brilliant, out of nowhere,' said Duncan Watmore, the Millwall forward, part of that winning Under-21 team. 'I think that was part of the idea that if we won, he'd be jumping in the pool in full tracksuit.'

A year before, Southgate had taken an England Under-21 side into the European Championships in the Czech Republic. Southgate had forged a team which included Kane, Loftus-Cheek, John Stones, Jesse Lingard and Jack Butland. Raheem Sterling and Eric Dier had also played in qualifying. They had been given a big build-up and seemed destined for great things. The tournament was an opportunity for Southgate to restore his stock in the game after being sacked by Middlesbrough. Yet they lost to Portugal, beat Sweden and then froze in big moments under pressure in the final game against Italy, just as England teams always do. They lost 3-1 and finished bottom of their group. Those at the tournament say Southgate seemed bewildered and lost. He was certainly far from being the England senior team manager. At 44, he was in classic mid-life crisis territory.

At the same age, Pep Guardiola had won two Champions League trophies and five league titles, three in Spain and two in Germany. Southgate was no bright young star in the firmament of the coaching game. Maybe he ticked management boxes at the FA. With his playing reputation, he might expect to pick up a desperate Championship club or manage in League One or Two for a while. In the aftermath of this tournament failure in the Czech Republic, Southgate and FA technical director Dan Ashworth agreed to meet journalists in the Clarion NH Hotel in Olomouc. Those present recall how ashen-faced and shocked the pair were by the setback. They hadn't seen it coming and, as such, didn't really have any answers.

'It was all a bit of a blur,' recalled Ashworth. 'When you're knocked out of a tournament it's horrendous. I can't remember exactly what my feelings were but I wouldn't be human if I wasn't thinking: "Have we got this right?" Ultimately I didn't feel that tournament was a defining moment. As long as we had a trajectory of proving there was some improvement across the age groups in various tournaments, there was always going to be a bad one and a good one.'

That said, Ashworth did not see what was coming in terms of Southgate's trajectory. 'I would be lying to you if I had said after that tournament that he was going to go on and be one of the most singularly successful England senior managers in history,' he said. 'Gareth is a wonderful human being, really open; he really wanted to learn and improve. He was really humble, has some brilliant attributes and he was still relatively new in his coaching career: he had three and a half years at Middlesbrough and two and a half years with the Under-21s. It wasn't about chucking the baby out with the bathwater. No, it was: "We believe long term he's the right person to be part of the organisation." No one could have foreseen he was going to be the best England manager and go on to the success he has, but he was a good human being with the right attitude, a good coach and a good leader in our organisation.'

The FA also sought outside help for him. Adrian Moorhouse was an Olympic gold medallist in 1988 over 100 metres breaststroke. After retiring from swimming, he set up a management and performance consultancy, Lane4. Teaming up with psychologists, Moorhouse brought science to the classic motivational pep talk and built a business, training executives at corporations around the world. Zneimer was one of those performance psychologists and when the FA called Moorhouse for help in 2014, he was seconded as the FA's head of people and team development.

Zneimer has degrees in sports science and sports psychology and an MA in human behaviour psychology, though that doesn't always stand you in good stead in football. When Southgate was an up-and-coming young player at Crystal Palace, he overhead his manager Steve Coppell talking to the club's star strikers Ian Wright and Mark Bright about him. 'He's got eight O-levels, you know,' said Coppell, who himself has a degree from Liverpool University. 'Don't know if I want them to know that,' thought Southgate. Sure enough, Bright shot back: 'Yeah, but can he fucking play?'

After his 2015 debacle in Slovakia, Southgate knew something needed to change. Perhaps it was desperation that made him open to new ideas, but quickly, Zneimer and Southgate became a team. Initially Southgate allowed him to observe a team meeting with the Under-21s before a European qualifier at Brighton against Switzerland.

Seats were lined up in rows and the players trooped in and dutifully took their places, and Southgate spoke to the team and explained his goals and ambitions for the week of training they were about to embark on. Tactical analysts presented video clips on Switzerland and Southgate talked at them, cajoling and exhorting. Players nodded when key points were raised. Polite silence was the order of the day, though he was spared the eye rolls and open contempt some managers experience. It was, say observers, far from dynamic.

'You see,' said Southgate afterwards to Zneimer, 'I'm not getting much back from them.'

'I'm not bloody surprised,' said Zneimer. 'You didn't ask a decent question. You're asking poor leading questions. "Do you think we do this?" "Do you understand what I'm saying?" These aren't open questions that encourage people to speak. And the way you've set it up' – Zneimer pointed to the rows of chairs, one behind the other. 'What does that say?'

Zneimer removed the lines of seats and turned it into a horseshoe, every chair looking in at Southgate. There was a second meeting half an hour later. Southgate stood in the middle of the horseshoe and this time he held a football. When he asked a question, he would chuck the ball at the player to whom he had addressed it. Immediately the mood was lighter, more playful and responses were more open. 'He was starting to think about engaging them in dialogue,' said Zneimer. 'Asking them: "What do you think?" and keeping quiet and letting them answer.'

Having engaged the team at one level, Zneimer's next challenge was to breach Southgate's reserve. At that stage he seemed uncomfortable sharing vulnerabilities. Maybe it was because generally in football that would be madness. Growing up in a suburban, steady home, Southgate had to adapt to the inner-city streetwise culture of the football dressing room when he was training as a schoolboy at Crystal Palace. Only strengths and achievements can be paraded there; failures are buried deep down, never to be examined. They only come up if another teammate senses a vulnerability and uses it to belittle you and so protect their own status in the hierarchy. You learn to keep problems private.

'I remember spending a long time persuading him that opening up about his penalty miss at Euro 96 would be a good thing for the players,' he said. 'He wasn't convinced. He would say that he hated that sort of thing. He wasn't comfortable disclosing.'

Zneimer persisted. He sensed that Southgate's weakness would release something in the players. Over time though, as Zneimer grew more trusted, Southgate listened more closely. Eventually though the moment came before an Under-21 game later that year, while the players were staying at The Grove Hotel in Watford.

And Southgate shared it all: rejection as a youngster at Southampton, coming through at Crystal Palace, missing the penalty for England, being sacked at Middlesbrough. The unwritten footballers' code was never go there for fear of piss-taking and disrespect. But according to Zneimer, you could feel an almost palpable change in the room. 'There was a dramatic sense of engagement with players in a different way,' said Zneimer. Psychologists use the phrase 'felt shift' when a buried hurt as yet unarticulated is brought to mind and the client is then encouraged to put it into words. It can often result in dramatic positive changes in the client's behaviour. Zneimer sensed something akin to that was happening in the room as Southgate opened up: 'He had moved away from being mentor to being on their level. It creates a different kind of bond.'

Of course, connecting with a bunch of 19- and 20-year-olds might be tricky for a 45-year-old if he relies too much on old war stories. This generation weren't massively cognisant of Southgate's lowest moment, despite its iconic place in English football history. 'Was it 1996?' said Watmore, now 30, when asked. 'I was two at the time, so obviously I don't remember it! Having said that, I was brought up with it. I knew about all England's major penalty misses, how close we got. I knew what a big story it was. Even though I didn't live it, I could feel how powerful that moment could have been, could stay with someone and hurt them. That's where a lot of respect came that got us all to open up.'

Southgate and Zneimer were now regularly getting the group of lads to break into small groups and talk about their lives, their worries, their hopes. 'I'd never done that before at club level,' said Watmore. 'He'd get us to split up into groups of three or four quite regularly. In a small group, you're more likely to be open than speaking amongst everyone. It could be about how you're finding club level, finding games, how you feel your game is, what's happening outside football and outside life.

'And that creates a bond with people and also just opens people up. I suppose by him doing that with his story, it was the cue for us to be open. He's a very intelligent man, speaks really well and genuinely cares. One of the main things I found, the first thing he'd do when he got to camp, he'd make sure he'd catch every single one of you, just walking around, nothing too formal and want to know how you are, how your family is, how you're doing as a person off the pitch. Obviously, he'd ask about club level and how you're finding that. But he really took an interest in you as a person, which in football doesn't happen that often.'

Which is why Toulon was such an important landmark for Southgate. You can deride the tournament's importance, but for him it had demonstrated that something darker lurked beneath England's failure. Something on which he had a unique perspective and that only being open to those wounds would allow healing. A vocation was being formed in his mind.

Meanwhile, back at Chantilly, CEO Glenn was briefing journalists on Hodgson's replacement. There were World Cup qualifying games scheduled for 4 September, but Glenn insisted he would not be rushed. More important to get the right decision rather a quick one. Arsène Wenger's contract with Arsenal was up the next summer and who knew? Maybe at this stage of life he might be persuaded. Sam Allardyce had galvanised Sunderland, saving them from relegation. Ashworth would meet left-field German candidate, Ralf Rangnick, a tactical visionary but one who would subsequently fail as interim Manchester United coach.

Glenn's initial press conference didn't go well. 'I'm not a football expert,' he cheerfully admitted. It wasn't necessarily a disqualifying factor for choosing an England manager and yet it was the sound bite that inevitably became the headline and invited the obvious response: 'Why the hell are you selecting the England manager then?!'

And beyond that unflattering headline, Glenn sounded clear-headed about what was needed. He talked about building success with the under-age teams, using St George's Park, the £105 million state-of-the-art (or white elephant, depending on your view) FA training centre in the middle of Derbyshire.

Alongside him on the selection panel were some actual football experts in Ashworth and FA interim chair David Gill, more famously known as one half of the double act that, with Sir Alex Ferguson, kept Manchester United as the dominant club in England for 20 years, an undoubtedly momentous achievement. Gill was the dominant voice in that trio and his great ally was Sir Alex, whose advice was understandably treated as having coming down from the mountain top inscribed on tablets of stone.

'Stressful,' is the word Ashworth uses to describe the process. 'In the role of technical director, changing and appointing a head coach is the hardest [part of the job]. If you sign a player and he doesn't work out, you can hide him. If you hire a head coach and that doesn't work out, there's no place to hide. With the England role you have the complexity of: "Should they be English? Should they have worked in England?" Fabio Capello was dropped in and had never worked in England. "Should it be an Arsène Wenger, a Pep Guardiola, who understands the cultural identity of England and our league, our media and players? Or do they have to be English?" There is definitely a sea of opinion that: "He must be English." Or "No, it doesn't matter. Get the best person. Go and get Diego Simeone." There is a different make-up and expectation and rules of engagement. And then, should he have had international experience before? Because it's a really different role, you don't really coach that much as they're in for 11 days on camp. That's a really different skill set and probably harder.'

Glenn was about to be pushed into a corner and would need a quick decision. He had assumed that while the FA searched for the big-name appointment they needed to get them out of a hole, Southgate would be more than able to hold the fort if necessary. Back home in Harrogate, that message filtered back to Southgate. 'They haven't asked me about that,' he told a friend. 'They definitely shouldn't assume I'll do it.' It was clear he was affronted, largely because the FA considered him a stopgap, not a serious part of the solution. Southgate was finally becoming fed up with being taken for granted. He was also considering going back into club management and didn't want to be considered a last-ditch stand-in.

But in truth, his decision was also because he was scared. 'I was frightened of failing in public again,' he said. He might have shared his Euro 96 shame with his Under-21 players, but he wasn't ready to do so in public with the nation again. That was a step too far.

Without Southgate to fall back on, Glenn and Ashworth's out-of-the-box thinking and data-led assessment of the best candidates would prove obsolete. They needed a manager quickly. Sir Alex's pal, Sam Allardyce, as recommended by Gill, was available and shared none of Southgate's tortured self-doubt.

The decision was announced less than a month after England's Euro exit. In terms of playing style, he was anything but a continuity candidate and far from the blueprint Sir Trevor Brooking and Southgate had advocated. Allardyce was no-nonsense in tactics as well as personality: don't mess around at the back, get the ball forward quickly, play to Anglo-Saxon strengths, exploit set pieces, work hard and show true grit. There seemed zero joined-up thinking in terms of developing a new England style.

Because Allardyce so easily fits the *Mike Bassett: England Manager* archetype as a large man of a certain age with a northern accent and the propensity to call a spade a spade, it's easy to stereotype him. The truth is he was onside with Glenn and Ashworth in many of their desired reforms and would embrace Zneimer's work. Allardyce was no dinosaur: he used data and specialist coaches at Bolton way ahead of the curve. Yet, as his downfall would prove, he did embody the trope of a super-confident, extroverted, bon viveur manager happy to hold court over, in this instance, a pint of wine, the detail that always stands out in the retelling of his demise.

Allardyce had one game as England manager, a 1-0 win in Slovakia before a video recording emerged of him chatting to undercover *Daily Telegraph* reporters, supping wine from a pint glass, as he mocked his predecessor Hodgson and offered advice on breaking FA transfer rules, with a £400,000 speaking fee also discussed.

Allardyce wasn't helped by the fact that a new FA chairman, Greg Clarke, had taken over days before his indiscretion came to light. Not only was it the worst first impression to make on your new boss, it presented Clarke with an opportunity. He hadn't been involved in the recruitment yet would have to carry the can for the new manager. If he wanted to make his own mark by having his man in the job, Allardyce's folly was an open goal.

As a dramatic day played out at Wembley, with the manager's future in the balance, a photographer trained his lens on the glass-fronted offices within the stadium when he alighted on the extraordinary sight of an office door open and the clear figure of Allardyce, shoulders slumped and head bowed, being addressed by Glenn and Clarke. It was clear how this was going. 'Allardyce's conduct was inappropriate of the England manager,' read the subsequent FA statement. 'He accepts he made a significant error of judgement and has apologised. Due to the serious nature of his actions, the FA and Allardyce have mutually agreed to terminate his contract with immediate effect.'

Watching this unfold in Harrogate, Southgate must have been inclined to ascribe the unfolding events to divine intervention. Only a few weeks before he had had an epiphany moment which had made him realise just how stupid he had been to turn down the FA's temporary job offer that summer. He had privately resolved never to buck a challenge like that again, though in this instance his self-enlightenment had come a little late. Now, incredibly, 67 days after Allardyce had been appointed ahead of Southgate, the job was available again. And more than ever the FA needed a steady stand-in to steer them through a storm.

CHAPTER 3

MIND GAMES

It seemed an odd film to be showing a group of elite footballers, more of a video nasty than your usual standard inspirational fare.

Gareth Southgate had been confirmed as England manager and for the first time since he had been invested with that full authority, he had his players together for a friendly against Germany and a World Cup qualifier against Lithuania in March 2017. He wanted to make an impression and he wanted to communicate his core values to them. The slogan plastered around the walls was 'Time for Change', Southgate now being in charge being the obvious reference point. But there was a deeper sense of rewriting England's story, which is why the players were now sitting in St George's Park lecture theatre with the lights dimming, preparing to watch.

The opening shots were of the Atlanta Olympics in 1996. It was a strange place to start. Some of the players weren't even born at the time and none of them would have a memory of those calamitous games for Team GB. Only one gold medal was won, by Steve Redgrave and Matthew Pinsent, in the rowing pairs. Britain had finished 36th in the medals table, behind North Korea, Kazakhstan and the Republic of Ireland. Unusually for an Olympic team, normally treated much more benignly than footballers, they were panned by the press and their return to Heathrow was more a walk of shame than a homecoming.

It was a seminal moment in British sport, prompting Prime Minister John Major to ensure that the newly founded National Lottery could partly fund Olympic sport.

The film's next scenes were perhaps more relevant to the England players but hardly likely to inspire. There was a shot of England departing the tournament in Mexico 1970 – 2-0 up with 22 minutes to play, they took off Bobby Charlton to rest him for the semi-finals and lost 3-2. To Germany. Then there was a flashback to the failures to qualify for the World Cup in 1974, the 1-1 to Poland at Wembley marking the end of Sir Alf Ramsey and in 1978, prompting Don Revie's flight to the desert to manage the United Arab Emirates. Then the players were watching the penalty shoot-out woes of 1990, 1996 (with a starring role for the manager), 1998, 2004, 2006 and 2012. There was Ronaldinho's free kick arching over David Seaman in 2002, a reprise of Brazil 2014 (out in two games) before finishing on the defeat that could still barely be named, so raw were the wounds: Iceland 2016. As an uplifting piece of cinema, it failed to meet its mark. The players were left wondering just where Southgate was going with this. It only reinforced the sense of doomed destiny that came with playing for England.

* * *

When Gareth Southgate got home the night he was sacked by Middlesbrough, it was well past midnight. His wife, Alison, was asleep in bed, as were his children, Mia, then aged ten, and Flynn, six. Alone in the kitchen he started to make lists: 1) return company car; 2) hand in mobile phone; 3) clear out locker at training ground. It doesn't really need a psychiatrist to work out that ordering banal areas of our lives when the bottom falls out of our world is a normal response to shock.

At 3 a.m., Alison Southgate came down to find her husband and was bemused to discover him writing. 'You haven't been sacked, have you?' she asked. 'Actually, I have,' Southgate replied.

The scene was captured by Joe Bernstein in *The Mail on Sunday* in an interview the weekend after the deed had been done. Middlesbrough had beaten Derby County 2-0 that night, were fourth in the Championship and a point off the leaders. Although the team had been relegated under Southgate, they had also finished 12th and 13th in the Premier League in his first two seasons. It would be fair to say the sacking came as something of a shock to Southgate and the wider world.

There is one very public Southgate failure that everyone remembers and which is referred to in hushed tones like a death in the family. And yet the Middlesbrough sacking hurt almost as much. 'Not as much as the penalty miss and not as much as being relegated,' he said. But he would later write that he felt 'humiliated'. Turning up for the school run to pick up his kids – Flynn was running round the playground shouting: 'My daddy's been sacked!' – was a chastening experience. Previously he had been the uber-cool football coach dad; now he was out of work.

The Middlesbrough sacking was one of the issues weighing most heavily on his mind when the FA pleaded with him to take over from Sam Allardyce on an interim basis. It's not that you necessarily need people cheering from the rafters when you take the England job, as they did when Kevin Keegan took over (though that didn't end well). But it's helpful if fans aren't actively disillusioned from the start.

Arsène Wenger had been on the summer shortlist and many craved a José Mourinho figure, so the current Under-21 manager, perceived as an FA suit, whose one senior job had ended in relegation and the sack, wasn't exactly what fans had in mind to reboot England.

'I didn't think the English public would welcome me in the role,' said Southgate. 'So I politely declined and passed on the offer.'

Some who know Southgate well might take issue with whether 'politely' is the correct word to use, although obviously Southgate would only ever be outwardly courteous in business dealings. Inwardly though he was angry that the FA had taken him for granted. That in itself though was perhaps cover for the deeper fear: that he wasn't good enough. The epiphany moment came when he watched his former Crystal Palace teammate Chris Coleman being interviewed just after he had declined the England job.

Coleman, who had been sacked by Fulham and Coventry, had taken the Wales job and not only led them to their first tournament since 1958 but all the way to the semi-finals of Euro 2016, in stark contrast to abject England. When asked whether he had advice for anyone else in a similar situation he had replied: 'Don't be frightened of going for things in life.'

Those words hung heavy on Southgate, having just turned down England. 'It felt like he was talking directly to me,' wrote Southgate. 'Unlike Chris, I'd chosen to back off. Some call managing England "the impossible job", which makes it sound as if there is no hope of a successful outcome, and I had fallen into that way of thinking. I had become so worried about what could go wrong that I'd failed to consider the opportunities.'

'I think there was an element of him being a good corporate citizen,' said performance psychologist Jonny Zneimer, who had been seconded full time by the FA from Lane4 as Head of People and Team Development. 'It was a case of, "There are two World Cup games coming up and there's no one else to do this." But there was also a moment the penny dropped. Gareth was thinking about what he could say to his own kids about taking opportunities and going for it.'

Allardyce resigned and Southgate was confirmed as interim manager on 27 September 2016. Zneimer recalled: 'I was sitting in Starbucks at St George's Park watching Sky Sports News saying that Sam had gone and Gareth appeared and said: "Jonny, I've been made England manager. I've taken the job."'

His first game was an unchallenging test against Malta at home, the only degree of difficulty being in that it was in 11 days' time. That was followed by Slovenia away, both World Cup qualifiers. In November came another World Cup qualifier, this one fraught with unpredictability: Scotland at home. That was followed by a friendly against Spain. The latter mattered less in competitive terms but could still prove terminal to Southgate's chances of getting the job full-time. Spain were not in their 2008–12 pomp, when they won two Euros and the World Cup, but with David Silva, Juan Mata, Thiago and Sergio Busquets they were quite capable of playing a Southgate team off the park at Wembley. A football lesson akin to Hungary's 6-3 win in 1953 would not have been a huge shock against a demoralised England.

At least Southgate had a head start. Allardyce had overseen a 1-0 win in Slovakia as his sole contribution to the national team and this was as benign a World Cup qualifying group as a prospective England manager could wish for. As such, Southgate's opening two games passed off without major incident on the pitch: a comfortable 2-0 home win against Malta was fine, though a 0-0 draw in Slovenia was gained only because of the excellence of Joe Hart in goal. Most felt England had been outplayed by a team ranked 67th in the world behind Panama and the United Arab Emirates.

The most significant moment in those games was his team selection, which would presage his first major decision with England. Wayne Rooney, the greatest player of his generation and leading England goalscorer of all time, was dropped against Slovenia. Legs tiring, body fading, Rooney had retreated to midfield and was increasingly peripheral at Manchester United. Southgate preferred Eric Dier and Jordan Henderson in holding roles and Dele Alli as his number ten, a nod towards what was to come in Russia 2018. 'As soon as you saw that, you realised the gaffer was someone not to be messed around,' said Danny Rose, who played left-back in Southgate's early games. 'He has this nice side but there is a side you don't want to cross.' The nation was about to become acquainted with this Southgate character trait: beneath the courtesy there is a stubborn streak that belies the 'too nice for football' tag.

Not that the Rooney decision seemed especially inspired. Neither Henderson nor Dier covered themselves in glory in that game, both making mistakes that could have cost Southgate an embarrassing defeat in his audition phase. Still, by November, a consensus was emerging that, by dint of having avoided quaffing a pint of wine with undercover reporters and having at least steadied a reeling ship, the job was now Southgate's to lose.

There was definitely a more relaxed feel to St George's Park as they prepared for Scotland and Spain with World Cup qualification on track. One observer recalls seeing the players crowded around a Subbuteo game that week. Introducing the Xbox FIFA generation to the old-school 20th-century table football game as an analogue throwback seemed a bold move, but there was some method behind the madness.

Coaches at St George's Park had recently inaugurated what was known as The Subbuteo Room. That particular day saw Southgate, Dier, Henderson and Adam Lallana immersed in deep conversation for an hour. Rather than actually playing Subbuteo, Southgate, Henderson, Dier and Lallana were running through the intricacies of how Spain press in midfield by busily moving around the figures. Southgate was keen for the players, coached by Jürgen Klopp and Mauricio Pochettino, to contribute given those two coaches were among the best at playing the pressing game.

Nick Levett was the talent identification manager at the FA at the time and along with Southgate had previously led the roadshow around the FA regions to persuade its members to switch to small-sided seven-a-side football for younger players to encourage technical skills, part of the joined-up thinking Sir Trevor Brooking had encouraged when he was FA director of development, had been trying to encourage.

'Subbuteo was a way of making the coaching more player-centred, rather than command and control,' said Levett. 'We wanted to engage people in the conversation rather than just telling them what to do. A lot of player meetings are coaches talking at players. We said, "Let's get out the Subbuteo table, get the figures out and talk about how we're going to press two against three." The players are the ones who have to make the decisions on the pitch. You're learning in 4D, having to work through the solutions. It was all based on [the academic discipline of] social learning theory, making sure people are part of the process. It wasn't just pulling something out of the sky and hoping it would work. There was science behind it.'

But it needed a win against Scotland to confirm the groupthink that Southgate was a shoo-in. On a crisp, autumnal Friday night against the auldest enemy, Southgate oversaw not only a victory but a fluid and exciting performance from an England forward line that boasted Lallana at his competitive peak, Daniel Sturridge and Raheem Sterling, with Rooney as a number ten. Three-nil up in 61 minutes, Wembley could enjoy a rare night of celebration after an awful year.

By now all that stood between Southgate and the job was avoiding humiliation to a technically superior Spain side in an era when Spanish football dominated. From 2014–18, the Champions League was won by either Real Madrid or Barcelona. When England had bombed out in South Africa in 2010, and Spain had won the World Cup, Brooking had specifically invoked their playing style, the Spanish investment in youth coaching and emphasis on technique rather than physique as crucial for the coming generations. It had informed his own document 'The Future Game', the 2010 FA blueprint.

Come the Tuesday night at Wembley against Spain, something seemed to have changed about England. They pressed their opponents coherently; Lallana was sparkling and Sterling thriving; Danny Rose and Nathaniel Clyne were pushing on like modern full-backs; Jamie Vardy was dashing in behind Spain's defenders, winning a ninth-minute penalty, which Lallana converted. Vardy added a superb diving header to make it 2-0 on 48 minutes. There was only one team looking fluid in their movement and comfortable in possession and it wasn't the tiki-taka maestros. The kicker came in two late goals from Iago Aspas and Isco that made it 2-2 and sullied the performance. Yet given the depths of despair felt against Iceland in June and the Allardyce debacle, that wasn't enough to suffocate the spirit of relative optimism.

And yet with England there is always a drama lurking around the corner. This one had actually occurred after the Scotland game and before Spain but only emerged in the aftermath of the Spain draw when *The Sun* printed pictures of a well-refreshed Wayne Rooney at the England team hotel, The Grove in Watford, on the Saturday night. Rooney had in fact begun the evening sharing a quiet drink with Southgate and Steve Holland. It seemed he was the sensible one, hanging out with the bosses, while younger players headed into London nightspots on a night off. Unfortunately, a wedding party was taking place at the hotel and Rooney, along with Phil Jagielka, were unable to resist the festivities. 'Roo's Big Fat Tipsy Wedding!' read *The Sun*'s front page, with accounts of how wedding guests were surprised to view England's record goalscorer 'stumbling around their party' like a 'comedy drunk', finally going to bed at 5 a.m. Rooney disputed those characterisations. He was there and drinking but his major crime, in his eyes, was to be caught on camera in an age in which the visual image frames public judgement. Saturday had been a night off for the players but training was scheduled for the Sunday afternoon. That said, many in the squad had late nights.

A very un-Rooney-like corporate apology followed. 'Naturally, Wayne is sorry that pictures taken with fans have been published today. Although it was a day off for the whole squad and staff, he fully recognises that the images are inappropriate for someone in his position. Earlier today Wayne spoke privately to both Gareth Southgate and Dan Ashworth to unreservedly apologise.' It would prove to be the end for Rooney. Behaviour like that from his captain and most senior player was anathema to the team culture Southgate aspired to build. It would prove to be the end for Rooney. He would play once more for England but only in the autumn of 2018 in a friendly against the US, which was pretty much a Rooney benefit to say 'thank you'. Southgate has since said he would have welcomed Rooney back in 2017, but by then the player had decided to retire from international football.

At this stage there seemed little doubt that Southgate had the job, though significantly, it was reported to be at a much lower salary than Roy Hodgson or Sam Allardyce would have commanded. And a break clause was said to have been inserted for Russia 2018. Southgate might be the man but the FA were hedging somewhat. The decision was publicly announced on 30 November 2016.

With the next international games in March, Southgate now had time to go away and think about what his England might look like.

'In a sense, coming [in] after the Iceland game, which was such a confidence-shattering experience, was a good time because how much worse can it feel?' he said. 'Maybe we can be a bit braver in what we push and try to introduce. Though clearly we were taking the team at a time where their confidence had to be rebuilt and you have to keep winning matches to buy the time to make the changes.'

With Zneimer having been seconded to the senior team after his success with the Under-21s and now Southgate and Steve Holland had been promoted, it was getting the old band back together.

Southgate now had a blank sheet of paper to reinvent England.

His conversations with Sterling, Kane and Dele Alli had convinced him that Fabio Capello's assertion that the England shirt hung heavy on the players was spot on. There was a negativity associated with playing for England. That had already begun to be addressed in the junior teams. 'That was the whole schtick of Dave Reddin [FA head of team strategy and performance],' said Zneimer. 'You want the players going back to their clubs saying what a brilliant time they had with England.' Southgate had called up some standby players after withdrawals in the autumn, but they had declined to come, preferring to take a two-week break. 'When St George's Park was built, Dan [Ashworth] and I talked a lot about the shirt feeling heavy, the pressure, all the things that you can allow to be narrative. But fundamentally, how do we get people to want to come at every age group to be with England and want to come back?' pondered Southgate.

It was clear the England team atmosphere was, if not quite toxic, extremely hangdog. England was becoming an optional career choice viewed by many as more a chore and unnecessary extra hassle. The idea that it was the ultimate honour was fast fading.

Some of the rebuild had already begun in 2012 when Dan Ashworth had been appointed FA director of elite development.

Ashworth's breezy optimism that an England renaissance could be achieved was not universally shared. In 2013, he spoke about the patience required for England to build up a new generation of players. Sports writer Martin Samuel summed up the mood in the *Daily Mail*: 'Only in the job a matter of weeks, Ashworth is already talking of a 15-year wait until changes in the English game begin to take hold. Judge me in 2028. Nice work if you can get it.'

'I remember talking about how youth development is no quick fix, that if it was quick and easy anyone could do it,' said Ashworth. 'Martin wrote the next day: "Get your excuses in early." You can tell him from me I've never forgiven him for it. You could sense [the mood of]: "Oh yeah!"'

It didn't get any better when Ashworth and Reddin tried to introduce a collective identity to the national teams at all age-group levels in 2014. With Southgate, then Under-21 manager, and Matt Crocker, head of player and coach development, at his side, Ashworth launched 'England DNA', the FA's vision of how international players would understand their history and culture, which spelt out a playing style that was possession-based but with a typically English attacking intent. An aspirational list of characteristics of an ideal English player was outlined: the ability to create, score and prevent goals, to travel with the ball, to be able to tactically manage international games, recognise and adapt to the state of the game and to perform effectively against varied playing styles and formations.

It's fair to say there was scepticism in the room at the corporate language, not least because the actual England manager, Roy Hodgson, wasn't even there. 'When we did the DNA it was, "Here we go again! Three grey men in three grey suits and yet another grey FA plan,"' said Ashworth. 'I did feel from a media perspective there was a huge amount of negativity. I remember coming out of that the next day thinking: "I wish we hadn't launched it." It was a big moment for me, Gareth and Matt Crocker. We had discussed: "Should we launch it, shouldn't we launch it?" You know you're going to get some stick. And we thought: "No, come on, let's be brave. Let's get on the front foot." We wanted to be fully transparent with the clubs and say, "This is what we'll be doing with your players when we borrow them." I was lying in the bath at St George's Park [after the launch] listening to someone on the radio – I think it was Henry Winter [then the *Daily Telegraph*'s chief football correspondent] – dissecting what we had presented and saying: "They're missing the point! They should be working with the Under-9s." I was lying in the bath thinking: "We don't have Under-9 teams at international level!" And getting really frustrated, going: "See! We should never have bloody launched this!"

'When we launched the specialist coaching model it was the same thing: [We were talking about coaches] in possession, out of possession, set plays and transitions. And [the response] was: "What're we gonna do? We've got the ball and now we lose it so now that coach is in charge?!" There was a general sense of ridicule. Now every club has set-play coaches.'

While Hodgson had been an arms-length supporter of those initiatives, now Ashworth and Reddin had a true believer in charge in Southgate. Together they were already trying to reimagine what an England team would look like. 'The FA was really clear that it had invested a lot of money in St George's Park and the remit [when I was appointed] was to bring St George's Park to life: make it the home of English football, make it somewhere people want to come and be proud to be coming. It was the catalyst for change and it enabled us to bring all the national teams and coach education together in one place. The vision was a vibrant hub of activity, so if you were on an A Licence course, you might bump into a national coach and the women's team manager might bump into the men's team manager. You could almost get a club training ground feel for the whole country and make them proud of coming. So it really excited me. Off the top of my head, England men and women were both ranked about 14th in the world [when I came in]. I thought: "Blimey, we've got some good players. We can definitely get higher than 14th. We've got the catalyst for change and a new exciting adventure.'"

Courtesy of Reddin, Southgate would have an unlikely confidant in those early days. Stuart Lancaster, another England coach who just so happened to live near Southgate in Harrogate, had been invited by Reddin to be on an FA advisory group. Lancaster perhaps wasn't the obvious go-to guy when trying to fix England: the England rugby team he coached had their worst ever World Cup performance, knocked out in the group stages of the 2015 tournament, which England hosted. Yet Lancaster, who until that moment had been widely praised for changing the culture of the England team into a more open, accessible group, was haunted by one particular moment. In their group game against Wales, England led 22-12 with half an hour to play at Twickenham. Somehow, a series of scrappy penalties had allowed the game to slip away. They trailed 25-22 in the final moments. Defeat meant World Cup exit was almost certainly assured. A point though would keep them in the fight and salvation arrived when England were awarded a late penalty. In rugby union, three points are awarded for a penalty and five for a try and as such there is an element of gambling as to how you deploy a penalty kick. You can kick for touch and then hope you're so close to the try line you can drive over to score five points and, in England's case, win the game. Or simply play it safe, take three points and, in this scenario, England would draw and stay alive. Captain Chris Robshaw famously elected to kick for touch and go for five points. The resulting England attack petered out, Wales won and England were out.

The memory of this still preoccupied Lancaster and as he was watching England play Iceland at Euro 2016, he had a crushing sense of déjà vu, reliving his own Waterloo against Wales. When the big moments came, the team panicked. He recognised the same fear on the pitch among the England footballers. 'It's about staying in the present in those pressure moments,' said someone familiar with the conversations between Southgate and Lancaster.

Lancaster said: 'The players start to think of the past and they begin to fear the future. "We could lose this game." The key, psychologically, is staying in the present.' Lancaster shared with Southgate the work of Gazing Performance Systems, specialists in mindset skills, who had worked with the All Blacks rugby team.

Gazing have a name for the kind meltdown suffered against Iceland: 'Red head, blue head.' Red head is when the blood is rushing to the brain and decision-making goes awry; blue head is keeping cool. Founded by Dr Ceri Evans, a former New Zealand international footballer and subsequently a psychiatrist, Gazing had been hired by the All Blacks rugby team because, rather like England, they had a huge reputation yet kept failing at crucial moments in World Cups. Gazing worked with the team in their 2011 and 2015 World Cup wins, so had good credentials. As it turned out, Southgate would use

Lane4 performance psychologist Zneimer and later Dr Pippa Grange on these aspects of performance. But the Gazing principles shone through. Fabian Delph, speaking at the 2018 World Cup, could have been reciting from the Gazing handbook when he said, 'A lot of the game is mental and how to keep a calm mind. We've looked at different ways of coping and it's eye-opening. It's just how to reset your mind if you make a mistake.'

But just as big as fixing the players' minds was turning the entire culture around. Although Reddin and Ashworth had started that work, Lancaster again was to point them towards a man who had helped to overhaul the England rugby team's culture. Owen Eastwood, a Kiwi with a Maori dad and an Irish mum, was the man they settled on. The death of his father when he was still a child had led Eastwood to write to the office of *Ngāi Tahi*, his father's Maori tribe. The sense of belonging Eastwood felt in their subsequent embrace of him remained with him in adult years. He recalls *Ngāi Tahi* sent him a single page listing his ancestors going back 20 generations, finishing with his father's name at the bottom. The covering letter described this as his *whakapapa*. As Eastwood understood it, it meant 'each of us are part of an unbreakable chain of people going back and forward in time . . . with our arms interlocked. We are unbreakable, together, immortal. We have passed down to us a culture that immerses us in deep belonging. We share beliefs and a sense of identity with those around us and that anchors us . . . *Whakapapa* points a finger at us and tells us you will not be judged by your money or celebrity or sense of self-pride, you will be judged by what you did for our tribe.'

This was grist to the mill for an England manager trying to mould a group of self-centred individuals into a team. Since 2006, Eastwood's business had been helping organisations understand their place in the world and he had worked with NATO High Command and the South African cricket team.

Now he, Reddin and Southgate were trying to redefine England. 'We got Owen to do an extensive piece of research to look into questions like: "What is the England team's culture? Where has it come from? What does it mean to be an England player in the 21st century?,"' said Reddin. 'There has been so much cultural change in the country that it looks so different now to 20 years ago, never mind 50 years ago.'

Eastwood was nothing if not thorough in his role. To understand why the three lions crest had become such a totemic marker for the England team, he went to the National Archives in Kew where a librarian wearing protective gloves brought out to him the first ever royal seal with the three lions, from 1197 and King Richard I, Richard the Lionheart. It was his family crest that became the English coat of arms.

Alongside that deeper work, Reddin had a more immediate goal. 'At that point, the England team had no clear purpose, vision, targets or principles to work with. I had a clear idea about how we could build the programme for change and Gareth and Dan Ashworth gave me their full support when I pitched it to them.

'From January to March 2017 I designed and led a series of workshops with a core group of staff including Gareth with others, such as Rhys Long, head of analysis, Bryce Cavanagh, head of physical performance, and the leads for culture, medical and team operations,' he wrote. 'The goal was to create a first version of a strategy and plan for the England senior team, which we could present to the players at the first international camp in March. It was apparent from our experiences in the autumn that the players (never mind the staff!) hadn't really processed the Euro 2016 defeats and would benefit from the confidence that a clear sense of direction could give them.

'In the March camp in 2017, we launched the strategy to the players under the banner of "Time for Change". There was an obvious change in Gareth taking over the manager role permanently, and we also wanted to convey clearly that we wanted the future to look different for the England team.'

When the team arrived at St George's Park, there was messaging pinned up on the walls of training areas and the spaces for downtime. This is standard sports psychology loved by the likes of Allardyce, reinforcing positive messages. There was a twist to this poster campaign, however. 'On the walls of a room, information was plastered everywhere: data pointing out England had only won one knockout game at a major tournament in almost 16 years,' wrote Lallana. 'The truth on how England had fallen short was pinned up for all the squad to see. It was a clever way of stripping everything back to reality. [As a football nation] we were miles off.'

And that is why the players were gathered around to watch the video nasty which had started with the ignominy of the Atlanta Olympics and then tracked all the England national team's various calamitous exits from major tournaments.

The plot twist was in the editing of the film. Intercut with those failures from Mexico 1970 to Iceland 2016 were shots of the British Olympic team, winning races and coming home from the Rio 2016 Olympics to a heroes' welcome. That was fresh in the memory, as the success in Brazil, where Team GB had come second in the medals table with 27 golds as opposed to the paltry single gold in 1996, had been a counterpoint to the failure of the England team in the summer of 2016. They had seen how the nation embraced the Olympians.

The finale of the audio visual homily came as the shots of English football failure faded away to be replaced by Harry Kane and Dele Alli scoring in the 2-0 win over France in 2015 and the Sturridge, Lallana and Gary Cahill goals in the 3-0 win against Scotland.

The credits rolled and Southgate took the stage. 'What are we worrying about?' he asked them. 'We talk about pressure but where is the pressure coming from? We haven't won anything for 50 years. In reality, there is nothing to live up to. It's been mostly terrible and you don't bear the responsibility of the past. You're your own generation. Why can't you write your own story, a new story?'

'What have we got to lose?' Lallana recalls Southgate saying. 'You weren't the players who had that legacy so why should we be weighed down by it?'

Then came the explanation for the Olympic footage. Twenty years ago the Olympic team were a joke, Southgate told them. And yet now they were heroes and the nation loved them. 'Why can't that be you? Why shouldn't you be the generation that changes it?'

People who were present say that by now he had a rapt audience.

Choosing his moment, he left them with perhaps the most subversive pay-off line you could imagine in an English football landscape long dominated by Premier League clubs.

'However well you do with your clubs, whatever you achieve, there is nothing that will ever match winning a trophy for the nation.'

It was a bold claim, Southgate parking his tanks on the Premier League's lawn in terms of player loyalty. And in 2017, it was an outlandish thought. Yet a new generation of players were about to buy into the belief that they could be the change-makers.

CHAPTER 4

TO RUSSIA WITH LOVE

After Euro 2016, after Iceland, when morale at the FA was rock bottom, Dan Ashworth presented a slide to staff. It outlined four broken elements that needed fixing for England to be successful again. One was culture, one was psychology and one related to DNA and playing style. The last was communications and media.

Those present felt their first glimmer of hope in a while. At least somebody had a plan. The low-profile, publicity-averse Ashworth is not the first person you would expect to place media on an 'essentials' list, but the analytical East Anglian had understood something about the organisation he worked for, and the national team he was trying to mend.

The FA had developed a relationship with television and newspapers over the years that was almost akin to Stockholm syndrome. In the 16 years since the millennium, it burned through seven chief executives and six chairmen, and media stings or pressure had accounted for many of the departures. At the same time, the FA kept looking to the world of communications for leadership talent. Brian Barwick (TV), Adam Crozier (advertising), Greg Dyke (journalism), Martin Glenn (marketing) and David Davies (press office) all came from it.

That was before you got to the influence the media had on the pitch. England managers' dysfunctional relationships with newspapers had been immortalised on screen (the *Mike Bassett* films, the Graham Taylor documentary *An Impossible Job*) and numerous players had spoken about their fear of incurring negative headlines.

Gary Neville described teammates being 'terrified' of the press. 'Too many players were frightened of what would be said or written about them, of making a mistake,' he wrote in a *Daily Mail* column. Steven Gerrard spoke of similar, admitting performances on the pitch – including his own – were compromised in crunch knockout games. 'I hate to say it, but your mind drifts to what the coverage is going to be like back home and the level of criticism you are going to get. You cannot stop yourself. "What if we don't get back into this? What will it be like if we go out here?"' he said.

Kieron Dyer, in his autobiography, would go even further. 'We're all scared in an England shirt,' he wrote. 'It's one of the main reasons we never achieve what we're supposed to achieve. That's the England player's disease. Sure, some are more scared than others. I sat next to a player on the bench once who had played for Liverpool and other leading Premier League clubs and the fans were giving the lads a bit of stick. He turned to me and said: "I hope I don't get on today."

'That was what it was like with England. That is what it is still like.'

Dyer's book came out in February 2018. Within four months his line 'that is what it is still like' seemed silly, as England footballers played darts and pool with journalists in a beach hotel and prevailed by performing without fear in big pressure moments: after a setback in a World Cup opening game, in a penalty shoot-out, at a tournament quarter-final. They were attracting coverage so positive that the press seemed less their captors than their cheerleaders.

But Dyer was not to know the plans to change how England communicated their story that were about to come to fruition. These were part of a holistic strategy envisioned by Ashworth and mapped out by Reddin. The pair understood that what happens in one moment on the pitch can be the consequence of a hundred factors and a thousand experiences off it; that the old idea in the game that you could separate the 'football bit' from the 'other stuff' was as outdated as screw-in studs on boots.

Greg Dyke played his part. 'A bull looking for a china shop,' said a former FA colleague – affectionately. The chairmanship of the man who brought Roland Rat and bingo to breakfast television before becoming director-general of the BBC was like Dyke himself: short and colourful. But it had a legacy. What attracted him to leading the FA was the opportunity to 'turn the tanker' of English football around and his way of doing that was to be bold and clear about the direction of travel. A few weeks after becoming chairman in summer 2013, he announced the goal was winning the World Cup in 2022 and that he was setting up a commission to examine the English game's key structural issues.

The 2022 target attracted derision, especially when it emerged a clock counting down the days to the Qatar World Cup had been installed in the national coaches' room in the football centre at St George's Park, but being clear and brave about objectives proved valuable. Ashworth began work as technical director just three months before Dyke's arrival and appreciated having something to work to. He recruited Reddin to do details and delivery and is generous in highlighting his work.

'Dave doesn't get the credit he deserves,' said Ashworth. 'It was about using things from other sports and asking, "What does it take to win?" If we're going to win in Qatar 2022, which was Greg's vision, what experiences do we need that are going to give the players the tools to help with the stresses and pressures of the tournament?

'That was anything from [gaining] experience of playing Brazil for the Under-16s. If the first time they play Brazil and those iconic yellow shirts is the semi-final of a World Cup, for players that's "shiiit", that's panic mode. Whereas if they had played Brazil two or three times in their youth career, drawn a couple, won one, it's not the same daunting task.

'It was the same with the media. If we can expose the young players to the media, the sorts of questions they're going to get asked, the number of media they'll face, we can put that as part of their development plan. As they came through the age groups we now had a more of a strategic plan for the media side of things.'

That involved trialling a greater openness at junior level and one of the first teams to allow cameras into their dressing room was the Under-21s – managed by Southgate – for an FATV 'day in the life' feature with kitman Neil 'Badger' Jones. There was an emphasis on getting young players to see beyond the pitch. 'We did discrimination workshops. Media workshops. Got outsiders in to tell stories, maybe someone who had served in wars,' said Steve Cooper, coach of England's 2017 World Cup-winning Under-17s.

Robert Sullivan was brought over from corporate affairs to head strategy and communications in 2016, in the wake of an undercover sting by the *Daily Telegraph* that led to Sam Allardyce departing by mutual agreement after only 67 days, one game and the odd pint of wine as England manager. A year later, once England qualified for the 2018 World Cup, Sullivan said to Greg Demetriou, 'Right – let's do this completely different.'

While Demetriou was still working on ideas, he and England's senior communications manager, Andy Walker, accompanied Southgate on a trip to the Super Bowl in Minneapolis, which also took in a Minnesota Timberwolves v New Orleans Pelicans NBA game. Attending the Super Bowl media day made a deep impression: all the players on risers, fielding questions about anything and from everyone, without a press officer in sight and the biggest star, Tom Brady, doing the most media of all. An England version at St George's before departing for Russia became the centrepiece of the new media plan.

Sullivan loved it. Southgate bought in immediately. Ashworth backed them. The hardest person to convince was Reddin, who was protective of time and always wanted to ensure players' days were tightly scheduled with enough time for such as recovery. But Reddin acquiesced and Demetriou and Walker pitched the idea to Kane and senior players before presenting it to the squad, explaining it reflected a new approach: relaxed and open, and media duties to be done as a collective rather than the old way of one player being expected to 'front up' to the press at a time. 'Trust us,' Demetriou and Walker said.

* * *

When Dan Ashworth left the FA two months after the 2018 World Cup, he gave a senior colleague a parting gift. A book. Ryan Holiday's bestseller *Ego is the Enemy*.

Ashworth once said the job of a technical director is to sit, like an axle, in the middle of a wheel and keep it spinning. The heads of all the departments are on the outside and the 'TD' just connects the spokes. Without one you cannot drive – but they do not do the driving.

He was a footballer, but not a special one – released by Norwich aged 17, having proved hard-working and athletic but limited technically as an academy right-back. He played semi-professionally for St Leonards, Eastbourne and Wisbech Town, and for West Florida Fury in the US while taking coaching qualifications all the way up to UEFA Pro Licence. At the age of 29, he was teaching PE at Darrick Wood School in Orpington when Peterborough United offered him a job.

'I was a teacher for three and a half years and took a risk to take a pay cut to work in Peterborough's academy and people said, "Oh, you're crazy, you're mad, giving up that security." I thought, "Yeah, but what's the worst that can happen? I can't cut it at an academy? I'll just go back into teaching," Ashworth recalled.

'I think I felt the same subconsciously, after six years at West Brom [when he was offered the FA technical director role]. I thought I could always go back [into the club game] if it didn't work out and I was just so excited about what St George's Park could bring, the opportunity to be an integral part of that. The England teams had not been doing so well. I didn't think through the threat, I just saw the opportunity.'

At Peterborough, Ashworth drove the minibus, washed kit and coached every age group, quickly rising from education and welfare officer to academy director. Barry Fry, the first-team manager, found him 'a very deep thinker'. His sessions were unconventional and he encouraged young players to solve problems for themselves. After three years in the academy at West Brom – whom he joined from Cambridge's centre of excellence – he was invited to be their sporting and technical director. Such roles were very rare in English football, though familiar to European clubs, and Ashworth told the Coaches' Voice, 'I didn't really know what it was!' But he soon realised it was about strategy, diligence, people skills and the ability to manage and organise – just like being an academy head – and he excelled. 'So many people still don't get it [what a technical director does]. They think it's a chief scout role,' he said. However, recruitment was an area at West Brom where he did excel – through an ability to go the extra mile which became legendary at the club.

In Buenos Aires, he scaled a fence to watch Claudio Yacob and would watch 300 games per year. He appointed a head of 'technical scouting', specialising in analysing talents using video, a role now standard at clubs but then (the late 2000s) almost unheard of. He filled a room with DVD recorders so almost any game shown on TV around the world could be captured and stored in West Brom's video bank. It became known as The Shire, inspired by where Hobbits dwell in *Lord of the Rings* – a mythic place where outsiders know not what goes on.

The FA's officer came at 'the right moment in my life to move'. He had helped West Brom return to the Premier League and become established there, while rebuilding their training ground and football structure, but scope for further improvement was limited. And the 'disparate' nature of the England youth system had always struck him. 'You would have the Under-17s meeting at Carden Park [in Chester], the 19s at Loughborough, the 21s somewhere else, the first team somewhere else.'

He saw a chance 'to help the country be proud'. Ashworth said, 'I hadn't played for England, I hadn't been a high-profile player; it was a once-in-a-lifetime opportunity.'

The 2018 Super Bowl trip was merely one in a series of visits to the US to learn from NFL and NBA, and following Southgate's friendship with Stuart Lancaster he developed a similar relationship with Lancaster's successor as England rugby coach, Eddie Jones, and in the run-up to Russia engaged with figures in cricket, athletics, boxing, swimming, canoe slalom and even short-track speed skating – the latter via his number two, Steve Holland, who spoke to Nicky Gooch, coach of the Olympian, Elise Christie, to garner ideas.

He also arrived at the tournament as a student on UK Sport's Elite Programme, a three-year course where fellow students included

Olympic swimming coach, Mel Marshall, and British Cycling's Paul Manning. Following the World Cup he would develop a particularly close connection with Sir Dave Brailsford, the INEOS head of sport and former British Cycling chief, and spend a weekend visiting McLaren Formula 1 at team principal Toto Wolff's behest.

The role of Cooper and other coaches of development teams was important too. In June 2017, as mud-spattered Harry Kane yomped across Woodbury Common, England's Under-20s, managed by Paul Simpson and featuring talents like Dominic Solanke and Dominic Calvert-Lewin, were preparing for a quarter-final with Mexico at their World Cup in South Korea. They won, then beat Italy, then Venezuela in the final.

Cooper's Under-17s – an incredible group involving Phil Foden, Marc Guéhi, Callum Hudson-Odoi, Connor Gallagher and other future stars – won their World Cup in India four months later. Internally, Ashworth branded these 'our winning teams' – examples to be learned from. The national coaches' room at St George's became what he always dreamed of: a hive of like-minded missionaries, sharing practices, discussing ideas, reviewing performance, supporting each other – and having fun.

'It was a brilliant time,' said Cooper. 'We met Mondays and Tuesdays and spent the rest of the week getting round the country to games and training grounds. We stayed at the hotel at St George's Park. Meetings would start at 8.30 a.m. and there'd always be an agenda, for example: "First two hours, Under-17s review. Next two, Under-19s review. Then we're going to do playing out from the back, then penalties." And we didn't just discuss playing style as a group. It could be something like periodisation. Culture was a big one.'

Southgate had been leader of this group of coaches, but in a 'first among equals' way, since managing the Under-21s and did not change after getting the senior job. He listened, he learned, and Cooper talked about what made India 2017 a successful camp, or Simpson told of the putting competition Aaron Danks staged in Korea to get the Under-20s used to nailing shots under pressure with penalties in mind. He went to Russia with a host of ideas for how to make England's set-up there different to previous tournaments – drawn not just from his own experiences as an international coach and player, but from those Mondays and Tuesdays at SGP.

Pippa Grang joined as the senior team's lead psychologist in late 2017 and a final, but crucial, part in the preparation jigsaw was data. One of Ashworth's biggest principles was improving and maintaining relationships with Premier League clubs and their managers, and this led, from Euro 2016 onwards, to clubs agreeing for the first time to share performance and fitness data with the FA – meaning that statistics on training and matches, plus injuries and wear and tear across a season, could be factored into Southgate's planning. The England travelling party that boarded a flight to St Petersburg on 12 June was the best prepared in history.

Their base was in Repino, a quiet beachside village on the Karelian Isthmus which used to be part of Finland. St Petersburg was 30 miles away and the Stadium Spartak Zelenogorsk, where they would train, six miles away. It was so sleepy that in season it looked out of season – and, out of season, you really doubted anyone came. England's hotel was the ForRestMix – simple, four stars and, yes, restful and in a forest. Mixed? Those would be the reviews on Tripadvisor. But what Southgate and Reddin loved was its seclusion, its simplicity and its space. Both the gym and swimming pool were huge and there were open areas, inside and out, that could be converted for the benefit of the players.

Bedrooms were personalised, with framed photographs set out

on bedside units, windowsills, and the small, wooden, stepladder-style desks with shelves angled against each room's walls. There was messaging in these: family, friendship, teamship, journey. For example, in Jesse Lingard's room, he found a picture of him with his mother, a picture of himself playing football as a child, a picture from a Manchester United charity night with Marcus Rashford, Paul Pogba, Romelu Lukaku and Stormzy. Framed was also a pencil sketch of himself. Among the photos in Rashford's room was one of him and Lingard, both sticking their tongues out and making faces at the camera. Among those in Danny Welbeck's was one of him and Lingard, arms round each other, in England training gear.

There was a common room for playing computer games – Fortnite was a favourite of the squad as was an indoor driving game – open not just to players but any staff. Basketball was a craze. The players played in the gym and on electronic basketball machines, again with staff joining in. The breaking down of boundaries extended to mealtimes, where there were no players' tables or coaches' tables and everybody sat with everybody. Meals were important to Southgate – when he became England manager he found meetings were often scheduled to take place over breakfast, lunch and dinner and abandoned this practice. Let's have those small windows in the day where we can put work away, relax and just *talk.* And enjoy team chef Omar Meziane's remarkable food.

There were special mattresses, to maximise sleep and even the table mats had Bobby Moore on them. Members of the FA staff were bowled over to discover, waiting for them in their rooms, handwritten notes from Southgate himself. The FA's social media officer, Jim Lucas, posted his on Twitter (now X). 'Jim. The more I see, the more important it is that when "attacking the tournament" we tell our own story. You're capturing that brilliantly. Keep doing it and I hope this

World Cup brings you unforgettable personal memories. Best wishes, Gareth,' it read.

The one Southgate left for Reddin was pithier: 'Well, here we go! I hated your planning documents, now I can't live without them!'

In the 'new England' culture, every margin of gain was important and worth investing in. 'Recces became important,' said Steve Cooper. Repino was announced as England's base unusually early – the previous October, before qualification was even assured – and even before then a 'long process' went into making the call, Southgate said.

ForRestMix, where normal rooms cost £80 per night, was only ranked third on Tripadvisor for hotels in tiny Repino and contrasted with the opulent, £500-per-night Auberge du Jeu de Paume, with its Michelin-starred dining, where England stayed during Euro 2016. But it would become the base future England billets were based on.

'[The hotel] was a Gareth/Dave decision. You'll remember all the debates from previous tournaments. They need to be in the city, they should be out of the city. They need to go for coffee, they shouldn't go for coffee. It was finding the balance between all of that. It was thinking less about the luxury of the hotel and more about "What do we actually need? What works for us?"' Sullivan said.

'Gareth, having been to major tournaments, just brought that smart thinking.' The FA's 'top brass' also stayed at ForRestMix – even the chiefs of the organisation shared the new mood of humility. 'We were in a Holiday Inn. Oh my God!' chortled then chief executive, Martin Glenn. 'I mean, Center Parcs wouldn't even get close. But the environment was pretty good. No one was trying to make a statement about grandeur, it was a good, fun hotel, well thought through, well scouted out. It just seemed to work from a location point of view. It was a happy camp, a buzzing camp.'

In Zelenogorsk, an even sleepier village than Repino with (for obscure reasons) a statue of a dachshund in the middle, the FA requested a six-metre fence be erected round England's training stadium – a facility ordinarily used by a local sports school. This was to thwart prying eyes, but didn't stop the English media, two days in advance, discovering Southgate's starting XI for the opening game in Volgograd. The big news was that, at left-wing-back, Ashley Young was preferred to Danny Rose.

Volgograd, a three-hour flight away in southern Russia, was boiling and sticky, the air fuzzed with mosquitoes that swarmed from the great Volga River. England's history was of being uncomfortable in hot conditions, and unsuccessful in tournament opening games. Their last victory in one of those was five finals ago, at the 2006 World Cup, and their overall record in opening matches going back to 1950 was a meagre played 17 won five.

Harry Kane was awkward in the pre-match press conference, thrown a weighty question about the two million who perished in the battle of Stalingrad (Volgograd's former name) in the Second World War, and responding with a rather unphilosophical 'history is what it is'. England's opponents, Tunisia, who sat back and looked to funnel breakaways through their maverick number ten, Wahbi Khazri, were out to cause discomfort too.

England dominated the first half. The Tunisians could not cope with the width of Young and Kieran Trippier, the running behind the lines from deep of Jesse Lingard and Dele Alli, and England's power and routines at set pieces. From Young's clipped corner, John Stones caught a header full on and Mouez Hassen, Tunisia's keeper, bent backwards and clawed the ball off his line but Kane, on the move and anticipating while others stood rooted, was there to volley in for 1-0.

Lingard miscued from Young's cross, Harry Maguire forced a save with a header, and Lingard hit a post. Yet at half-time it was

1-1. Under a cross, Kyle Walker stood his ground and instinctively threw out an arm as Fakhreddine Ben Youssef tried to come from behind him to attack it. The back of his elbow clipped Ben Youssef's ear and Wilmar Roldán, the Colombian referee, signalled penalty. VAR upheld the decision – which seemed flimsy in the context of the wrestling that the Tunisians did to stop Kane reaching high balls in the other box.

But Ferjani Sassi dispatched the spot kick and England were suddenly in a familiar position: hit by a sudden, left-field setback in an opening match they were expected to win. Pressure started weighing. Passing grew untidy, aimless crosses sailed through Tunisia's box, free kicks were hit without conviction. A decent Southgate substitution regained some momentum – the silky but powerful Ruben Loftus-Cheek replacing a tiring Alli.

And in the first minute of stoppage time, Trippier hit an out-swinging corner and Harry Maguire headed it on. At the far post Kane guided a header into a small gap between Farouk Ben Mustapha – Tunisia's substitute keeper – and the goal frame: 2-1. The levels of guile and control in Kane's body movement, planting himself then swivelling his hips to get the ball from behind himself to his target area, were exceptional. To execute at such a pressure moment was breathtaking.

* * *

Southgate leapt out of his dugout, right-hooked the air above his head and roared while pumping his fists. It was the celebration of someone who knew exactly how significant Kane's goal was. 'That 91st-minute winner was a huge thing. Draw against Tunisia and forget all your pre-tournament work, you're back in crisis. We played really well, murdered them for half an hour but were only 1-0 up and they got a goal from nowhere,' said an insider in the camp. 'Until Harry scored, you're thinking here we go again.' Said Glenn, 'Had that been in 2016, in the Iceland game, we'd have been shooting from 30 yards out, panicking. Instead it was "get it on the floor, get it out wide, get good crosses in. Keep calm and carry on."'

England travelled straight back to Repino, as they were to do from other far-off locations like Samara and Nizhny Novgorod.

The priority was recovery. Cool climate and quietness was one reason for choosing Repino and those who did not feature in a game could go to Zelenogorsk for a light, tailored training session. The others could recover in the ForRestMix swimming pool, where Cavanagh had some unusual aids in store.

The unicorn is actually the national animal of Scotland. Yet, looking for a way to enliven recovery work, Cavanagh procured a set of white inflatable unicorns, replete with purple hooves and rainbow manes and horns, and had the players who figured in Volgograd race each other across the ForRestMix pool. Lingard posted pictures on his Instagram and so did Lucas on the official England social feeds. His caption: 'If you can't have an inflatable unicorn race after a win, when can you?'

The images went viral. It just looked so much fun. When congratulations poured in for Rosenblatt, he generously tweeted, 'This is all the work of @Bryce_Cav I only helped him take the [unicorn emoji] out of the forest.' To which Cavanagh replied, 'That was the most important part. #unicornwrestler.'

The vibes continued into press activity. At the Cronwell Park hotel, a two-minute minibus shuttle from ForRestMix, some more of the blue-sky ideas for media relations were manifested. Sullivan empowered his team – Demetriou, Walker, Jo Plummer, Anna Bush and James Webb – to create something that would break down the old barriers between players and the press, with no expense spared. The whole first floor of the Cronwell was commandeered for England comms. There were two press conference rooms, a buffet restaurant for journalists, a coffee station, a working area – and the ultimate sixth form common room. It contained a mini bowling alley, pool tables and a dartboard. Beside the latter was a whiteboard for keeping scores with a challenge set up – every day a member of Southgate's squad would play a member of the press in a three-dart competition. The prize was the 'Charlie Sale Memorial Trophy' – in homage to the ex-*Daily Mail* diarist, who took Joe Hart to task throughout Euro 2016 for his bumptious refusal in a press conference to talk about a darts contest the players had, or for that matter give anything else away.

One of the ideas was for interviews to take place out in relaxed fashion out in the open rather than the traditional way of huddles in closed off rooms, or players sat before journalists on a formal press conference stage. There were white sofas with St George's Cross cushions where a Kane or a Jordan Henderson would lounge, yakking to reporters sat on similar chairs, while other interviews took place nearby. A chat between Walker and Sunday newspaper reporters even took place standing at the bar. One Friday, before England's second game versus Panama, Harry Maguire was doing a written briefing and Jamie Vardy some broadcast interviews nearby. Vardy finished first and sidled over, announcing he wanted to ask a question. 'It's Jamie Vardy from the Vardy Express,' he said. 'How big is the diameter of your head?' Maguire's nickname was born – 'Slabhead'.

The coverage engendered was so positive it was giddy.

'We did a lot that was different and there was even more we wanted to do,' Sullivan said. 'But just the recognition that [doing media] was important helped change how the players felt about being there and changed how the public felt about the team. And guess what? When the public are behind the team, you buggers have to change your narrative.'

The sudden comfort, in each other's company, felt by media and players alike, was something Wayne Rooney had dreamed of during his England years. When Rooney became captain, one of his first acts was to treat the press to lunch at Wing's Chinese restaurant in Manchester in an attempt to build bonds. At a Football Writers dinner, he made a passionate speech about the need for the press and England teams to work in partnership, a quote from which was on the cover of Demetriou's plan: 'The younger players now have to understand that the media are a massive part of football . . . the media has a huge influence on the game and, especially on the young England players, they are the ones who have to go out and perform under huge pressures . . . at this moment in time there is a huge gap between the media and the players. The quicker both come together and meet in the middle, the better it will be for English football.'

As England captain, often Rooney found himself at odds with what at the time was an attitude of caution within the FA towards communications. 'In 2015, when France played at Wembley following the Paris [terrorist] attacks, before the pre-conference I remember sitting in the office with Roy [Hodgson] and Martin Glenn, disagreeing with the FA's briefing.

'We knew, because of the sensitivities, there would be difficult questions that should be answered carefully and clearly but the FA advised we say the events in Paris were tragic but not for us to talk about. I said, "No, we're all adults, we have to say how we feel." We had to speak from the heart. People would have seen through rehearsed answers,' he recalled. Getting away from the 'them against us' relationship the team and media had at tournaments was something they talked about when Southgate became manager.

The openness players spoke with in Russia came not just from the change in FA comms strategy but the work on sharing they had done with Pippa Grange, and before her, Rebecca Symes and Jonny Zneimer. It came from the culture work with Owen Eastwood, with its emphasis on taking ownership of their story. Other elements played their part. The press pack itself was younger and less cynical and certain club managers who filled players' heads with suspicion about the press – like Sir Alex Ferguson and Kenny Dalglish – were gone.

But the biggest factor was Southgate himself. 'All the transformational plans our department had would have been met with a flat "no" by certain past England managers,' Sullivan said. 'But the combination of Dan saying [media] is important and Gareth coming in allowed them to take place.'

Southgate, the ex-*Sunday Times* columnist and ITV pundit, had inherent conviction the press could be turned into a positive part of England's tournament experience and at the NBA game he attended in February in Minneapolis was courtside with Chris Wright, an Englishman who worked with the Timberwolves for 26 years before becoming chief executive of their soccer franchise. 'One of the things he wanted to talk about was how to prepare players for media focus and access,' said Wright. 'He was amazed by the amount of access the media get on game day.'

After England's final World Cup warm-up against Costa Rica, Southgate had tried to explain why he was so keen for players to be open, whether in front of journalists or in team meetings. There had been concerns among some about potential racism in Russia and Southgate had encouraged conversations around that. The players were also encouraged to take the lead in unit meetings – something commonplace in rugby, and which Reddin was particularly keen on.

'We're asking them to open up quite a bit on their own feelings about things and we've discussed the possible situation over racism which was an important connection between the team,' Southgate said. 'We open up tactical discussions and they know they can have an input and suggest solutions. They have a voice and I want them to have some ownership. They have a say in the way we work and that's healthy for their growth.'

While Lingard and Pickford raced unicorns in the pool the day after beating Tunisia, their manager went for a run. He did so most days. He put his music on and struck out along the road running from ForRestMix alongside the beach. He was going well – on course to beat his personal 10 kilometres record, he claimed – when he clipped a step and stumbled over, landing on his right elbow. He got back on his feet quickly but looked at his arm. It was pointing in a funny direction. He called England's doctor, Rob Chakraverty, and waited for help, pulling down his cap to avoid being recognised by passers-by. The knock to the elbow had dislocated his shoulder. The next time the players saw him, he was walking into a team meeting wearing a sheepish grin – and a black medical sling.

The FA's senior delegation were enjoying some culture on their day off and were in St Petersburg's famous Hermitage Museum surrounded by art treasures hoarded by Catherine the Great when Sullivan's phone rang. *Are you sitting down? Well, the manager's broken his arm.*

'It felt like the classic England moment. Creating a crisis for ourselves. There was a conversation as a media team: "What do we do about this?" But Gareth was stoic, he was "Get on with the job." We needed a way of defusing things and Eddie Keogh [the England photographer] had taken pictures of Gareth addressing the squad in a sling. We looked at those and I said let's just release the photos. "Boss is back at work" type of thing,' Sullivan said.

Southgate had doubts. Would he look weak and not able to do his work properly if images of him in the sling were released? 'I said, "No, it's the opposite. It looks like you're getting on with it,"' Sullivan recalled. 'We released the photos, he did a press conference, made a self-deprecating joke and the story moved on.'

Turning up at the Cronwell, Southgate greeted reporters with a grin and made fun of himself. 'I might not be celebrating any goals as athletically in future. The doc has made it clear that punching the air is not an option,' he quipped. Journalists and their editors, having been undecided whether this was a crisis or not, went with the fun side of things in their reporting. 'Sling it to win it' was the headline in *The Sun*.

For Sullivan, 'Shouldergate: The Crisis That Never Was', encapsulated Southgate's deftness in communications. 'Before doing media he'd meet our team. "What are we talking about?" he'd ask. If non-football stuff was likely to crop up, Greg, Andy or me would talk him through it and say, "Here's the FA position." He'd ask intelligent questions. He'd say, "How important is it?" Then he'd go and blow everyone away in his press conference,' Sullivan said.

The agreement was that the media team and others in the FA would try and handle off-field politics – at the start of his reign it was Sullivan who appeared alongside then FA chairman Greg Clarke before a House of Commons select committee – so that Southgate could concentrate on football. But when he did have to address issues away from the pitch, he was to prove a master. It came from breadth of character, and experience.

Just look at Southgate's time at the FA, says Sullivan. He has traipsed around the country, selling new ideas in kids' football. He has negotiated with the Premier League, helped drive the early strategy meetings about DNA and St George's Park. And in his early days as head of elite development he sat at an ordinary workstation – near Sir Trevor Brooking's office – in the open-plan offices at Wembley, in the midst of all the ordinary staff. 'If he walked into Wembley, even now, he would know people on every team and be able to ask them specific questions. This is a guy who once sat at a desk in the same office as everyone, tapping away on his PC. There's a personal loyalty from a lot of people in the organisation to him and he gets the whole FA ecosystem,' Sullivan said.

'He's big on identity and that knowledge of how everything at the FA fits together, and the thread from grassroots football through development teams to the senior side has helped him tell a rounder story about English football.

'I'm not going to claim that any of us said, "Gareth, what we really need is for you to be this kind of voice for societal change." But we did encourage him to communicate in a wider way than just football matches and he has taken that and developed that in his own style.'

The success of the 'boss is back to work' line on Southgate's shoulder furthered a strategy that shapes Three Lions comms to this day. There was an internal debate about how to position the England team, and the marketing department, then headed by future FA chief executive Mark Bullingham, came up with ideas around work. The line around squad announcements became 'let's get to work'. Imagery of players in the gym would be accompanied by captions like 'the boys at work'. It fitted Southgate's sensibilities perfectly and was a conscious attempt to address the old criticism of England teams as full of overpaid slackers who do not care.

* * *

In Nizhny Novgorod, England met Panama, whom Belgium found hard to break down in their opening game. John Stones scored after eight minutes and by half-time England were 5-0 up, with Stones adding another, Kane lashing home two penalties, and Lingard popping a gorgeous curling effort into the top corner. The final score of 6-1, after Kane fortuitously completed his hat-trick, was England's biggest ever World Cup victory. The team who went out in Brazil after six days were through to the next round in Russia in exactly the same time span.

The group returned to Repino for more darts, unicorns and serene training sessions. Southgate dispensed with his sling. The final group match, versus Belgium in Kaliningrad, was a dead rubber and Southgate rotated, resting Kane and seven other first-choice players while giving minutes to all the back-ups. When Danny Welbeck came on as a substitute for Trent Alexander-Arnold with 11 minutes left, it meant England had used all 20 of the outfield players in their squad.

Clever? Having experienced the frustrations of life as an unused player at the 2002 World Cup, Southgate knew spreading the minutes around would boost morale throughout the squad. Nobody would be sat in a corner of a squad meeting, feeling a month away from their family was in vain. Strategic? Perhaps. Belgium beat the weakened line-up 1-0 to win Group G – a dubious reward for it meant they progressed to the side of the draw including Brazil, France, Portugal and Argentina. Whereas England's path, now, was a second-round match with Colombia then a quarter-final with the winners of Sweden v Switzerland.

Before the Panama match, Raheem Sterling penned a moving piece for The Players' Tribune about himself, his family, his upbringing, his motivations, his hopes. About what he had suffered, what he had overcome and the misperceptions about him along the way.

He told his story.

The article ended like this: 'If you grew up the same way I grew up, don't listen to what certain tabloids want to tell you. They just want to steal your joy. They just want to pull you down.

'I'm telling you right now . . . England is still a place where a naughty boy who comes from nothing can live his dream.'

And two days after the Belgium defeat it was Dele Alli's turn to do media in the Cronwell Hotel. He talked about the impact of Pippa Grange ('she's an amazing person, everyone listens to her when she talks') and of the motivational 'Euro 96 to a new dawn' video that Southgate showed the squad. 'We can't worry what happened in the past. It's a new team, new day, new manager. We've come here with the mentality we want to win,' he said.

Afterwards, a journalist was in the car park outside when Dele appeared, looking for the shuttle to take him back to the ForRestMix. They started chatting about Fortnite. The reporter's 11-year-old son loved Fortnite and the goal celebrations inspired by the game Dele was known for. Coincidentally, the boy FaceTimed his father in the middle of the conversation and asked to say hello to the player.

Dele took the phone. 'What, is this actually Dele Alli?' said the kid, incredulously. 'Yes,' Dele smiled. Seeing the boy had headphones on, Dele asked, 'You playing Fortnite? How're you doing?'

A discussion ensued over tactics, weapons and strategies – ending only when Dele was reminded he had to go.

The boy and his dad would never forget it.

The shirt had seldom looked lighter.

* * *

Jordan Henderson looked so calm, in his bubble, going through his rehearsed routine. To the penalty spot he strolled, doing keepy-uppies, head down, looking at the ball and not the mass of enemy supporters behind the goal. He put down the ball, stepped back, waited for the whistle and breathed. Up he came: a sweet strike just like in practice, in the corner and to the goalkeeper's left. But in shoot-outs, when the Three Lions are on your chest, you have to know it won't always be your day.

This wasn't Henderson's day. David Ospina, Colombia's goalkeeper, had faced a Henderson penalty playing for Arsenal against Liverpool in 2015. He had very nearly saved it and now, even before Henderson reached the ball, was on the move, springing in the right direction. He shot out his left arm and with a granite wrist was able to keep his hand stiff enough to push the powerful shot away.

Fine margins. Henderson's kick had been a perfect save for one thing – it was two feet off the ground, at the ideal height to save. In 2015, when Ospina got a hand on the ball but could not stop it squirming over the line, Henderson had gone lower.

So, there he was: Southgate's vice-captain, England's most vocal player on the pitch – a totem of the team, failing at the very moment his country needed him to succeed. Penalty traumas from down the decades whirled through England supporters' minds. You thought of England's shoot-out record in tournaments – won one, lost six. They were the only nation on the planet to have taken part in three World Cup shoot-outs and lost them all.

So, Henderson turned and began walking back to the centre circle. It was then that something unprecedented happened. Henderson straightened his back, raised his chin and stared straight ahead, walking calmly – almost proudly – to where his teammates stood. Kieran Trippier shook his hand, then Harry Kane. 'You wouldn't know that his penalty had been saved,' said Ben Lyttleton, author of the seminal *Twelve Yards: The Art & Psychology of the Perfect Penalty.*

So many things went into a shoot-out finally going right for

England, in the Spartak Stadium on 3 July 2018 – and one of the biggest was what Henderson did at exactly the moment it was going wrong.

* * *

Penalties had been England's curse stretching back to 1990, when in their very first tournament shoot-out the team, managed at that point by Bobby Robson, lost to West Germany in a World Cup semi-final. Consider this. When their team lined up against Colombia in Moscow, there were English men and women who had reached 22 years of age, been married, had children, and voted in two general elections, yet had never been alive when their country won a shoot-out at a finals.

The only English triumph on penalties was against Spain in the quarter-finals of Euro 96. Four days later, in the semi-finals, came the defeat to Germany that hinged on Southgate's infamous miss. The accidental way Southgate ended up as a penalty taker that day – volunteering only through a sense of duty after being approached by manager Terry Venables and his assistant Bryan Robson a few seconds before the shoot-out began – encapsulated England's lack of rigour, down the years, regarding penalties.

Before that shoot-out he had only taken one penalty in his life – and missed. Afterwards, his distress was such he lay awake all night worrying about the backlash 'and it was frightening'. Teammates had not been able to assuage his fears. He told the German writer Ronnie Reng, 'Stuart Pearce had said to me, "Gareth, tomorrow I'm going home to feed my horses. I'll look at them and say, 'We lost to Germany on penalties again.' And they'll answer, 'What do we care? Give us some carrots now.'"'

World Cup 1998: out on penalties to Argentina. Euro 2004:

semi-final heartbreak against Portugal in the shoot-out. At Euro 2012, it felt England were not just beaten on penalties but humiliated when Italy's Andrea Pirlo spooned a dismissive Panenka over Joe Hart in riposte to Hart's attempted gamesmanship. Then there was World Cup 2006, when the 'golden generation' fell in another shoot-out to Portugal.

The Portuguese were so confident of that happening they even played for penalties for the last hour of the game while having a man advantage after Wayne Rooney's sending-off. Extraordinarily, England's manager, Sven-Göran Eriksson, had admitted to Portugal's keeper, Ricardo, before kick-off: 'My players are scared of penalties.'

Eriksson had actually flown in a performance specialist – his friend, Marc Sagal, an American who worked with the US military, Olympic athletes and high-end business clients. But Sagal arrived only two days before the Portugal game and Eriksson was too nervous about press ridicule to make Sagal's involvement public.

When Dan Ashworth became the FA's technical director, he knew all the projects to improve England, from grassroots reform to DNA, would be seen to count for nothing if the senior team could not change its fortunes from 12 yards. The first step was the holistic efforts to affect mindset which began with the work of Lane4. 'With psychology, everybody goes, "Can they take it?" [a penalty]. That's it. One of the units is delivering under pressure – but delivering under pressure is not just taking a penalty. That's a big pressure moment but it's dealing with the pressure of a tournament, dealing with the pressure of being away from your family. And psychology and mental wellbeing and culture are all aligned. So, we got Owen Eastwood to come in and do something around what does it mean to play for England and wear the badge?

'To strike a successful penalty you've got to go and see that guy in the corner, the psychologist? No, it's about delivering psychology through the whole staff. We're all responsible for psychology, we're all responsible for mental wellbeing, we're all responsible for culture,' Ashworth said. Southgate's soul-baring was fundamental. 'He's a brilliant leader, he's really good at connecting people, he's really good at bringing people into the conversation, making people feel valued. And brilliant at building a team and making people feel part of the team, whether that's the head of security or Harry Kane,' said Ashworth.

Ashworth commissioned a study into shoot-outs led by England's lead analyst, Steve O'Brien, and overseen by lead data scientist, Rhys Long. It dug into every detail. The elements of a successful penalty, from where a shot is placed to how long is taken between the whistle and striking the ball. The preparation and information goalkeepers need. Behaviours, like the long walk to the spot or how and where the takers should stand while waiting before and after their kicks. Other aspects such as what the coaching staff should do while the shoot-out is under way and what the manager should do before it starts. There were some striking findings, like the extent to which England tended to rush their spot-kicks compared to more successful nations. In tournament shoot-outs, English players started their run-ups an average 0.28 seconds after the referee's whistle, not far off the time of a sprinter leaving the blocks. No country's takers were hastier.

Entering the picture here is a perhaps surprising figure – a Basque professor of managerial economics and strategy at the London School of Economics called Ignacio Palacios-Huerta. The pioneer of penalties research, Palacios-Huerta, an Athletic Bilbao fan, started analysing shoot-outs as a way to verify the Nash Equilibrium – proposed by the Nobel laureate economist and mathematician John Forbes Nash, immortalised by Russell Crowe in the movie *A Beautiful Mind*. According to Nash, in a zero-sum game – where a win for one player means a loss for the other – the best approach is to vary moves unpredictably but his theory is so complex, economists have found it hard to test in the real world. Palacios-Huerta figured a football shoot-out was an ideal scenario for proving Nash: a zero-sum game for two players with simple rules and easily observable outcomes.

His first paper on shoot-outs was published in 1999. He followed in 2003 by examining more than 1,000 penalty kicks in major national and international competitions then in 2010, with a colleague, conducted a further study into almost 3,000 penalties from games between 1970 and 2008. His data verified the Nash Equilibrium. By 2014 he had updated his analysis to include more than 9,000 penalty kicks. His work was used by Barcelona and the Netherlands and its first significant use in English football was by Chelsea in the 2008 Champions League final. He and Avram Grant had a mutual friend and Palacios-Huerta's vast database revealed a glaring fact about Manchester United's goalkeeper, Edwin van der Sar: for penalties, van der Sar usually dived to his right.

In the shoot-out, Chelsea's players kept putting the ball to van der Sar's left and scoring, and had John Terry not slipped and put his kick against the post, Palacios-Huerta would have been the backroom hero of a Chelsea victory. Then came sudden death and van der Sar, realising what Chelsea were doing, pointed to his left as Nicolas Anelka stepped up for his kick. Spooked, Anelka became the first to ignore Palacios-Huerta's advice and sent his shot the other way, and van der Sar saved.

Palacios-Huerta is even able to use regression analysis to detect trends in the habits of takers and goalkeepers, helping predict when a particular player is going to shoot right, left or down the middle and doing similar with keepers' movements. England's analysis team contracted him to help with preparation for tournaments but his involvement remains so secretive that until a request was made to speak to him for this book, members of England's communications department had never heard of him. The request was declined by the FA, who are protective of his data, which was once again part of Southgate's armoury at Euro 2024.

Even more important to shaping Southgate's practices were Steve Cooper's Under-17s. In May 2017, they lost a European Championship final on penalties to Spain, converting just once in the shoot-out, leaving Cooper determined that spot kicks would never again hold back his outstanding young side. They had a World Cup in October and two warm-up games in September, the first a 0-0 draw with Brazil in Shrewsbury. At Cooper's behest there was a shoot-out after the game, to help players to practise. England won 5-4, but some leading lights in the team declined to take kicks. 'The next day we had a review meeting. I said, "Lads, we're not going to let this get the better of us. When we go to India [for the World Cup] we're going to have a meeting about penalties. I'm not letting this get the better of you and your England careers. We're going to face up to it,"' Cooper said.

In Mumbai, the team's psychologist, Emma Rowe, led a workshop. 'She was brilliant,' said Cooper. 'We divided the shoot-out into four parts: the bit after the whistle at the end of the game including the selection of takers, the standing on the halfway line, the walk up, the penalty. We went through it and put a bit of data on it as well. Like everything now, it's data and human behaviours. That meeting was really powerful – because [penalties] was an elephant in the room.'

Players were asked which of three categories they belonged to. One: somebody who would always want to take a penalty (striker Rhian Brewster's hand shot up). Two: somebody who might take a penalty but felt unsure. Three: those who see penalties as their worst nightmare. Most belonged to the middle category, but a couple admitted being in the 'nightmare' one. Cooper thanked them for being open and said, "There's no shame here, lads; the only way you could let people down is by not being honest and putting yourself in the wrong category.' There followed a discussion about emotions and reasons with Cooper's staff taking notes.

The meeting seemed to lighten mental loads and the squad had a structured penalty practice at every training, with rankings kept and Mike Marsh, Cooper's assistant, in charge of compiling a list of best takers and going round players at the final whistle to tell them the 'batting order'. England's second-round game with Japan duly went to penalties and they won – smashing home all five spot kicks. It felt like a seminal victory for an England side. 'There are all these little mini journeys on the big journey,' said Cooper who presented the Under-17s' penalties work to Southgate as part of his tournament review.

Cooper was part of the team of age group coaches brought to Russia to assist the England seniors. Their role was to scout opponents and support crucial work being done at the tournament by O'Brien and fellow senior analysts, Mike Baker and Dan Parker. Southgate and his staff scouted the Group G opposition while a list of teams England might meet in the knockout stages was divvied up between Cooper, Simpson, Marsh, Aidy Boothroyd and Keith Downing. In advance of the tournament they studied these sides on video. Cooper got Colombia and travelled to Russia already knowing plenty about their coach, José Pékerman, and his players after watching all 18 of Colombia's qualifying games.

Cooper attended Colombia's three Group H matches, even staying at the same hotel as the South Americans when they played their last game against Senegal in Samara. He sat with Downing, who had

Senegal, and it was amusing: if the game was a draw or Colombia won, Cooper would be flying to Repino to present to Southgate, but if Senegal were the victors, it would be Downing. Cooper remembers how incredibly organised the process was: '[Our analysis] was all on the same template, the same coding windows, everything was up to speed. I even remember how planned and prepared the travel was to get me everywhere, like you had your own travel company. Rhys Long was, "Okay, we'll need you here and here," even down to telling you what kind of working space you'd have at different locations.'

Cooper's findings on Colombia were fed to a hub at St George's Park, staffed by analysts and coaches. He suggested which clips to show and they turned the whole thing into a slick presentation. The day after Colombia defeated Senegal 1-0, he was up at 2 a.m. to fly to St Petersburg and be driven to ForRestMix, where a coaches' room and mini analysis room were set up. He remembers, in his presentation, describing Colombia as having a 'flamboyant style' – which Steve Holland liked, and used in his training sessions before the match. He ran through Colombia's system, how they played in the different zones, what they did in transitions, the characteristics of every player in their team. 'The irony of it all was James Rodríguez got injured and it was a secret whether he'd be fit or not, and he was the key to so much of what they did,' said Cooper. 'In the game Colombia played a diamond – and they'd never played a diamond before.'

Penalties were the responsibility of England's goalkeeping coach, Martyn Margetson, and attacking coach Allan Russell. They had players practise their techniques so much that each morning at the Spartak Zelenogorsk stadium, the groundsman had to lay out a new penalty spot because the previous day's spot was worn out. Used in the practice was a special penalty-taking net, with target areas marked for takers to hit, brought from St George's Park. Russell and Margetson oversaw the rehearsal of all aspects of a taker's routine, from leaving their teammates on the halfway line to striking their kick. Each player's routine was personal to them – what was important was that it was honed and stuck to. Before every kick, Jordan Pickford was to walk from the box and hand the taker the ball. Not only was it psychologically important to receive the ball from someone friendly, the ritual would also break up that dreaded long walk to the spot.

In the analysis room at the team hotel on the eve of the Colombia clash, Margetson sat painstakingly writing out notes on every potential Colombian penalty taker and taped these to a water bottle. He went through the list with Pickford, who would take the bottle on to the field and keep it near him during the shoot-out.

England were superb in the match, but the game was to be decided by a penalty shoot-out. Southgate moved calmly between his players with the list. Individually, he went to each taker, putting his arm round their shoulder, showing them the piece of paper, reassuring them of the plan. He gathered his players and staff for a huddle, crouching in the middle of it and going round the circle, making eye contact, as once again he reinforced what had been talked about in preparation. One of the cardinal rules: 'Relax, take a breath, and as soon as you hear the whistle, don't go immediately.' Then Southgate went back to the touchline and put his arm round Holland, who put his arm round Margetson, who put his arm round Russell and so it went until there was a long line of England, stretching from manager to unused substitutes, standing on the side. England's takers stood on the halfway line as near as possible to them – knowing the data showed that such proximity was also linked to being successful.

Kane scored, firing a low, unerring shot to Ospina's right. Marcus Rashford scored, striking his penalty so crisply it sounded like a Tiger

Woods 300-yarder thwacking off the driver. But Radamel Falcao, Cuadrado and Luis Muriel had rammed in Colombia's first three penalties without giving Pickford a chance. And then up stepped Henderson. And missed.

Henderson's purposeful, proud walk back to the halfway line was as planned as every other element of England's shoot-out. It told the rest that things were still okay, that there was nothing to fear, not even missing. 'Gareth Southgate told his players that penalties were a trainable skill that could be improved,' said Ben Lyttleton, and for Young, an England player since the Steve McClaren days, this was a whole new level of preparation.

'A lot of people weren't really talking about the different steps of taking penalties,' said Young in the FIFA film, *The Long Walk*. '[Under Southgate] there were penalty shoot-outs at the end of every training session. And it wasn't just the penalties that we practised. It was being together on the halfway line, it was standing to get an advantage right on the centre circle, our goalkeeper picking up the ball and giving it to us as players.

'Left out was a piece of paper. You put your name on it where you wanted to go in the shoot-out and where you were going to put your kick.' He had written down that he wanted to go first or second and 'straight down the middle!' and was statistically identified as one of England's five best takers, but having been substituted in extra time it meant the 'batting order' changed but, no sweat, Southgate had the stats to show who should take it instead. After Henderson's miss, Mateus Uribe stepped up for Colombia and crashed his shot against the bar. Next for England was Kieran Trippier. Striking the sweetest strike, he found the top corner. 'He did something that we rarely see players do for England. Score, in a penalty shoot-out, when the pressure is on, when the chips are down, when the stakes are at their highest,' said Lyttleton. 'And that is the moment the momentum of this shoot-out flipped.'

Colombia's next taker was Carlos Bacca. Pickford looked at his bottle. Bacca struck his shot hard and centrally, slightly to Pickford's right, at a difficult height. But as the Colombian's boot met the ball, Pickford was already springing, forward and decisively to his right, and he shot up a ramrod left arm to palm it away. His celebration was an almighty fist pump. And so it was left to Eric Dier. The plan had been for Jamie Vardy to take the fifth penalty but Vardy had tweaked his groin, meaning Dier was suddenly promoted from the reserve to top five in the 'batting list.' You would not have known it. Dier sauntered up and, as if it were just another moment in training, stroked England into the quarter-finals. And it was gone. The ghost of penalties. 'If you could choose to win that way you would choose it every time,' Southgate told television, grinning. 'We're trying to write our own history, I've talked to the players about that. They write their own stories. We didn't have to be bowed by the pressure of the past. They've done that.'

Russell, a Scot, initially did not comprehend what winning a tournament shoot-out meant to England. Then he walked into the coaches' room. There was Ashworth, in tears.

* * *

As Dier's penalty hit the back of Ospina's net, players charged across the pitch, the coaching staff hollered and hugged like World Cup winners – and Ashworth jumped to his feet in the stand. His phone went flying from his pocket and smashed on the floor, the battery coming out. 'My goodness me it was emotional,' he said.

When Ashworth looks back over his six years at the FA, the point he wants to emphasise is teamwork. 'Collective effort,' he said. 'We had some brilliant people in the organisation who came up with so many ideas. Some of them were rubbish but many were great. We generated a culture where people could say, "What about doing this? What about going on a camp?'" Or: what about taking a Spanish economist, a Scottish ex-striker, a Welsh coach, a putting mat, a water bottle, and years of practice, psychology, analysis and personal experience on the manager's part – and mixing it all together with a tiny dash of luck to break tournament football's longest curse?

Teamwork was the main characteristic of what England were doing on the pitch. In the group stage, Southgate's side made 25 uninterrupted passes before scoring their sixth goal against Panama – the longest sequence for a World Cup goal since 1966.

This was DNA in action. Playing through the thirds, players able to handle the ball. There was a balance to Southgate's side and a lack of stars – Kane apart, and he did not *act* like a star. A far cry from Iceland, from Cape Town. Albeit, as England's final two games in the competition would show, there was still a level of football above where they were.

* * *

Between the group stage and the game with Colombia, England's players had a day off. Many saw their families and some played golf. Lingard, Rashford, Danny Welbeck and Trent Alexander-Arnold went to a theme park. They ran screaming from a roller coaster after thinking their seat belts were broken before dissolving into fits of laughter when realising they were okay.

For Lingard, the Sweden quarter-final was emotional. Since his childhood his mum had battled depression. She would drop him at school and go straight back to bed and stay there until the end of the day and this continued into his adult life. Initially, she could not travel to Russia, but when the teams lined up in Samara he looked at the section for players' families and friends – and there she was. It gave him goosebumps. 'I was dying for her to be there and she came to the quarter-finals and that just made me so happy. Because in her situation . . . she found that motivation to come and see her son play at a World Cup. I told her I'm really proud of her, that it's brave what she did,' he said when opening up about his personal and family struggles in *The Diary of a CEO* podcast, in 2023. And reflecting on his England journey for this book, the former Manchester United player described Russia as one of the sunniest chapters of his career. 'Gareth was top. That World Cup was top and Steve Holland was a top guy, and it was perfect,' he said. 'They were really happy times. Gareth made it family orientated. The rooms had pictures of our mums, our families and in the free time we could do what we want, see our families, go to a theme park even. It was about enjoying it and sometimes you've got to get away from the football side and do the normal side of things – like when you go to a theme park with your boys and have fun.'

England's first World Cup semi-final in 28 years was against Croatia in Moscow's Luzhniki Stadium. The cost of flights and tickets spiralled, with one fan telling the BBC they had spent more than £7,000 attending the game. It did not stop England supporters travelling in huge numbers. As many as 10,000 descended on Moscow, singing that familiar chorus: 'It's Coming Home'. There would be problems with that – and with assertions in the English-speaking media that Zlatko Dalić's team would be tired, having had extra time and penalties in consecutive knockout games. 'England the biggest winners as exhausted Croatia edge out raucous Russia' was the goal.com headline after the Croatians' shoot-out victory over Russia in their quarter-final.

England could not have started the match better, Trippier arcing a free kick into the top corner after only five minutes. For a period, they were dominant, ran free. Dele found Lingard, who rolled a pass through for Kane and he should have scored twice, yet put his shot too close to Danijel Subašić then knocked the rebound against the post. But even before half-time the weather of the game was changing.

In midfield, Luka Modrić, Ivan Rakitić and Marcelo Brozović were playing keep ball with each other, manoeuvring England around and bringing their team into threatening positions. Every movement of Ivan Perišić looked terrifying. Mario Mandžukić seemed able to occupy the English back three on his own. Dalić's veterans appeared to be playing in fast-forward, Southgate's youngsters in slo-mo.

Perišić scored, with an opportunistic volley from Šime Vrsaljko's cross. Then Perišić hit the post. Then Ante Rebić went close. England clung on for extra time but at the start of its second period, Perišić sent the ball goalwards with a header, Stones switched off and Mandžukić shot through Pickford's legs to score. Stats are not everything but they do provide little Polaroids and here are some from the game: Kane lost the ball 21 times, Sterling completed just nine passes, Pickford kicked long 40 times. A cruel video went round on social media of all Henderson's hoofs and hacked passes. Crowed Vrsaljko, 'The all-round perception was that this is a new-look England who have changed their ways of punting long balls upfield, but when we pressed them, it turned out they hadn't.'

That was not all the Croatians were saying. Modrić told ITV that England 'should be humble and respect their opponents more' and said in another post-match interview, 'All these words from them we take, we were reading and we were saying: "Okay, today we will see who will be tired."' And when Dalić's assistant, Vedran Ćorluka, passed English journalists in the mixed zone, he offered them a cutting observation. 'It's not coming home,' he said without breaking stride.

Croatia had found glitches in the system. By using two quality, aggressive wingers (Perišić and Rebić), they forced Southgate's wing-backs to defend, meaning England's formation became 5-3-2. This provided opportunity for Vrsaljko and Croatia's other full-back, Ivan Strinić, to move up and even sometimes infield. Often, in that battleground where England lose so many big tournament games – midfield – it was five v three in Croatia's favour. And without the right supply the free-running trio of Lingard, Dele and Sterling were suddenly caged.

However, speaking to English Sunday newspaper reporters on the night, he seemed quite capable of the right analysis. Yes, Croatia had success against his system 'but the biggest issue was not keeping the ball. Fundamentally we have to keep the ball better,' he said. He noted how 'under pressure' his players regressed and 'went a bit safer'.

Russia had been a great journey forward – but there were many miles of road still to travel.

For Ashworth, it was the end. Two months after the World Cup he became Brighton's technical director. He was 47 and felt that after six years at the FA he was at a fork in the road. 'I felt if I committed to the next cycle – it was four and a half years because the Qatar World Cup was in December – that would have taken me to ten years at the FA. And at that point I would feel, or be perceived as, institutionalised,' he reflected.

Looking back on Russia, he feels no less proud now than he did when flying home from the World Cup in 2018. 'You go there to play seven games,' he said. 'I remember saying that to you lads at the start and some of you laughed. Well, the seventh game wasn't the one we wanted, it was a third/fourth play-off – but we did it.

'The margins are so small, but when we did the tournament debrief and asked, "Did we do everything we possibly could to prepare?" the answer was at least 90 per cent yes, and that's what your job is to do.'

Southgate? 'Gareth came of age but never lost his humility, his connection with people. He wanted to keep on learning – so he didn't come home from that tournament and say, "Look, I got to the semi-final of a World Cup." That's not him.

'I just saw somebody enjoying himself. And of course you enjoy yourself when it goes well, but we had a group of staff and a camaraderie.

'I still go back to it and that was the best four or five weeks of my life. Sorry, Sian!'

CHAPTER 5
YOUNG HEARTS RUN FREE

'¡Así, así, así gana el Madrid!' ('That's how Madrid wins!') bawled the Real Madrid midfielder, clambering into the away end to get as close as he could to the ultras, who returned his clarion call. '¡Vamos!' he yelled before being dragged away. Jude Bellingham, by his standards, hadn't dominated the game, though the delicacy of touch to bring the ball down to set up the crucial Real Madrid goal was just another exquisite moment in his scarcely credulous season.

It wasn't so much that Bellingham was the best player on the pitch. You could argue that another young Englishman, Phil Foden, was even better over the two legs of the Champions League quarter-final. What was more noticeable was the charisma and leadership of a 20-year-old in his first season at Real Madrid. Michael Owen, a Ballon d'Or winner when he moved there, spoke about 'feeling like an outsider' and how he 'struggled to assert his personality' in the highly politicised Real Madrid dressing room. David Beckham talked about how nervous he was on his first day. He spent weeks settling in and years before he ventured to speak Spanish in public.

Bellingham's Spanish that night would not merit a GCSE A*, but in terms of demonstrating his affinity with fans, his centrality to their cause and the fact that he had become the biggest character in the best team in the world, it spoke volumes. Bellingham is Real Madrid's poster boy. Only Vinícius Júnior is up there with him, but when the team looks for a leader, it is Bellingham who steps up. The weekend after that game, having knocked Manchester City out of the Champions League, Bellingham would play the biggest club match in world football against Barcelona. He had already made a huge mark on El Clásico in October 2023. It's meant to be intimidating travelling to Barcelona as a €100 million Real Madrid signing, but Bellingham scored from 20 yards to equalise there before being in place to hit the winner in the 92nd minute.

He celebrated in the corner like he always does, arms outstretched in the mode of the Christ the Redeemer statue in Rio de Janeiro. On this occasion he eyeballed the small band of travelling Real Madrid fans high in the top tier. Behind him Antonio Rüdiger shouted: 'Again! Do it again for them!' meaning the Madrid fans. So, he did.

It maybe isn't a deliberately Messianic celebration but it has that effect. The 20-year-old from Stourbridge, son of police officer and 'non-league football legend' Mark – his police identification number was 1966 – and human resources manager Denise is simply announcing to the world that nothing fazes him.

In the Barça fixture at the Santiago Bernabéu a few days after that win in Manchester, there would be yet more from Bellingham. There were just the first grumblings in Madrid that maybe he wasn't being quite talismanic enough, having not scored in six games: not enough water turned into wine of late. In this game, in which a Real Madrid victory would pretty much ensure they won La Liga, they twice went behind. But Bellingham popped up at the end to score the winner in the 91st minute. It's just what he does. This time he was so excited he eschewed his trademark celebration and linked arms with Lucas Vázquez to square dance around the corner flag.

First experiences at Real Madrid aren't meant to be like this. It takes time to adjust, to build a reputation. At the press conference to announce his signing back in the summer of 2023, club president Florentino Pérez wanted to convey the sense that Bellingham was born for Madrid so finished his speech: 'Welcome home, Jude!' It seemed bombastic at the time, but Bellingham simply walked into the building and pretty much took over.

After a couple of months at the club, Alfredo Relaño, editor of hugely influential and famously demanding Spanish sports tabloid *AS*, wrote: 'Bellingham is a huge success and as a midfielder who plays like an attacker, he genuinely reminds me of Alfredo Di Stéfano. The elegance in his gait and the manner in which he uses the ball, his ferocity and indefatigability in battle, he's half artist, half warrior. He's the organisational focal point for the attacking game and yet still able to be the goalscorer finishing chances.' There is no higher praise at Real Madrid: Di Stéfano is the legend who bestrides the club in the way in which Sir Bobby Charlton does Manchester United. From there it was difficult to up the ante but some journalists tried, reaching for the Diego Maradona comparison when Bellingham scored an astonishing goal after a mazy run in Naples in the stadium named after the world's greatest player.

His La Liga debut was in the stadium many think the most intimidating in Spain, Athletic Bilbao's San Mamés. He scored of course, a slightly fortunate scuffed shot into the ground, which bounced over the goalkeeper in a 2-0 win. He stood steely-faced just yards away from a wall of red-and-white-shirted Athletic fans, stretched out his arms and stared them square in the eye. It caused predictable apoplexy and a cascade of shrill whistles. He grinned only when his Real Madrid teammates joined him but, just in case the Athletic fans hadn't quite got the message, as the celebrations broke up, he turned to face them again and repeated his gesture. By now the fury was off the scale. Bellingham seemed not to care.

At Birmingham City, they knew. The youngest ever to play for the club at 16 years old and the youngest ever to score – another fortunate, scuffed, deflected shot – he gave them one unforgettable season before moving to Borussia Dortmund. But in the highlights reel of that season it isn't so much his goals that stand out, nor the precocious weaving around grown men, shrugging them off and leaving them stranded. It's a moment against West Brom at home when he crunches into Nathan Ferguson. The crowd roared in appreciation and Bellingham, a Blues fan from birth, picks himself up and, gesticulating with his arms, demands still more noise from the home fans in a derby game. Many players never develop the confidence to enthuse fans like that. Bellingham had just completed his GCSEs. In a relegation fight, Bellingham was their leader.

It didn't look promising early on. 'Jude didn't want to play a lot of football,' recalled mum Denise, remembering his early years. 'He didn't seem to be interested. If you gave him a ball, he'd throw it. He didn't seem to want to kick it. It just seemed nothing happened until he was six and then something clicked.'

'I never really enjoyed it,' said Bellingham. 'I just did it because my dad wanted me to. I really enjoyed the racing at the start, the cat and mouse games. But the actual football I didn't really love.'

This isn't the standard origin story of great players. Foden would irritate his family by always having a ball at his feet, even in the kitchen and living room, from his toddler years upwards, always trying to learn new tricks. For Bellingham it needed an epiphany moment. 'One weekend it just clicked and then that was all I wanted to do all the time.'

Bellingham was destined for Birmingham City's academy once he had caught the football bug. Dad Mark scored more than 700 goals for Leamington, Stourbridge and Halesowen Town at the highest end of non-league football. And it was Birmingham City's own head of academy, Simon Jones, who gave him the moniker 'non-league legend'. Bellingham senior was already well known to Jones. Indeed, the academy chief's first memories of Jude are of an overexcited three- or four-year-old scampering around his dad at a non-league cup final in which his dad Mark was playing. As such, it was a natural fit for Bellingham to join City's pre-academy, where the best seven-year-olds begin their football journey, a precarious one which will result in just a handful becoming professionals.

It was 2010 and England were experiencing their South Africa meltdown with Fabio Capello; Sir Trevor Brooking had just launched his 'Future Game' document, envisaging a generation of English players comfortable and creative in possession to some hilarity and a few more raised eyebrows. England didn't really do creative playmakers.

And, in 2010, Southgate was touring the country attempting to persuade local FA youth leagues to adopt seven-a-side and nine-a-side matches for children. 'Whenever you go down into smaller numbers in a game, there are more touches, more shots, more dribbles, more engagements with the game,' said Nick Levett, who at that time was the FA national development manager, meaning he had responsibility for how youth players were coached. 'So you get coaches encouraging kids to express themselves and you get more creative players.'

'I remember one county league chairman saying publicly on stage: "I don't care what you think about small-sided games. I've got a baseball bat in my car ready for you,"' said Levett. 'I can still picture him saying that. Another county chairman said: "We'll bring in nine-a-side games over my dead body!"'

'That could be arranged,' whispered one of Levett's colleagues, a former England international (not Southgate) to him. They needed that dark humour to sustain them but often it was Southgate's presence that got them over the line. 'Gareth joked he was my warm-up man,' said Levett. 'He would open up and talk about the ideas and because he was open, passionate, spoke about his kids, the people bought into it. He's incredibly articulate. Gareth was brilliant at opening doors in some of the leagues where they were against it.'

In 2012, the FA voted in favour of the changes. Levett and Southgate had succeeded in their mission. But some youngsters, like Bellingham, had already benefited from early adopters of small-sided games. His first matches for Stourbridge Juniors were seven-a-side football. Now he would move on to Birmingham City's academy. But even here change was coming to English football and Bellingham was an early beneficiary.

* * *

In all the long list of the England national team's humiliations, the 3-2 defeat to Croatia at Wembley in November 2007 holds a special place. Perhaps because of the pouring rain that night which necessitated manager Steve McClaren deploying an umbrella on the touchline, which invited the unforgettable 'Wally with the Brolly' headline in the *Daily Mail.* Or the fact that England, having gone 2-0 down but then having pulled the game back to 2-2, still managed to mess it up and allow Croatia to score again.

The upshot was they failed to qualify for Euro 2008, McClaren was sacked and the ill-judged Fabio Capello adventure began. Richard Scudamore, Premier League chief executive, was at Wembley that night. Strictly speaking, this wasn't his mess to own. That said, he was well aware that in the furious blowback about to be directed at the

FA, he would be caught in the crossfire. The national team was being undermined by the 'greed is good' league, critics argued. English football knew the price of everything and the value of nothing. And who cares about investing ten years in developing a young English boy when you could pick up a better Croatian for a few million?

Equally, the rules around youth development in England were antiquated. Incredibly, they restricted the amount of days on which boys could train. That was a well-intended child protection measure to prevent burnout and excessive travel. But all the research indicated that there was a correlation between the amount of time a child touched the ball and his future skill level. In Spain, a similar youngster would spend a couple of hours a day playing with his club; in England, he was limited to a couple of sessions a week and a game. Premier League clubs wanted reforms anyway, to recruit from around the country rather than within a specific area. (Again, a rule imposing a 90-minute time limit on travelling to academies was rooted in good intentions, protecting children from too much, too young. But it meant, unless you uprooted your family, you were stuck with your local team.)

So Scudamore knew this was a nettle he had to grasp and appointed Ged Roddy as the Premier League's director of football development. 'You can plot the traces of the EPPP. I can date it,' said Scudamore. '[It was] 21 November 2007, England v Croatia, 2-3, in the rain. I was there with a number of people. We went ballistic. That's when we went away and recruited Ged and said: "We've got to do something to get the thing back up."'

Roddy's job was to push through reforms that would somehow strike a balance between keeping smaller Football League clubs happy, many of whom relied on finding and selling a Bellingham to survive, and allowing kids access to the best coaches and facilities.

What emerged four years later in 2011 was called the Elite Player Performance Plan (EPPP) and the road to get there for Roddy was pretty much as difficult as Southgate's and Levett's had been. The unique competing parochial influences of English football meant it was almost impossible to keep everyone happy that the compromise agreed upon was not without issues.

Yet crucially, from 2011, clubs were permitted more time coaching young kids. The best children would have more ball contact time. Many clubs partnered with elite local schools, some of them boarding schools, so that training could fit around lessons every day rather than being a twice-a-week bolt-on evening activity requiring long journeys. Those who lived outside urban conurbations could board. For others, like Jadon Sancho, it would mean moving out of an inner-city environment at 14 and into Watford's club accommodation and attending an outstanding state school, the Harefield Academy in rural suburbs. Later, when he would join Foden at Manchester City, he was at St Bede's College, a private school, part of the Manchester City academy. Chelsea organised private tutors to school their boys so they could fit work around training. Clubs like Chelsea and City, with the best facilities, would be a Category One academy, which naturally attracted the best boys. Birmingham City, still highly thought of, became a Category Two academy. But Bellingham's family were not only Blues fans. Dad Mark knew football and that Jude was in good hands under Jones.

That said, when Bellingham graduated to England teams, he was in a distinct minority coming from a Category Two academy. 'I first got called up for England as an Under-14 playing for the Under-15s,' recalled Bellingham. 'So I was nervous, thinking: "I'm really good at Birmingham, against the teams that we play against. But how do I compare to the boys from City, Chelsea, Tottenham, Arsenal and

United? I go there, do really well, find it comfortable and you have that realisation I'm not far off some of these if not better. So I go to the next camp at St George's Park, so that's getting more serious, now you're closer to playing in a game. And I remember doing really well in the sessions and showing people it doesn't matter what club you're from or what category your club is in, you can go and make an impact and show you're better than some of the boys from the higher academies.'

That was in 2016, a red-letter month for England football. It was Southgate's first as permanent manager of the senior side – and Bellingham's first international game, a 5-2 victory over Turkey for Kevin Betsy's England Under-15s. Bellingham, who came on as a 60th-minute substitute, was just 13 years and 171 days old. He joined a very good team. In the match, played on 17 December at St George's Park, Chelsea's Cole Palmer was striker, Aston Villa's Morgan Rogers left-winger, and Newcastle's Tino Livramento the right-back in Betsy's starting eleven. In midfield was Yunus Musah, who would go on to play for the US against England in the 2022 World Cup. Introduced into the game at the same time as Bellingham was fellow sub Jamal Musiala, another talent with dual nationality who ended up a Bayern Munich and Germany star.

'I didn't quite play as much as I wanted because I was a younger one and I was still quite small for that age group,' said Bellingham. 'I took it as a learning point, tried to use it as something where I could come back in maybe a couple of months' or years' time to show I was there for experience first time but now I'm here to be the main man.'

Bellingham wouldn't have known it, but he was one of the first to benefit from FA technical director Dan Ashworth's determination to make the England age group teams a crucial part of a young player's development. 'We had looked at what Spain do, Clairefontaine [the national youth training centre] in France. It's actually quite cyclical. France win the World Cup so everyone has to do what France are doing. "Oh, the Netherlands are doing well, so everyone copy them. Germany are the ones,"' said Ashworth.

'We wanted to take the best bits [from all]. At the time the FA didn't have an Under-15, Under-18 and Under-20 team, but when we looked through the German players [whose FA ran teams in those age groups], they were getting double the [junior] international caps on their route through to seniors compared to the England players. National teams only get 55 days a year with the players. How could we get more experiences for our young players? Ultimately by having an Under-15s, Under-18s and Under-20s, that gives you an extra three years' worth of experiences, another 150 days of those players getting international experiences. So why wouldn't we run those teams? But historically, England had not.

'But the Premier League is different to the Bundesliga. English academies are different and the rules are different [as is] our culture and our DNA about how England play compared to Brazil or Spain. You can't say: "Let's play like Brazil." You have to understand what you've got, get the best ideas from other sports and nations and try to get some alignment on what is right for English players.

'One thing I remember vividly from our research is that [trophy-winning national] teams rarely come from nowhere. Spain were quarter-finalists, semi-finalists, finalists, winners, also with their youth teams. Germany were banging on the door of finals and then they'd win. The only two that came from nowhere, that won once and never won again: Greece and Denmark.

'So we were saying senior winners have won at youth levels and been in and around the latter stages at a number of tournaments before they actually got over the line. And St George's Park was a crucial nexus for that development. Firstly, it meant young players had a consistent venue at which to turn up, something that would prepare them for the seniors. And secondly, because all the national coaches were located in one place.

Rebecca Levett (née Symes) was the FA's senior performance psychologist at the time and worked with the coaches on the psychology of player management. 'You'd have all the coaches for the Under-15s right through to Gareth sitting in sessions, which was important when we were trying to link up the pathways,' she said. 'Historically, I think that link between all the age groups hadn't necessarily been there. Dan's big thing was that the only thing that changes is the size of the shirt [as you go through the age groups].'

Previously, many clubs had put pressure on young players not to accept England call-ups. Their reasons were multiple: some of it was the age-old club v country prejudice and clubs hated sharing control. But on other occasions they feared youngsters had too many games or they were unimpressed with how the FA had previously treated *their* players. Ashworth set out to transform that perception.

Ashworth wanted England to be the '21st club' – equal or better to any of the 20 in the Premier League in terms of standards. 'He was big on visibility in the clubs, not just at games; go and see them train, go and meet academy managers, coaches,' said Steve Cooper, the former Nottingham Forest manager who coached the Under-17s at the time. 'Another of his things was – we're not regional coaches, we're national coaches. So, if there's a game in Bournemouth and even if you live in Wrexham, you go to it. You go and get round the country,' Cooper said.

First impressions for the England Under-15s were particularly crucial if Ashworth's strategy was to work. 'That first welcome meeting when the Under-15s come in is really important,' said Rebecca Levett. 'The coach needs to be able to get their language, their tone right, to be able to help the players feel comfortable.' She was a coach to the coaches 'helping them to think about what they are going to say, and how they want to frame it. When the coach delivers that, the psychologist isn't front and centre of that, but they might have helped to shape and influence the coaches to work out how they might deliver something.'

Nick and Rebecca Levett – the surname match is not coincidental, they are married and met while working at the FA – were part of the first FA staff to have contact with Bellingham. 'The first wave was when Jude came in and the camps were based on fun games to bring people into an understanding of what being competitive was about,' said Nick Levett, who by now was the FA's talent identification manager. 'They would play games, whether that was how many cups they could stack in 30 seconds or how many balloons they could keep off the floor. I did work on that with [coach] Kevin Betsy and the sports science team. It was a case of saying: "If we want creativity and decision-making, what environments do we need to create to allow that to emerge?" A game-based workshop for 45 minutes was developing skills we thought a senior international would need.

'An evening table tennis competition will drive competitiveness. Some players would say: "I don't want to play." "Okay, why's that?" It becomes the start of a conversation. You're just collecting data on humans. How do they engage with situations and people? They would have development plans, so we could feed back to clubs.'

Indeed, some clubs were enthusiastically partnering with the FA because they could see that exposure to the international environment helped their players. 'We were already seeing elements of leadership emerge,' said Nick Levett. 'We had Jamal [Musiala] and Jude, who came in a year early, and I still remember Jude being a year younger but still demonstrating really good social skills and leadership.'

Bellingham recalled: 'When I came back [to England Under-15s] a year later, I thought: "I'm showing from the first day why I deserve to be maybe captain of this group or an important player." We got to the games and they sit me down, tell me that they see me as a great leader for this age group from what I've shown in workshops and in training. I get given the armband for my first game against the Netherlands, make a couple of assists, play really well and really enjoyed it. From then on it was like, "This is my group; this is the team I want to really improve."'

For Ashworth this was ideal. He had young players emotionally invested in England. Not only that, they were also developing lifelong relationships with other players who might be their colleagues in the senior team. That said, this all sounded great in theory. Ashworth desperately needed to demonstrate it worked in practice.

* * *

Dan Ashworth turns in his home office to point out the shirt on the wall: it is from the England Under-17 World Cup winners from 2017. Foden was the star of that team. Sancho played, as did Morgan Gibbs-White, Marc Guéhi, Conor Gallagher, Callum Hudson-Odoi and Emile Smith-Rowe. Alongside Ashworth's shirt is more memorabilia from that year. In June 2017, the England Under-20 team with Dominic Calvert-Lewin, Lewis Cook, Dominic Solanke and Fikayo Tomori had also won their age group World Cup in South Korea. A month later, in Georgia, in the Euro Under-19s, England won again with Aaron Ramsdale, Mason Mount and Ryan Sessègnon in the team. Joint-top goalscorer was Stoke-born Ben Brereton who would go on to be a national team star, only at

Copa América for Chile, where he was Ben Brereton-Díaz, courtesy of his Chilean mother. If 2016 had been an *annus horribilis* for England, 2017 was going down as an *annus mirabilis*. It came at a good time for Ashworth. His England DNA had been laughed out of town, his pleas for patience adjudged a cynical attempt to cling on to his job and his tenure had seen the 'out in two games' 2014 World Cup and the Iceland debacle in 2016. Here, however, was evidence that, in the rebuilding of English football, the foundations were being attended to.

'I look back at 2017,' he said, pointing to the shirts and trophies. 'Did it save us? I'm not sure I'd go quite as strong as to say it saved us but it just made everybody go: "Oh, okay! There might be something here." And sometimes in your career and life you just need a moment where you get a little bit of luck where everyone starts to believe there might be something in this. And if we had gone out in those tournaments in 2017 and [in Russia] 2018, we probably would have been finished.'

Instead, Bellingham joined the England junior set-up that was growing rapidly in strength. The Under-19s were recent European Championship semi-finalists and the Under-20s had just beaten the Netherlands, Germany and the US, then Nigeria 8-1 and Iran 4-1. But everybody in the national coaches' room at St George's Park knew the pick was Cooper's Under-17s, a treasure chest of talents: Sancho, Guéhi, Hudson-Odoi, Smith-Rowe, Gibbs-White and the most exquisite of the lot, Manchester City's Foden.

Since coming together that August, Cooper's new crop had reeled off eight consecutive victories. These included a 6-0 thrashing of Belgium and a 5-0 win against Croatia in Pula, the game where Borussia Dortmund first scouted Sancho. And – how about this – an 8-1 defeat of Germany. *Away.*

Cooper, a former League of Wales defender who became one of UEFA's youngest Pro Licence holders when he completed the course at 27, is a deep thinker about how the game should be played and taught. A formative influence was Pep Segura, an ex-Barcelona B coach and title winner in Greece who joined Liverpool's academy as technical manager when Cooper was coaching their Under-12s. Before meeting Segura, Cooper thought he was in a good place with his work, but the Spaniard, he said, 'opened my eyes'. Segura's biggest message was about vision: that a coach must be able to close their eyes and imagine their team playing. Have clarity and ambition – then build a methodology to get there.

Finding himself out of work after Brendan Rodgers overhauled the Liverpool academy, Cooper sat in his kitchen thinking harder than ever, refining his game plan and the steps to teach it. He created a presentation that wowed Ashworth and Southgate when he joined the St George's Park staff as youth coach educator, contributing ideas to the England DNA project. In 2014, aged 34, he became England Under-16 coach and stepped up to the Under-17s the following year.

'It was a brilliant time. Gareth was the Under-21 coach and head of development teams. He was like the academy manager while coaching his own side. They appointed Dave Reddin as head of performance, who was fantastic and said let's go through everything and talk about how we want an England team and camp to be. There was a change of coaches. I came in, Neil Dewsnip came in, Dan Micciche, Keith Downing, Aidy Boothroyd, Gareth brought Steve Holland in . . .' Cooper recalled.

'Dave made a room at St George's Park called the national coaches' room. Gareth worked out of it as well. We would meet every Monday and Tuesday all day and then go off round the country.

Dan was big on relationships with the clubs. [Previously] it wasn't brilliant. England wasn't perceived the way it should be. What had happened – having been at Liverpool and on both sides of it – was EPPP came in and the Category One academy clubs were operating on this level up here whereas England were down there.'

Initially, some clubs were more welcoming than others. But Chelsea were particular supporters of the new England push on youth, seeing international experience as a key part of their youngsters' development, which was important, given the torrent of talent spewing from the club's academy at Cobham.

Ashworth was bold in 2015, pulling England out of the Victory Shield. Traditionalists hated the decision. The historic competition had been played between boys from England, Scotland, Northern Ireland and Wales since 1925, initially using Under-15 teams, then Under-16s, and helped launch the careers of Stanley Matthews, Wayne Rooney and Bobby Charlton. However, Ashworth wanted to change the programme for the youngest England footballers, bringing talents in a year earlier and providing a wider range of experiences. 'We got slaughtered for coming out of the Victory Shield,' Ashworth recalled. '"Arrogant English, too good to play Scotland, Wales and Ireland." Right? That's not it. There are two reasons we pulled out of the Victory Shield. It was many players' first experience of international football and it was live on Sky, so imagine your first trial, you're playing for England and you're live on television. That's not great for the egos of players and parents. I didn't like that.

'Secondly, the majority of the players playing for Scotland, Wales and Ireland are the same players the boys were already playing in the academies. So, we were pulling players out of the West Brom Under-16s against Stoke Under-16s, all of which are full of English, Irish, Welsh and Scottish players . . . and playing them again! We're using that 11 days to play against the same players they play against every week. Instead, how about we go to Florida and play against the US, Brazil and Portugal? Now, you tell me what you'd rather do as a young player? Which experience would be conducive to becoming a first-team player? But, no, "Arrogant English Pull Out".'

Had he been born two or three years earlier, Bellingham's introduction to the international game might have been on a sodden field in Belfast against teammates from the Birmingham academy, the pressure on, the TV cameras there. Instead, by the time he passed through England's Under-15s and Under-16s, his experiences included away games against Japan in two different countries, a mini-tournament in France where he faced Brazil, Argentina, Portugal and Ivory Coast, and beating Italy in Italy via a penalty shoot-out.

'There was a backlash when he left the Victory Shield, but the following summer we were in Sarasota playing Brazil, Portugal and the US,' said Cooper. 'We completely revamped the games programme. With everything we did, it was "What's the objective?" The Under-17s, 19s and 21s are competition years, so there was a big emphasis on reaching and winning tournaments with them. The Under-15s is a talent ID year. The Under-18s and 20s go round the globe, playing South American teams, African teams, Asian teams, to get the experience.

'In international breaks, it was normal to play a double-header. Bring Hungary to St George's Park, play them twice, go home. We scrapped that and said: "Let's play tournaments." The idea was to become the master of a four-team tournament – because at a finals, the first thing you have to do is get out of your group of four. Win the first game. But if you don't win the first game, what needs to happen? Goal difference, game management.

'We'd play for "The St George's Park Cup" or "The So-And-So

Memorial Trophy". You'd have penalties. There'd be consequences all the time. You were still giving young players minutes and opportunities but there was a purpose to it all the time.'

Bringing in Mike Rigg as head of talent identification, Ashworth directed effort and rigour into finding the best youngsters and bringing them into the England fold. Previously, the system was casual, relying on recommendations from academy coaches at clubs and England were losing out on talents – Declan Rice and Jack Grealish went through the Ireland system, Rice even playing friendlies for the Irish senior team before being retrieved for England just in time.

Matt Crocker, an unsung hero of the operation whose role was akin to that of a club academy manager, drove a 'plan-do-review' model and worked on aligning all the age group teams, in culture and playing style. Whether teams embodied 'England DNA' principles was monitored closely. 'We got to a point where, because you were always going back and presenting to your fellow national coaches, it created a real belonging: this is what we're doing, we need to change the game here, we need to change the game in England. Let's stand up for this. It was almost a sense of mission,' said Cooper.

'You didn't want to stand up in front of the national coaches and have them say, "Why are we going long from those goal kicks?" Or, "You've come away from the plan." There became a real attitude of "This is what we're doing." We're putting England first, the DNA first. And we started to win. That pushed everyone on again.' Part of the review process involved grading young players after every camp. How were they in the games, in training, in terms of everything else? The ratings were A, B, C and A*. Three times a year the national coaches convened for a grading meeting where they discussed the emerging A* players. So, when Southgate called Bellingham into England's seniors at 17 he was doing so, not blind, but with the full knowledge of all the whens, wheres and hows that Bellingham had excelled on the pathway.'

Southgate's engagement was novel. 'Fabio [Capello] couldn't give a monkeys what was going on,' said Nick Levett. 'Sven [Göran Eriksson] had a bit of a passing interest but never anywhere near Gareth. He was invested in grassroots, and he had been crucial in connecting the whole pathway. Before that, the only person who had that connection was Trevor [Brooking] and he drove a lot of the reforms and ideas through.'

Cooper recalled: 'Gareth was always interested anyway, but from the moment Phil Foden walked into the Under-16s at 15, every national coach would know about him. One, because he was brilliant. Two, because he was always A*, and the discussion was, "How do we get the right programme for him?"' Others who were A*s every time included Mount, Reiss Nelson, Trevoh Chalobah, Sancho, Bukayo Saka, Guéhi and Palmer – who played a remarkable 30 times for England Under-15s but from there until Under-21 level was used sparingly because of injuries and Manchester City's desire to protect his developing body.'

Bellingham's potential was well known from when he was 13, and was guarded carefully. But that was standard. 'There was an awareness where players were in their journeys. With the 17s they'd be doing their GCSEs. Bukayo did his during a European Championship,' Cooper said. 'The 17s is a huge year for a young footballer: GCSEs, am I going to get a pro-contract, and can I get in the England team? The People and Teams department were important in helping coaches understand them all individually.'

The approach of tailoring programmes to individuals applied to Bellingham. First, he was invited to join training camps for players born in 2002. He was a 2003 birth but already so precious that it was deemed the older age group would do more for his development. So, before that Under-15s debut he had already gone through the process of making himself comfortable in England surroundings.

Bellingham's progress was so rapid that his first tournament final was with the seniors – Euro 2020 – but junior tournaments were integral to the growth of other talents. Within five years of winning the 2017 Under-17 World Cup in India, no fewer than six of Cooper's victorious squad were senior internationals and preparation, coaching and culture work that went into the tournament provided inspiration for England teams.

It started in earnest a full 103 days before the finals, on 17 July, when staff met at St George's Park to review information from recce trips and agree on the 'what' and the 'how' – their goals for the tournament and working culture. Emma Rowe from People and Teams oversaw a 'RACI' programme to give everyone clarity and ownership on their roles. RACI stands for Responsible, Accountable, Consulted, Informed, right down to which analyst live-coded the opposition during games and who provided referee analysis on Matchday 1. Nobody boarded the nine-hour flight for acclimatisation in Mumbai with any doubts about what, at any moment, would be required of them. England's group opponents were Mexico, Chile and Iraq. Chile, opponents in the all-important opening game, were video-scouted across 12 matches, with Cooper watching four of them himself. Working to Ashworth's specialist coaching model, one assistant, Mike Marsh, looked at the South Americans from an in-possession vantage while one, Lee Skyrme, studied them from an out-of-possession point of view. Mexico were scouted across nine games, Iraq six.

Issues players would face included travel (there was another nine-hour flight from Mumbai to England's base in Kolkata and a five-hour flight back from a quarter-final in Goa), the average 33°C with

75 per cent humidity and sanitation. Hundreds of pounds were spent on producing Three Lions branded signs warning players to wash their hands, which went up all over the Novotel Residence hotel, in Kolkata, where the team were based. The planning was so detailed that England budgeted for six people to get ill at some point, but in the event the only casualty was an FA Councillor, who got a dicky stomach. The drive to keep players healthy included bringing their own chef and a schedule of tablets for all sorts, including gut health.

Strategies were devised around sleep. India is four and a half hours ahead of UK time and understanding that late into the evenings his youngsters would be messaging friends, partners and family back home, Cooper took the pragmatic decision to let them lie in. Wake-up time for players was midday and training was at 4 p.m. All games were in the evening, in any case. Schoolwork was factored in. At the Euros earlier in the year, Callum Hudson-Odoi and Jonathan Panzo sat GCSE exams the day before the final, where England lost on penalties to Spain and now some players were doing A-levels while others were studying on vocational courses. In the English system, all players of compulsory education age require one hour of education for every school day missed through football and a retired head teacher from Southampton, Kevin Batchelor, accompanied the squad as education officer.

People and Teams produced a 'Rooming Matrix' to decide who shared with whom. Throughout the season, players were paired with different room-mates to build strong relationships across the squad and in preparation for the Euros and World Cup, and were invited to privately write down a minimum of three players with whom they would like to share the matrix – a complex spider's web of arrows pointing from individual to individual – which ensured everyone roomed with someone they felt comfortable with. Foden was with

George McEachran, Sancho with Angel Gomes and Hudson-Odoi with Guéhi.

The team-building work included a powerful evening, at the team hotel, where room-mates presented their tournament shirts to each other in front of the group. Cooper made a speech about how proud he was of every person in the room, and the fun. Rowe had asked players privately to sum up every teammate in a word or short sentence and Cooper read out the descriptions, while they were projected on a screen. 'It was powerful,' he said. Warm and affecting. For example, Gomes – 'crazy, funny guy, always laughing'. Joel Latibeaudiere – 'he makes us better by making everyone feel calm'. Guéhi – 'proud and passionate, he really believes in everyone'.

Chile were thrashed and Iraq dispatched by the same 4-0 scoreline and only Mexico troubled England in the group stage. But that game also ended in victory for Cooper's team and then came Japan in the second round and that seminal victory on penalties.

In an entertaining quarter-final, where the sides traded chances, England were on a different level to the US in terms of decisiveness, winning 4-1, with Rhian Brewster scoring a hat-trick. That brought a semi-final against Brazil and a chance to demonstrate the wisdom of changing the youth games programme to accumulate experiences against such opposition. Cooper's kids had faced the Brazilians in a friendly in Shrewsbury only six weeks previously and showed no inhibitions, with Foden outstanding, Brewster deadly again and Smith-Rowe coming off the bench to provide the striker – who completed another hat-trick – a slick assist.

Psychology played its part. Again, borrowing from rugby, the eleven beginning a game and the players on the bench were rebranded as 'starters' and 'finishers'. A poster put up on display for the players set out the principles for 'finishers' (substitutes), things like 'we prepare like we're starting', 'we're ready to make an impact if we come on' and 'we don't let our emotions negatively affect our preparation or the team'. Smith-Rowe embodied all this.

Displayed in the meeting room at the hotel was quite an artwork, a Rowe creation. It was a 'Belief Wall' where across ten large sheets of white paper, glued together, he traced a winding path, heading diagonally upwards towards a destination: the World Cup final. Along the way were marked stages of the journey, the group games, the knockout matches. And beside these were written snippets: interview quotes from Cooper and the players, facts from match reports, comments on social media. There were ones from Michael Owen and Gary Cahill, wishing the team luck and a special message from Southgate which began, 'Your performances have been fantastic. Not only the wins but the way that you've played, the belief that you've got. You look like an England team.'

Said Cooper, 'The lads loved it – it was an amazing piece of work, all about building belief. It became a thing. "Have you seen the wall? Seen what so and so said? Well, this is us, lads." When I presented to the coaches after the tournament, Gareth loved it.'

Before the final against Spain, Cooper played his squad a video of their best moments, emphasising their growth together. They had become a beautifully honed team: he can show footage of patterns of play in training sessions many months before the tournament and then clips of identical patterns of play in games. In their biggest one, in front of 67,000 fans at the Vivekananda Yuba Bharati Krirangan Stadium, and with the match shown live on BBC2, they did not disappoint.

Sancho had been recalled by Borussia Dortmund after the group stage, but with Foden hitting heights that made him a shoo-in for the player of the tournament award, it barely mattered. In a 5-2 victory there was the symbolic landmark of England having more possession than Spain in a major game and so many things about the victory were sweet. There was vengeance for Spain beating Cooper's side in the Euro final and England had to come back from 2-0 down. Morgan Gibbs-White scored, having suffered racial abuse, and the last goal was scored by the unsung but deserving Guéhi.

For the celebration photos, the young players turned their shirts around so they wore their numbers on their chests. It produced an endearing, iconic image – but not one that went down too well at St George's Park. Southgate was not a fan. 'In the review, I got stick for it. We won the World Cup and I'm getting hammered in the coaches' meeting!' said Cooper with a laugh. 'But I said the tournament had been all about the players making decisions and giving them ownership and if that's what they wanted to do, I don't think I'd have chanced it. I don't regret it at all.'

A little tale about Foden. While acclimatising in Mumbai, England played New Zealand in a warm-up game and the Manchester City tyro took a bang on the head. There was no concussion but as a precaution, Ish Rehman, the team doctor, said he should sit out of the contact part of the next day's training to be safe. The session began with a warm-up, then there was a technical exercise. After those Cooper said, 'That's you, Phil, you're done,' and Foden went off. The group carried on, completing a good stint of contact work.

Cooper takes up the story. 'Every night we got the GPS and I said to the physical coach, "Are the numbers okay?" And he said, "Come and look at this!" The highest runner, the player who got the most physical outcomes from the training . . . was Phil. Then we looked at the camera footage.

'When we excused him from the rest of training, what he's done is he's got a ball, drifted on to the next pitch, and he's booting it up in the air, chasing it, doing dribbles, trying to hit the crossbar and hitting it every time. Then pulling the ball down when it came back to him. That's Phil. He just loves football. Every time I walked past his room, the door would be open, and he'd be playing two-touch with George McEachran.' Just talking about Foden makes the eyes of this football man shine. 'He was brilliant in India,' said Cooper. 'The best teammate as well. Loved his team, loved his coaches. Just a really, really nice kid.'

* * *

Michael Zorc, the former German midfielder, is one of the most respected figures in European football. He was the sporting director of Borussia Dortmund from 2006 until 2022. Back in 2018 he sat around the table with around ten English journalists, all of whom were desperate to know just how this Bundesliga club was so good at talent identification. They had become the gold standard at graduating teens from all around Europe into their first team and selling them on for record transfer fees. Sancho was there and the reason for the English interest but there was also a young striker called Erling Haaland about to join, as was Jude Bellingham.

'Go back say five to ten years, there was a time that English clubs signed German players and had a team of scouts to do that,' Zorc said. 'There was a lot of discussion here: "It's all about money; it's too early for them to go from Germany to England." But in the meantime we have the feeling that the education and development of youth players in the English academies is quite good, to be honest. The teams don't only spend much money on transfers or salaries but also on infrastructure. When you see these youth academies – for example, Manchester City – you can't compare it with the German standard. It's much higher.'

Victory, in terms of improving the quality of young English players, it seems really did have a thousand fathers. 'EPPP was a huge part,' said Ashworth. 'Ninety per cent of development takes place at clubs and there was a huge push and emphasis on developing your own players. It was almost the perfect storm. There was definitely the opportunity here for someone to go in and get a group of staff around them and really try and push England back up the map for football. I'm a proud and passionate Englishman as well and I wanted to hopefully be a part of something that would help the country be proud.

'Ged Roddy [the architect of EPPP] was brilliant; it's been a game-changer for English football and clubs. But you can't launch an EPPP plan and six weeks later have a raft of players in your first team. And we had to form relationships with the clubs. You have to get player release to go into these tournaments and win European Cups and World Cups at youth level. The players that are in the system now, some of them were winners in an England shirt, and that was always the aim. Give people the confidence and belief that you can win in an England shirt. And whether that starts at the Under-17 European Championship or the Under-21 European Championship, when you rock up to Gareth or whoever the first-team manager is, you believe as an Englishman and with the England badge you can win a tournament. And that takes time.'

Not everything is perfect. Some Football League clubs complain that EPPP means that big clubs simply profit off their hard work and take their best players at 14 or 16. [Compensation structures are in the EPPP regulations, but many clubs would claim they don't cover their investment.] Some clubs such as Brentford simply abandoned youth development, preferring to pick up rejects from bigger clubs at 16 and 17 and develop a B team comprised of Under-23s. Birmingham City only benefited from their Bellingham years because the family had a loyalty to the club: he signed a pro contract on his 17th birthday, which allowed them to pocket a €25 million transfer fee from Dortmund. And another 5 per cent of the €100 million fee Real Madrid paid for him. However, had he simply not signed that contract, he could have moved at 16 for very limited compensation. And not all families in football are as honourable as the Bellinghams.

But the overall goals are being achieved. It is noticeable now how many senior England players speak about their formative teenage years making friends and winning trophies with England. 'Jude Bellingham was in the first Under-15 team I worked with and Jordan Pickford was in the first Under-21 group I had [as was] Jack Grealish and James Maddison,' said Rebecca Levett. 'They've transitioned through. Phil Foden was in the second group of players that I had, players that were playing in the Under-19s and the Under-17s are now playing in that first team. I think the success of the senior team now isn't just down to what was done at the senior level, I think it is the result of the entire pathway and that was Dan's great vision all along, the whole point of what he was trying to create, to futureproof the teams.'

* * *

If you weren't an experienced Pep Guardiola watcher, you might have assumed there was something seriously wrong with Foden's spectacular goal at the Bernabéu against Real Madrid in that Champions League quarter-final. Finger jabbing, face creased with aggression, Guardiola strode on to the pitch to clutch Foden's face with such vigour that he not only squished Foden's cheeks but even made his ears flap. Just Guardiola's way of showing affection.

Perhaps it is because he sees something of himself in Foden. Guardiola was sidelined initially at Barcelona because he was too small.

Foden can relate, according to Mark Allen, who was Manchester City's director of academy during the player's formative years. 'Phil wasn't the biggest. Physically there was no way he could compete,' said Allen. 'But he was smart enough to work around that. His frustration came when he saw players in his group being promoted into older groups. While he had the ability to do that, it wasn't wise nor prudent to push him into overage groups where it was significantly more physical. I had several conversations with him about that.'

Guardiola would be the coach that benefited from and empowered the most famous 21st-century example of youth development when his Barça team became the best in the world, perhaps of all time. It included graduates from the same Barça academy that had honed him. Lionel Messi, Xavi and Andrés Iniesta were its home-grown stars, but Carles Puyol, Sergio Busquets, Pedro, Gerard Piqué and Victor Valdés were key components. All would win the World Cup, either with Spain or Argentina. So, in many ways, you couldn't have asked for anyone better than Guardiola to oversee England's finest talent in a generation in Foden.

And yet in those early Foden years, it didn't seem that Guardiola would ever trust him in a midfield that contained David Silva, Kevin De Bruyne and Bernardo Silva. Game time was initially limited. Home-grown academy players looked great in theory but were swamped by expensive imports.

But when David Silva left in 2020, his moment had come and Foden is now the poster boy for the Premier League Category One academies set up in 2011. He has been through the club system and the England age group teams.

There was a fear expressed some years ago that the newfangled academies would machine-tool technically proficient players that lacked charisma and aggression. It didn't turn out that way with

Bellingham – 'half artist, half warrior' – and Foden. 'Although Phil's a product of the academy, he's also the last of the street footballers,' said one of his friends and advisers. Foden will show you the concrete playground next to the bookies where he played his childhood games, vying with older cousins and teenagers as an underdeveloped eight-year-old. It was bollards rather than jumpers for goalposts, but nevertheless an old-school development plan more akin to the 1950s than the 2020s, instilling the aggression required to play with older boys and the 100mph playing style of a box-to-box player. He has the best of both worlds. He is an academy product with the heart of a street kid – both Bellingham and Foden can look after themselves on the pitch if necessary.

And that Champions League quarter-final between their respective clubs in April 2024 was significant. For Foden, it marked a major game in which Guardiola put his faith in him as his central creative playmaker. Against him, playing a different version of the number ten role, was Bellingham. Blink and you might have missed it, but (probably) the two best teams in world football, coached by the two best managers, were entrusting their creative attacking output to two young Englishmen. England had come a long way from Sir Trevor Brooking's 'Future Game'.

CHAPTER 6

WHAT'S THE STORY?

Joe Gomez offered his hand in greeting to Raheem Sterling, who was seated and ready to eat. Those present say there was nothing unusual in the interaction. Gomez wasn't gloating and didn't show any signs of aggression. With England there is always the chance that club rivalries can surface, but Gareth Southgate's squad seemed to have put those bad old days behind them. But Gomez and Sterling had been on opposite sides in Liverpool's victory over Manchester City on the Sunday evening. Here they were 24 hours later, supposedly meant to be best friends after having confronted each other on the pitch a day earlier. Southgate has always recognised the players need time to decompress before they get their England heads on, especially after a fixture as intense as that one.

It was the time of peak City–Liverpool rivalry. The head-to-heads between the clubs, even in November as this one was, almost felt like title deciders as neither side lost many other games. The previous season, Liverpool had failed to win the league with an incredible 97 points, missing out to City by a point. In 2019–20, City had started the season poorly so the Anfield game already seemed a last opportunity to rein them in, given that they were on course for another 90-point season. (They would of course go on to win the Premier League in the Covid-affected season with 99 points.)

As such, Sterling must have been more on edge than normal. City had lost 3-1 and Gomez and Sterling had clashed in the final minutes, though nothing notable; they merely squared up to each other. As such, Gomez's gesture on the Monday night seemed a reasonable reconciliation. Southgate worked hard on throwing club rivalries aside once you crossed the threshold at St George's Park, yet here something had gone awry.

'You still the big man then!' said Sterling as Gomez held out his hand. Suddenly Sterling leapt from his seat and was grappling with the Liverpool defender, seemingly attempting to get him in a headlock. There were only around 15 players in the dining area and initially some laughed as food scattered, thinking it a good-natured prank. Harry Maguire and captain Harry Kane, senior players, were among the first to realise it wasn't benign and were on the scene, pulling Sterling off Gomez, who hadn't responded. Players were stunned. Gomez bore a scar near his eye from Sterling's jewellery. It had come from nowhere and left the entire squad blind-sided. This was the anathema of the united camp they had worked to create.

The incident was fleeting, perhaps 15–20 seconds, but the repercussions ran late into the night. A team meeting was convened. Southgate needed to restore order. But Sterling appeared deregulated. He sensed the mood of shock. Either he assumed he was going to be kicked out of the squad and sent home and wanted to make a pre-emptive strike or perhaps he just needed space. The FA provide chauffeur-driven cars to ferry players from their homes to St George's Park and there are always a few on standby. Sterling now booked one to take him back to his Cheshire home. Some say he was gone for 20 minutes, others recall it being a longer period, closer to an hour. All those nights under canvas on Woodbury Common in Devon with the Royal Marines and the togetherness engendered in Russia looked to have been in vain.

Sterling was on his way to the motorway when Jordan Henderson called. The Liverpool captain wasn't even on England duty, missing this meet-up because of injury. But having been a teammate at Liverpool, he was perhaps best placed to connect with Sterling. Whatever was said, it did the trick. They spoke and Sterling turned around and headed back, averting an even bigger crisis. Had he walked away, it would have been hard for Southgate to pick him again. Yet even if the initial crisis had been averted, now the pressure was on Southgate. How would he deal with the blatant disregard for the group's culture by one of his star players?

'Players will complain if there's strict discipline but they sure as hell will complain if there isn't,' Southgate would say later. Asked to identify his core value for the team, he said: 'Respect is huge. It's not just respect for me, it's respect for everybody, the team ethos, the lady on reception, your teammate. If you're coming off the pitch, respect for the teammate that's coming on, that encapsulates timekeeping, encapsulates preparing professionally for a game. It's the bedrock of everything really.'

This was the opposite of that. Joe Gomez was 100 per cent the wronged party, as Sterling would later confirm. And now Gomez held Sterling's fate in his hands. Southgate involves senior players in group decisions and had Gomez not opted for forgiveness and magnanimity, it would have been hard for Southgate to accept Sterling back into the fold that week. 'As a manager you need to see that the group are prepared to work together,' said Southgate. 'Everyone is comfortable and in the right place. My priority is the care and wellbeing of all of my players.' But Gomez made it clear he had no problems about Sterling returning to the squad, which made Southgate's job a lot easier.

But the press day less than 48 hours later was less comfortable.

'We have a very young squad and we're in a sport where emotions run high,' said Southgate. 'Raheem explained that for a brief moment his emotions ran over and it would be correct to say that wasn't the same for Joe. These things happen in football. Then you have to find a way for the group to move forward and it needed time for emotions across the board to calm down. We have excellent senior players who played a part in bringing everyone together. Then you have a decision to make if there needs to be something further which is right for the group moving forward.'

There was something further. Sterling would be dropped for the game against Montenegro on the Thursday. Sterling himself was contrite, posting an apology. 'Joe and I have had words and figured things out and moved on,' he wrote. 'We are in a sport where emotions run high and I am man enough to admit when emotions got the better of me. Me and Joe are good; we both understand it was a five-to-ten-second thing; it's done, we move forward and not make this bigger than it is. Let's get focused on our game on Thursday.'

'I love all my players,' said Southgate. 'We're like family and all families have disagreements. The most important thing is that you communicate through the disagreements and work through them.'

Jordan Pickford picked up the theme. 'In life it's normal; you're going to have your ups and your downs, whether it be at home with your family or your club or with England,' he said. 'Life is never straight and narrow. It's about how you come out the other side of it.'

It was as good a recovery job as could be expected in the aftermath of a melodrama. Yet few reckoned the line would hold. Some were saying Sterling would never accept his punishment, nor trust Southgate again. Others that the manager had been too weak.

The confrontation might have only been a matter of seconds, but looked like it had destroyed three years of hard work.

* * *

'It's the amygdala hijack,' said Rebecca Levett (née Symes), who was team psychologist to the England Under-21s. 'They're two little almond-shaped bits in the brain in the limbic system. It's the "Theory of Challenge and Threat States in Athletes". When we're in more of a threat state, physiologically everything tightens up. Everything starts to constrict, so your heart is having to beat faster, there's less room for the blood to be pumped round the body because everything's narrowing, which means the oxygen doesn't get round as effectively and doesn't get into the muscles.

'From the brain's point of view, what happens is when we get into that real threat state, the amygdala hijack, your red brain, the emotional part, takes over. We know that the oxygen gets diverted to the emotional centres, and your prefrontal cortex – which is your logical thinking part of the brain – effectively shuts down because the oxygen is not being diverted there. It's when your fight or flight response basically takes over. That is a really helpful system when used at the right time, but unfortunately what happens nowadays is that that system still kicks off in response to ego, reputation – "what do other people think about me?" It's when the system is kicking off at unhelpful times; that's what you've got to navigate.'

She was speaking in the context of sports performance, not the Sterling–Gomez showdown, another way of putting the Gazing work of Red2Blue into words. There were good scientific reasons why England had often gone to pieces on the pitch and made incredibly poor decisions. She was pretty much describing the reaction of England players in the Iceland game. But the relevance of the science is more universal and related back to just why the confrontation was so damaging. The work Southgate and his team had done with psychologists, initially Jonny Zneimer and then Pippa Grange, was among their most important. And Sterling had been the team leader.

When Southgate took the England job, Zneimer and he talked a lot about their work with the Under-21s and how they might transfer it to the senior team. There was a worry that senior players, with bigger reputations and more established careers, would be more resistant, though there was a natural generational shift occurring anyway and the squad was relatively inexperienced, so potentially open to new ideas. Everyone had recognised the need for change. When he became Republic of Ireland manager, Jack Charlton, the 1966 World Cup winner, had written a note about his philosophy for international football: 'Make them want to come – winning helps.'

'This was the schtick from Dave Reddin,' said Zneimer. 'We want the players to go back to their clubs saying what a brilliant time they've had.' But Zneimer and Southgate wanted to push deeper so that it wasn't just about fun but about trust. And the two were natural bedfellows anyway. 'Trust is a good word,' said Southgate in the run-up to Russia 2018. 'We're proud to represent everyone but the guy next to you is the most important one. You've got to be there for him, you have to support him, you have to be available when he needs to pass the ball, you have to be covering his back if he slips and makes a mistake.'

Charlton had engendered team spirit with the Republic of Ireland through big nights out in the pub. That made them want to come in the 1980s. Work hard, play hard was the mantra and he achieved extraordinary results. The level of scrutiny applied to the average England international made that impossible even before the invention of the smartphone. And anyway, many players were teetotal and almost all were very careful about how much they drank. Southgate had to find another way.

Owen Eastwood's work on culture meant the management team were already thinking about how important storytelling was, that to have a sense of your future, you needed to understand your past. That was framed within the England story. But Zneimer and Southgate believed it to be the case for individuals as well. If you wanted to know where you were going in life, it was important to understand how you had ended up where you were.

'We had been talking about the power of storytelling and Gareth saw something in a museum that summer [of 2017] on a holiday in California which inspired him. He said: "Jonny, this is exactly what we've been talking about." I think previously he wasn't sure it was part of the manager's role, but he really switched on to that.'

Zneimer had previously worked hard to convince Southgate to share his penalty miss story and failures with the Under-21s. He now repeated that with the senior team. 'It took a long time to persuade Gareth of the empowering effect that his story would have on the Under-21 team,' said Zneimer. 'He was talking about getting Steven Gerrard or David Beckham in to talk to the players, thinking the team would relate more to them.'

If the football dressing room is generally a closed space, where vulnerabilities are not commonly aired, the England dressing room amplified that reticence, the mix of club rivalries meaning players were even less inclined to give anything away. How to break through that barrier? Through 2017, a degree of consistency grew around the players selected and they began to work on encouraging them to tell their stories. Zneimer had been introduced to the senior players by Steve Holland. 'I've worked with José Mourinho, Guus Hiddink and Carlo Ancelotti,' said Holland. 'But I've never done anything like the work we've done with Jonny. And this is the work that could help us win something.'

That was a good start but trust is hard to establish. 'It's not a comfortable space for us to be at times, but I think it helps build togetherness,' said Southgate. 'You get a closer connection.' Describing how the team were responding, he said: 'They are having a go at things you ask them to, when sometimes you think: "They're not going to go for this!" At times they are painstakingly putting up with things I throw their way.' Having a young squad helped. 'They're possibly more malleable and open to suggestions. But [announcing] any meeting, you see a certain look! And we're asking them to open up quite a bit. And we're starting to hear some of their own stories and background, which is important.'

Southgate had to lead the way. 'Who goes first is vital in how they share their story,' said Zneimer. 'The level of vulnerability is crucial. That's why we get the leader to share first. They set the parameters of disclosure. It's role modelling and Gareth did it brilliantly. He made it psychologically safe to share. And made it okay to be incomplete, to struggle, to have fears, to be ridiculed, to create a culture of openness, honesty and an increased level of accountability.' But if the leader going first was important, whoever went next was just as crucial.

* * *

Raheem Sterling's story is compelling. During the World Cup in Russia it would come out in detail. But during the early days of Southgate encouraging the players to share, Sterling was a leader, one of the first to speak openly. 'It was because we were going in a new direction,' said Sterling. 'I felt at those times that it was the right time to try to use your short experience to voice your feelings. I feel like in football, everything that I'd learnt before just came from what the coaches told us. I felt like this was the first time that coaches shared stuff and were asking for our thoughts on things and how we see things. I just started to express myself.'

His example allowed others to step forward. When he put it down on paper, for The Players' Tribune, his starting point was intriguing. 'Can I trust you? Can I tell you my story, and will you really listen? If you read certain papers, maybe you already think you know me. Maybe you think you know my story, and what I care about. But do you really?'

Sterling's father, Phillip Slater, was shot dead when he was two. 'That shaped my entire life,' wrote Sterling. He lived in the Maverley district of Kingston, Jamaica. Soon after, his mum, Nadine, took the decision to leave Raheem and older sister Kima-Lee to travel to England to gain a nursing degree. She wanted more for her family. For the next few years the kids lived with their grandma in a three-bed bungalow. 'I remember watching the other kids with their mums and just feeling really jealous. I didn't fully understand what my mum was doing for us. I just knew that she was gone. My grandma was amazing, but everybody wants their mum at that age,' wrote Sterling.

When his mum did bring them over to England, her choice of home was auspicious: Wembley. Sterling would grow up watching the new stadium arch rise from the ashes of the Twin Towers. 'I grew up in the shadow of my dream. *Literally.*' Nadine worked as a cleaner to pay her way through her degree. 'I'll never forget waking up at five in the morning before school and helping her clean the toilets at the hotel in Stonebridge. I'd be arguing with my sister, like, "No! No! You got the toilets this time. I got the bed sheets."'

And he didn't immediately settle in England. 'I was so naughty that they kicked me out of primary school. Technically, they didn't kick me out. They just told my mum that I needed to be in an environment with more attention.' Indeed, at the age of eight he had been moved to a school with reduced class sizes and specialist help for children with specific emotional needs. He was assigned a mentor, Clive Ellington, who had done well in the motor trade, rising from technician to manager, but figured there must be more to life and had begun to volunteer to help young boys in Brent. Ellington recalled meeting a cheeky youngster and asking: 'What are we going to do to make you happy?'

'He was a young child who always smiled,' said Ellington. 'But when he played football, he absolutely beamed. The way to connect with him was to understand his love. He wasn't playing for a club so I said: "What do you do on Saturdays?"'

'Clive asking me that simple question was a turning point in my life,' Sterling wrote. Sterling came to sign for his first club, Alpha and Omega FC, the team connected to the church fellowship in Kingsbury. His mum, a church-going Christian, would doubtless approve and Sterling would grow up to share her faith. But football was predominant in those days and Ellington was key, filling as much of a father role as is possible for a mentor. 'Going to football, coming back from football, with him in the car, it was just [talking] all about life,' said Ellington. 'There was a rawness and an innocence about him. He just didn't know how to lose. When you're a young child and you're much more talented than any other player at the club, losing was not an option and a lot of my work was based around understanding the world that he was about to go into. He just didn't know how good he was, just didn't know it at all.'

Soon he would understand better. QPR came calling and his mother persuaded him to reject Arsenal, with the logic that he would stand out at the smaller club. He did. His coach Steve Gallen joked they became 'Raheem Park Rangers.' Kima-Lee would accompany him on the three buses it required to get across to QPR's training ground near Heathrow Airport. 'I was a nurse and single mum and if I had to go to work because I'm on rota, because we were a family and we could see the passion he had for football, when I couldn't make it she would take him to training,' said Nadine. 'Which is love.' Sterling would never forget the selflessness of a 17-year-old young woman looking after her little brother. Ten years later he would buy her a house for her 27th birthday.

At 16 he left for Liverpool, partly because they were a huge club and Rafael Benítez was very persuasive. But also because he knew it was a good time to leave north-west London behind. He actually lived on the fringes of Stonebridge, rather than in the midst of the estate, yet at that time it had become a byword for violent crime. Manchester City would follow with four Premier League titles and an FA Cup win accumulated before the move back to London and Chelsea. His importance to Southgate though was not just in the 18 goals he would score under him – including the vital one against Germany in Euro 2020 and the penalty he won against Denmark in the semi-final. Where Sterling led in sharing, others followed. 'I don't think it [our background stories] was spoken about a lot and part of me was accepting everything in my journey. I have never tried to not accept the past. I always tried to share my experience. And it wasn't like my experience was the most valuable. It was just one view that if I was to speak in that way, [then] other people can see that it's okay to open up and accept that.'

Southgate, said Sterling, was key to enabling that, more than the psychologists: which the psychologists would say is exactly how it should be. The manager was to lead.

'I would say [it was] Gareth: from minute one he had his vision of the national team and the step-by-step on how we get there and the initial bits were these conversations, these meetings, understanding the players and the group and getting their views on how we move forward in various different aspects – whether it was in media or on the pitch. I think it was definitely him that started that group thing.'

'Sometimes there's a perception of these players from not really knowing them or their back story,' said Southgate. 'We judge on a very public stage and often the persona on the pitch is not the exact person off it. It's normally closely aligned but it doesn't tell the full story. So we've said, "Look, get your story out there, let people know."'

Over time, several players would go public with their stories, perhaps more comfortable owning them having shared them privately.

'My upbringing, where I grew up, you had to survive,' said Kyle Walker before the 2022 World Cup, speaking of his childhood on the Lansdowne Estate in Sharrow, Sheffield. 'I wasn't aware of what was actually happening. If I look back on it now, I think, "That was actually quite bad." There was a fire on the estate which was bad. Or someone hanged on the stairs when I was going up on my landing. Those two were probably the ones that stick in my mind. I was 12, 13. The police blocked it all off on the landing, and it was right next to my house. Someone put petrol through the door at a neighbour's house, chucked a match in and that was it.

'The kids got out, the caretakers caught them on some blankets and the mum threw them out, but she couldn't get out. I don't tend to think about it now. I wouldn't say it's part and parcel of growing up, because no one should experience that. But it gives me that motivation to actually go and prove people wrong.'

There was also agency in owning your story. 'If you grew up the same way I grew up, don't listen to what certain tabloids want to tell you,' wrote Sterling. 'They just want to steal your joy. They just want to pull you down.' Sterling bought into a more optimistic vision of the nation. 'England is still a place where a naughty boy who comes from nothing can live his dream.'

Southgate concurred. 'It's not a comfortable space for us to be at times, but I think it helps build togetherness. Trust is good and also you get a closer connection.'

Or as Zneimer said: 'Storytelling builds trust through vulnerability. In learning your teammates' personal highs, lows and struggles, you can connect with them at a deep personal level and with the team as whole. That results in individuals committing to each other, trusting one another and going the extra mile during performance especially under pressure.

'But storytelling can also be about the team's shared ambitions and collective purpose: "What excites us about being a team? How will we know when we've achieved our shared goals?" It starts to form in the film of your imagination; it primes you for a successful environment.'

For anyone still unconvinced that the holistic approach that includes well-being is performance enhancing, Sterling's testimony is worth a listen. 'I felt like that was kind of a release for me when I came into the national team – the first time I relaxed, in the sense that I just felt I knew exactly the direction I wanted to go in with the national team. And I felt part of something that was clear how we're going to do it and that we're doing it together, and that was the first time going in with the national team that I felt like it was a relaxed environment. It wasn't there's home [over there] and this is the national team. It was like no, when I go there, I'm going to have just as much fun there as I do at home. It started to become a relaxed environment.'

* * *

Sterling wasn't missed for England's game against Montenegro.

His teammates won 7-0. With England there is always another act to the drama, however. When Gomez had been introduced as a late substitute, some of the Wembley crowd booed. Whether this was pantomime reaction or something more malicious was hard to tell. Playing for England sometimes does feel like performing on the Shakespearean stage in the 17th century, where the crowd get to throw rotten fruit at those they decide are the villains. The modern incarnation would be a reality TV show where social media picks the goodies and baddies.

Southgate had attempted to draw a line under the issue by bringing Gomez on, only for the wounds to be reopened. 'No England player should ever be booed when they're wearing the shirt,' he said. 'I don't get it.' It wasn't the last time he would have to address the issue of his players being jeered by their own fans.

'The reason I wanted to get Joe on the pitch was that he's been with us in September and October and we've not got him into the games. Also, I know I'm going to start Raheem on Sunday and get him back on to the pitch as well. It was important for both of them to get back on and show everybody we're all in this now.'

Later, in the bar and restaurant concourse housed behind Wembley's main stand, which is kept back for players and their families, Gomez's parents, agent and friends left as a group to go down to a lower level of the stadium. England manager Gareth Southgate had invited them to spend some time with them despite his extensive media duties.

Everyone at the FA felt their pain keenly, as did Sterling. 'To all the England fans, I wanted to leave things as it was, but tonight I have to speak again: it was hard for me to see my teammate get booed for something that was my fault,' he posted. 'Joe hasn't done anything wrong and for me to see someone who keeps his head down and works hard, especially after a difficult week, for him to be booed when he came on tonight was wrong. I've taken full responsibility and accepted the consequence. I felt as though I had to say this.'

Sterling would play in the 4-0 win against Kosovo that Sunday. And he would prove to be pivotal at the delayed Euro 2020 in the summer of 2021. In fact, it seemed his relationship with Southgate had not only survived but thrived.

When the BBC Radio 4 *Today* programme asked Sterling to edit a special edition of the show at Christmas 2021, he asked Southgate to be a guest. 'If anyone asks me what it's like with the national team, I always say it's a big credit to you because I was one of the individuals who felt the pressure from the outside world,' Sterling told Southgate. 'From when I first came in, to now, you can see how enjoyable it is. Everyone can't wait to come [and] will be speaking on text. I don't think it was quite that, previously. Players felt a huge weight on their shoulders. But the thought process you put into it, to lift the weight off our shoulders and give us the best possible chance to win . . . from me and the boys, I just want to say: "Thank you."'

It didn't sound like a player consumed with anger at the way he had been treated. The Gomez spat might have seemed like a moment that would break three years of team building. With hindsight, it became a demonstration of the importance of those sessions. The nights under canvas on Woodbury Common had not been in vain. The relationships and levels of trust meant this group could navigate even extreme disputes and still reconcile.

CHAPTER 7

THIS IS ENGLAND

The villages of Rangemore and Hanbury Woodend had turned out in force, lining the streets for hours before the team's departure from St George's Park. Townsfolk from nearby Burton had swelled their ranks. By the time the England team bus was leaving their base, set amidst idyllic East Staffordshire and Derbyshire countryside, to head to Wembley for the national team's first major final since 1966, the country roads outside were thronging with people in the July sunshine.

There was the atmosphere of a Jubilee street party or village fete as locals crowded along country lanes on grass verges bordered by green hedgerows. The team coach had to edge its way out carefully to negotiate the crowds, so unexpectedly huge were they. As they drove away, well-wishers continued to line the lanes for at least a mile, cheering with England flags waving. It was an entirely wholesome scene, which overwhelmed the players. 'Wow,' said one on the team bus. 'These are the best! Did that just happen?!'

Veterans of Euro 2016, like Harry Kane, Raheem Sterling and Jordan Henderson, might have been recalling the video Southgate had shown them when he was appointed manager, which had suggested that they too could be treated like the Team GB Rio Olympic heroes. Here it seemed was the culmination of Southgate prophecy, a nation rallying around a team that had embraced multiculturalism and decency. The rural setting evoked the genteel, village England referenced by George Orwell's 'old maids biking to Holy Communion through the mists of autumn mornings' in his definitive 1940 essay, 'England Your England'. Or even William Blake's 'green and pleasant land' referenced in 'Jerusalem', England's unofficial anthem.

Baroness Casey, the crossbench House of Lords peer who was later asked to review the day's proceedings, summed up the mood well. 'This was a team of role models which the whole country could be proud of,' she wrote. 'They cut across so many divides and represented the St George's Flag as a flag for everyone. They had a manager that stood up for the values we hold dear. They were in a major tournament final at their home ground at a time when the country was being released from Covid-19 restrictions and beginning to put a year of immense national difficulty behind it. We all wanted to get behind the England team, celebrate them, our country and our national game.'

At the same time, at Wembley Stadium a different kind of street party was brewing. 'It was as like a war zone, I've never seen anything like it: vandalism, yob behaviour, broken glass, highly drunk people, [a] very horrible atmosphere for a lone female. Police barely seen,' said one onlooker.

Another reported: 'Bottles and cans [were] being thrown at people, children [were] cowering behind parents, trees [were] being ripped up and thrown.'

All day, crowds had been gathering across the country but mainly in London. Pubs were open at 8 a.m. and immediately full. A Greater London official on duty at Wembley recalled: 'I walked into the control room about 9 o'clock and there were England fans drinking as I walked in. It was really, really early on and the alcohol was flowing. And I thought, "This is going to be a hard day."'

'I have never seen drunkenness like this so early on in the day,' said one London Underground official, a veteran of major finals and New Year's Eve celebrations.

Leicester Square in central London was also filling up and one fan, Charlie Perry, was about to gain global fame of sorts. He was filmed openly snorting cocaine to cheers from onlookers. No police intervened. 'I'd been on the piss since half eight in the morning and had had at least 20 cans of Strongbow,' Perry would tell *The Sun*, adding that he had also 'banged a load of powder. It was the biggest day of my life. There were no rules that day. I was off my face and I loved every minute.'

Context is everything. The Euro 2020 final was delayed and played in July 2021 because it had come after 17 months of extraordinary Covid restrictions on the population which had disproportionately affected young people and their natural inclination to socialise. The Euros had become England's coming-out party, a celebration of national significance almost akin to the end of the Second World War as the country emerged from an existential crisis. At the start of the tournament, Wembley crowds were restricted to 22,500, but by the final that had been increased to 67,500. Given that parties had effectively been banned for a year – an unthinkable proposition in England, at least since 17th-century Puritan rule – it was predictable a youthful explosion was imminent, though perhaps not necessarily in the manner in which Perry chose to express it.

In the spirit, he said, of attempting to cheer people up after Covid, he had taken a firework flare, pulled his trousers down and inserted it in his anal passage to set it alight. 'There was a bit of a competition to do stuff so I just thought I'd put the flare up my bum,' he said. 'The flare burnt for about ten seconds or so around the cheeks, I didn't feel a thing because I was highly intoxicated.'

Perry was one of those who would then make his way to Wembley Stadium. By midday there were already 10,000 fans on the pedestrianised approach to the stadium, Olympic Way, commonly known as Wembley Way, but still no visible police presence: Brent Council officials and London Transport staff were nominally in charge.

At 11.45, a single-decker bus travelling along Fulton Road, which transects Wembley Way, had been surrounded by boisterous fans who had clambered on the roof. At this point, extra police were summoned to rescue the bus. 'The bus incident was a massive red flag,' said a Wembley official. 'I was getting calls that there were lots of people out there and it was apparent it would grow.'

By 1.45 p.m., disorder was so bad that an FA official requested more police support but was informed that there were now so many similar situations in the capital that their planned deployment couldn't be brought forward ahead of the 3 p.m. scheduled arrival.

Perry was one of hundreds about to take advantage of the anarchic scenes. 'Obviously I didn't have a ticket,' he said. 'I had gone in as a gibber [football gatecrasher] before, so I knew how to get into the stadium.' He bribed a steward to get through initial Covid checks at the outer fence but still had to breach the turnstiles. 'To get in you have to go round the back of someone who already has a ticket. I gave them £100, and went behind them.'

Others though weren't prepared to spend that kind of money. The outer perimeter fence was meant to filter out ticketless fans and conduct Covid checks, but at 5.25 p.m. a group of 100 men charged and breached it. 'Large groups of fans were observed working together to attack specific points and cause breaches. This would then draw in response teams, stewards and police, allowing these fans to charge an area far further away.' It was the first of several breaches of the outer fence, including concerted assaults on the VIP entrance.

Such was the chaos that authorities had to suspend the initial Covid and ticket check at the outer fence because the crowd density was now so dangerous, which inevitably meant hundreds more ticketless fans swept in. Manchester University's Professor Geoff Pearson wrote: 'Thousands of highly intoxicated fans were now left very close to the stadium but with no means of watching the most significant match in their lives.'

Many were tailgating fans with legitimate tickets, as Perry had, but others were targeting the most vulnerable entrance points. 'Every time the stewards opened the disabled gates to let [a] wheelchair user in, they were met with a rush of non-paying people charging the gate, barging past and pushing disabled people and stewards out of the way. I had to physically guard [my son] to get in through the gate,' said a parent carer. Another ticketless fan tried to impersonate a steward with a hi-vis jacket and separated a wheelchair user from his father in order to trick his way through a gate.

The players' families were not immune. Horrifying scenes of fans rushing gates saw Harry Maguire's father, Alan, caught up in the stampede and crushed in a pile of bodies, causing him to break his ribs. Other players' families arrived in their seating area to find their places taken by intoxicated, abusive fans. Andrea Mancini, son of Italy manager Roberto, found his seat occupied by a fan disinclined to cede possession and ended up having to sit on a stairwell. One hour before kick-off, the walk to the stadium was akin to a post-apocalyptic scene where law and order has completely broken down. As one journalist showed his credentials to enter the stadium and was fastidiously frisked by a group of stewards, he had to point out to them that a few yards away a fan was brazenly scaling the eight-foot high fence, clambering in to make a dash for the turnstiles gates.

Inside the stadium you would have been oblivious to the fact that police were by now having to surround the ground to prevent a baying mob from storming turnstiles. The atmosphere inside, doubtless fuelled partly by cocaine and alcohol, was as febrile as anyone could recall. By kick-off there were probably 15–20,000 ticketless fans in the stadium in addition to the 67,500 capacity.

The stadium DJ, who had already popularised Neil Diamond's 'Sweet Caroline' as an England tournament anthem, warmed the crowd up with Atomic Kitten's 'Whole Again'. Since Russia 2018, a small but hardy group of fans had lionised Southgate by adapting that song's chorus to: 'Southgate you're the one! You still turn me on! Football's coming home again!' It was as weird as it was tongue in cheek and not wholly successful in that it was usually only a handful of fans singing the chant. Yet here, as the Euro final loomed, a raucous stadium took their cue: 'Southgate you're the one!' 80,000 fans roared. 'You still turn me on!' The stadium that witnessed his moment of infamy now hailed him, his Palm Sunday moment. Only a few weeks previously the team had been booed by some for taking the knee and Conservative MPs were saying they couldn't support England, yet now he was a step away from canonisation.

* * *

The road to that moment at the European Championship final in the summer of 2021 was arduous, though not in terms of the results. Aside from a 2-1 reverse in the Czech Republic, England dominated, scoring seven goals at home to Montenegro, six in Bulgaria, five against the Czech Republic and Kosovo at home and another five in Montenegro as well as four against Bulgaria at Wembley and Kosovo away. The football was increasingly straightforward: England were simply a very good team who were far too strong for most. Yet the political and societal convulsions in the run-up to that delayed Euro 2020 would make Southgate's job more fraught than ever.

Indeed, the path to the simple gesture of taking the knee to express opposition to racism during the tournament really began in December 2018 when Raheem Sterling was racially abused by Chelsea fans while playing for Manchester City. There was the usual flurry of outrage, but Sterling then did something extraordinary the following morning, which encapsulated the changing power dynamic between media and footballers. 'You can see by my reaction I just had to laugh because I don't expect no better,' he posted on Instagram.

However, what followed next was revolutionary in terms of challenging mainstream media's treatment of race. He highlighted two articles MailOnline had written on two different Manchester City players buying homes for their parents. Tosin Adarabioyo, who is black and had yet to play a first-team game, was featured under the headline: 'Young Manchester City footballer, 20, on £25,000 a week splashes out on mansion on market for £2.25m despite having never started a Premier League match'. The headline for Phil Foden, who is white and 18 at the time, was 'Manchester City starlet Phil Foden buys new £2m home for his mum'.

'Two young players, both starting out their careers, both have done the right thing, which is buy a new house for their mothers,' wrote Sterling. 'Look how the newspapers get their message across for the young black player and the young white player. This young black kid is looked at in a bad light. Which helps fuel racism and aggressive behaviour. So for all the newspapers that don't understand why people are racist in this day and age, all I have to say is have a second thought about fair publicity. Give all players an equal chance.'

It was an extremely powerful statement which caused crisis meetings at the *Daily Mail*. There was a back story, which related directly to Sterling. When he had also bought his mum a house, *The Sun* had featured it on the front page, unhelpfully shortly after the Iceland debacle. Sterling wasn't even close to being the worst player at Euro 2016 but it felt like he was being lined up as the old-fashioned scapegoat. 'Obscene Raheem!' screamed the front-page headline. 'England failure steps off plane and insults fans by showing off blinging house,' read the sub headline. The use of word bling, associated with black culture, seemed an obvious reference to his ethnicity, though *The Sun* would deny that in a statement. Within the story, Nick Kay, 32, from Cheshire was quoted, saying; 'They should rename the team Blingerland. Any normal person would hang their head in shame after how they performed in France, but these guys come home and show off about how rich they are.'

Clocking the tone of that press reaction, Foden's agent, fearing something similar from *The Sun* when Foden bought a house, had briefed a *Mail* reporter to ensure the story came out in a different light. The Adarabioyo story had been picked up from a BT Sport documentary on the phenomenon of rising wages for young footballers. This was all pre-Covid and before the murder of George Floyd by Minneapolis police officer Derek Chauvin in May 2020, the height of lockdown. The Sterling racism incident had come a week after a banana skin had been thrown at Arsenal's Pierre-Emerick Aubameyang. A central pillar of English football's boldest progressive claim, that it had eliminated the racism of the 1980s from the terraces, looked to be crumbling.

As such, the fact that racists seemed emboldened throughout Europe was on the agenda even before England stepped out in Podgorica, Montenegro, for their Euro 2020 qualifier in March 2019. What followed shocked everyone except Danny Rose. He had been racially abused as an England Under-21 player in Serbia in 2012.

'I sort of prepared myself for what happened,' he said. 'It happened in Serbia so I thought there was a possibility it might happen again and it did. I looked up straight away in the first half and I know the exact time it happened.'

As early as the sixth minute, racial abuse was aimed at Rose, with Sterling and Callum Hudson-Odoi, a 19-year-old making his first start for England, also targeted. The abuse grew louder as the game progressed, as England thrashed their opponents 5-1. Rose would be booked in injury time, something which initially annoyed Southgate, worried about potential suspensions due to unnecessary yellow cards.

'I didn't realise that earlier in the game, on the other side of the pitch, there had been racial abuse going on,' said Southgate. 'So when we got in the changing room, I'm having a go at Danny for getting booked. And I had to apologise on the plane [home], because it emerged that this had been going on. I didn't like the fact that the boys felt they couldn't mention it in the changing room at half-time or report it. For me, it was: "God, this is awful. How is an environment [allowed] where our players are abused on the pitch and they don't even feel comfortable to report it or feel anything's going to happen?" Even now I know we would all worry: "Even if we report it, is anything going to be done about it?" But at the very least this had the team where we were united on how we saw it. And we could send a message to young kids watching. I think the lads maybe didn't realise how powerful that would be.'

Some football would briefly interrupt political machinations that summer when England competed in UEFA's newly created Nations League tournament. Though it was a new competition cobbled together on Microsoft PowerPoint to keep TV execs happy, England had beaten 2010 World Cup winners Spain and their World Cup semi-final nemesis Croatia to qualify for the last four, so there was demonstrable progress. And when you haven't won a trophy for 50 years, it's best not to be too choosy about which you take seriously. The semi-finals took place in Portugal and England were a VAR armpit away from reaching the final when Jesse Lingard scored in the 83rd minute, a goal which would have made it 2-1 to England against Netherlands. A foretaste of tech trouble ahead came when, after lengthy consultation, it was disallowed and Netherlands then won 3-1 in extra time. England did at least win another penalty shoot-out in the third/fourth place play-off against Switzerland, a game of so little importance it was a contender for the penalty shoot-out with least jeopardy ever.

Even in Portugal though, there was a stark reminder that aggressive nationalism and the England team are often uncomfortable bedfellows. A new generation of younger England fans had been involved in clashes with local police as they took over bars in Porto's town squares with old generation chants about the Second World War and taking on the IRA. In the pretty, historic streets of Guimarães, where the semi-final was played, they gathered on Rua Paio Galvão by the Dom Afonso Henriques Stadium and sang, drank, urinated in bottles and generally intimidated locals. On seeing a woman appear, they struck up 'Get your tits out for the lads!' and 'You've got chlamydia!' followed up by a song proclaiming they were 'England 'til I die!'

Stephen Yaxley-Lennon, known as Tommy Robinson, a convicted criminal, racist far-right leader and briefly adviser to the UK Independence Party, was at the game and was filmed punching a fan. Among the flags England fans carried, several now bore the insignia of the Football Lads' Alliance, a confederation of unofficial football fans groups formed in the wake of the 2017 Islamist terror attack on London Bridge. They proclaimed themselves defenders of English culture; others called them Islamophobes and Robinson had enthusiastically attended a march. Southgate was now having to dodge questions on Robinson amidst his press briefings.

Another kind of far-right expression, this time of an eastern European bent, would follow them to their Euro 2020 qualifier in Bulgaria in October 2019. UEFA had ordered the Levski Stadium in Sofia to have a partially reduced capacity against England because of racist chanting at previous games, which was a huge red flag, given England's experience in Montenegro. Pre-match media briefings tend not to help. Local journalists adopt the indignant stance of a nation subjected to crude and malign stereotypes when racism is raised while some English journalists seem to revel in English exceptionalism, the anti-racism stance being a mark of just how brilliant and better England is than the rest of the world. The rest of the world, however, is bemused and puzzled by such a bold take. Southgate typically attempts to steer a path through all of this by suggesting that while the UK has its own racism issues, he and his team will confront abuse by walking off, if necessary.

This time it was to no one's great surprise that racists targeted England debutant Tyrone Mings from the start, as well as Sterling and Marcus Rashford. The game was halted in the 27th and 43rd minute, announcements being made saying the game would be halted if racist chanting persisted. There did seem a belated effort from Bulgarian authorities to remove the worst offenders from the stadium, or, at least, a group of black-shirted ultras left. Ivelin Popov, the Bulgarian captain, was seen remonstrating with them to desist, though amidst a flurry of denials, he was a rare hero among the Bulgarian delegation, most of whom hadn't heard anything.

At half-time, the England team debated whether they would come out for the second half. 'The lads decided to stay out,' said Kane. 'They wanted to play. They wanted to carry on.'

'For myself and a few others, it was, "you come off and they win,"' said Sterling. 'You stay on the field. If someone can't deal with it mentally in that minute, we can have a break and report it. But I don't feel like we should pack the game up and finish, we should intend to win that game so that it rubs salt in their wounds.' Sterling scored twice as England won 6-0 but the idea of equating a football score as a totemic victory over racists seemed to trivialise the issue.

That said, the unity of the England team, the clear anger the likes of Henderson so eloquently expressed on behalf of teammates and the fact that the entire squad co-ordinated anti-racism messages on social media in the aftermath made an impression. Often black players understandably end up being the de facto spokespersons on these issues; on this occasion the load was shared and the team, already well liked for its football, was in danger of belying the self-obsessed footballer stereotypes; even becoming admired for its leadership off the pitch.

Sterling adds: 'I think we had a conversation on the coach and it was "how do we go forward with it?" It was more the senior players at the time that were going over it. And obviously them asking questions to a few of the other ones, whether it was to Mingsy [Tyrone Mings] or myself, and trying to get a group understanding of what we could do as a group. When that happens, do we walk off the field? You heard some that said yes, some that said no, if we walk off that kinda makes them win. The decision we came to in the end was that if it did get too much, it was something we would definitely consider as a group to come off the field. I think it was like a vote and talking it through and how everyone viewed it. It was just our way, how we were going to deal with it. We got to the point where if it got like that, we would walk off, it didn't matter what game it was.' *The Sun*'s barbed Blingerland pun of 2016 seemed a caricature from a distant past.

***

Southgate has always been a keen observer of people and is recognised as a great communicator. Less appreciated is that he is a talented writer. If he wasn't a footballer and was happy to live on a fraction of the wages, he could make a fine sports writer. Most football books are conversations with a player from which a writer hopefully hones coherent words. The most intelligent players are excellent verbal communicators but, having left school at 16 and not developed the discipline, few are natural writers. Southgate is. So when he sat down to pen his *Dear England* essay to fans, he did so alone, without a ghostwriter. He recorded the words initially, being interviewed by The Players' Tribune, but he alone edited the transcript of that interview into his letter.

Southgate's open letter to England fans on the eve of the European Championships in the summer of 2021 came after a year of social tumult. In the moments the nation wasn't arguing about Covid, lockdown and Brexit, it was busily reporting a neighbour's minor breach of unprecedented rules or angrily defying those regulations. And a fresh national pastime emerged: discussing whether Britain was a country full of unreconstructed racists or an idyll of multiculturalism. No nuance was allowed. Everyone had to pick a team.

George Floyd's murder in the US on 25 May 2020 had resonated globally and led directly to the protest on 7 June in Bristol which saw a statue of slave trader/philanthropist Edward Colston dragged from its plinth, which previously sat in pride of place in the city centre. It was dumped in the harbour, from which his slave ships set sail in the

17th century to build the wealth that funded the numerous schools, poorhouses and churches he built in the city.

The following weekend, fearing the nearby Cenotaph was to be defaced, the Football Lads' Alliance, old crews of football fans generally in late middle age, organised a counter-demonstration. In a highly unusual development and ironically demonstrating how historical prejudices can be overcome, Bristol City and Bristol Rovers fans united for the day. (Only a Bristolian could truly understand how seismic that development was.) Fans of Swindon Town, Cardiff City and Newport County, some of whom might have previously only ever travelled to Bristol with the intention of confronting Bristol hooligan crews, joined the counter-protest. Their banner insisted they were: 'Not Far Right: Just Ordinary People'. Aside from the Welsh clubs represented, the other fans were precisely the kind of people who follow England away from home: traditional conservative patriots from old working-class backgrounds and predominantly followers of smaller teams that had no expectations of competing abroad in UEFA competitions (Liverpool and Manchester United fans flaunt their disregard for England as another way of indicating how much bigger they are than such provincials).

Into this maelstrom stepped Southgate with his own attempt to define what England meant in 2021. As in 1996, sometimes his sense of duty leads him to grasp a nettle when others might leave it untouched. Few writers have felt bold enough to attempt to pull together the threads of this peculiar nation since 'England Your England' was written by George Orwell in 1940.

Given that Orwell had struggled with 'the diversity of it! the chaos' (and this in an age prior to large-scale immigration), it was a bold assignment Southgate set himself. Orwell wrote of 'the clatter of clogs in Lancashire mill towns, the to and fro of lorries on the Great North

Road, the queues outside the Labour Exchange, the rattle of pin tables in Soho pubs . . . How can one make a pattern of this muddle?' Southgate would try where Orwell broadly failed.

No fan of international sport, which he famously described as 'war minus the shooting', Orwell did mention the pub and the football match as defining features of English culture, but he didn't have an England team to reference in the same way Southgate would because that shared identity didn't really exist. England might have played their first game in 1872, but they didn't bother entering a major tournament, the World Cup, until 1950: they assumed global tournaments were beneath them, which tells you a lot about England. Television wasn't a mass product until the 1950s and the World Cup wasn't broadcast live in the UK until 1958, a tournament in which England failed to win a game. The first big televisual communal experience which Southgate references in his essay would have been the 1966 World Cup final. It is notable that it was the Union Flag that fans flew back then to celebrate the team, not the cross of St George.

When Orwell wrote in 1940, the England team was a niche hobby for a minority of committed match goers in a relatively new sport whereas Southgate could draw on more than 50 years of the nation watching England on TV. 'We saw during Russia 2018, with the street parties, the barbecues and with every drop of beer thrown into the air in celebration [that] when England play, it's not a few thousand – or even a few million – watching on subscription. You are representing more than 50 million people. You remember where you were watching England games. And whom you were watching with. And who you were at the time.'

'Why do we care so much?' Southgate mused, reflected on rushing home from school as an 11-year-old to watch Bryan Robson score a goal in 27 seconds in a World Cup qualifier against France in 1982, England's first World Cup game for 12 years after two ignominious failures to qualify.

Perhaps because there are actually very few institutions that define the English: they don't have a parliament like Scotland, Wales or Northern Ireland. Their law is shared with the Welsh, as is their cricket team, and their language with the world. Their patron saint, St George, who is lustily invoked by England fans – 'Keep St George in my heart/Keep me English!' – was a Greek from Turkey shared as a patron saint with Malta, Catalonia and Ethiopia among others. The borrowed flag was probably adopted by English soldiers in the 13th century. William Shakespeare, who was born and then died on St George's Day, immortalised 'this blessed plot' and wrote the best-ever pre-match team talk for Henry V, which included the line 'Cry God for Harry, England and St George!' But rhetorical flourishes alone, even from a literary genius, do not an identity make. In popular culture, only the England rugby team and, above all, the football team are just for England.

And yet symbols of Englishness are often disdained. Labour's Emily Thornberry was briefly fired from the Shadow Cabinet in 2014 when she posted the photo of an Essex house adorned with St George's flags, because it was assumed to be sneering at them, though it was in fact posted without comment. That she was MP for Islington, the supposed epicentre of left-wing elites, commenting on Essex, the spiritual home of Margaret Thatcher's children, didn't help her cause. Orwell, despite being on the same political side, had little time for 'left-wing intelligentsia' and the fact that they saw 'something disgraceful in being an Englishman and feel the need to snigger at every English institution'. He aspired to bring 'patriotism and intelligence together,' as would Southgate.

Yet the manager's vision of England was difficult for the political right to quantify. On one level, he pressed all the right buttons for them. 'The idea of representing "Queen and country" has always been important to me,' he wrote. 'My sense of identity and values is closely tied to my family and particularly my grandad. He was a fierce patriot and a proud military man, who served during World War II. Growing up, the Queen's silver jubilee and royal weddings had an impact on me.'

He reveres the armed services. 'Because of my grandad, I've always had an affinity for the military and service in the name of your country – though the consequence of my failure in representing England will never be as high as his. My grandad's values were instilled in me from a young age and I couldn't help but think of him when I lined up to sing the national anthem before my first international caps.' Indeed, he says he sings especially loud for fear of offending his grandad, should he display insufficient gusto.

However, Southgate's inability to keep to a predetermined script of what patriotism should be would come to irk many right-wingers. 'I have never believed that we should just stick to football,' wrote Southgate. 'I know my voice carries weight, not because of who I am but because of the position that I hold. I have a responsibility to the wider community to use my voice, and so do the players. It's their duty to continue to interact with the public on matters such as equality, inclusivity and racial injustice, while using the power of their voices to help put debates on the table, raise awareness and educate.'

The left-wing singer-songwriter Billy Bragg, whose song 'The Few' addresses English football hooliganism, once wrote that while 'the national flag is associated with football violence . . . we need to find a way to overcome that reticence and repossess the symbols of what it means to be English. What we lack is a confidence, not so much about who we are, more about whether it's okay to celebrate being English. We need to stop being embarrassed about our home and find a way to celebrate the things about it that we love.'

Southgate, like Bragg, would attempt to wrap himself in a flag that embraced both patriotism and progressivism, a task many Conservatives considered ill-judged at best and a cloak for Marxism at worst.

'I am confident that young kids of today will grow up baffled by old attitudes and ways of thinking. For many of that younger generation, your notion of Englishness is quite different from my own.' Southgate would often remind journalists that in England age group teams, the majority of the teenage squad had dual heritage and could opt to play for either England or another country.

'I understand that on this island, we have a desire to protect our values and traditions – as we should. But that shouldn't come at the expense of introspection and progress. It's clear to me that we are heading for a much more tolerant and understanding society, and I know our lads will be a big part of that. It might not feel like it at times, but it's true. The awareness around inequality and the discussions on race have gone to a different level in the last 12 months alone.'

Some would find it bizarre to find anything disagreeable in that. Yet Southgate's essay had come just a week after the England team had adopted a gesture which would become an extraordinary source of division in the fallout of the post-Covid world.

* * *

On 14 August 2016, San Francisco 49ers reserve quarterback Colin Kaepernick declined to stand up for the ritual playing of the US national anthem prior to an NFL game. Few noticed. He wasn't in the starting squad and so wasn't in club colours. But by the time he had repeated the gesture for three games, he was asked about it by local journalists. 'I am not going to stand up to show pride in a flag for a country that oppresses black people and people of colour,' he said. 'To me, this is bigger than football. There are bodies in the street and people getting away with murder.' His comments came after a number of incidents that summer when white police officers had shot dead black suspects of crime, many of whom turned out to be entirely innocent. In the case of Joseph Mann, a mentally ill homeless African-American man acting erratically with a knife, police offices were recorded saying: 'Fuck this guy. I'm going to hit him,' as they attempted to run him over, before chasing and shooting him dead.

Nate Boyer from Tennessee, who had briefly also been an NFL player but then served in the military in Iraq and Afghanistan as a Green Beret, a member of the US special services, was an outraged 49ers fan. He felt Kaepernick was disrespecting the military although, on re-reading his interview, he realised there was more nuance in Kaepernick's position. He wrote an open letter explaining his stance. 'Even though my initial reaction to your protest was one of anger, I'm trying to listen to what you're saying and why you're doing it,' he wrote. The letter went viral and resonated with Kaepernick, who arranged a meeting, where the pair discussed the issues. 'We didn't even have opposing opinions necessarily,' said Boyer later. 'We just had opposing experiences, opposing emotions, opposing reactions to the flag, the anthem itself, the symbols of America based on what we've seen and done in life.'

Boyer told Kaepernick that he felt remaining seated during the anthem was too divisive. And so it was a US Marine, who loved his country and revered the flag, a man superficially with zero woke credentials, who came up with the suggestion of taking the knee instead. It was meant to be a more conciliatory protest located in the prayerful tradition of Martin Luther King, the civil rights leader who had popularised peaceful protest in the US, having been inspired by Mahatma Gandhi and ultimately by Jesus Christ's teachings on loving your enemies.

All of this occurred in the run-up to the polarising Donald Trump–Hillary Clinton election of 2016 but went largely unnoticed in the UK. It would only become an issue there following the murder of Floyd, when Premier League players had begun taking the knee on their return to football that month. #BlackLivesMatter had become the slogan of the day and by then Kaepernick's simple gesture of taking the knee had become a global symbol and appropriated by the Black Lives Matter political movement.

Therein lay the issue for many. Premier League shirts and Sky Sports and even the *Daily Mail* had been branded with #BlackLivesMatter to catch the wave of social feeling, but early dissent was indicated from pundits such as Gary Neville and Jamie Redknapp who, while supportive of the players, didn't seem to want to be associated with that political organisation, not wearing the slogan. And though difficult to pin down, as a decentralised international movement with several local incarnations, the original US arm of Black Lives Matter had called for a revolutionary overthrow of the established order, defunding the police and disrupting the nuclear family, while its leader had expressed sympathy for Marxism. None of which are political positions you would expect the average highly paid Premier League footballer to endorse, nor did it seem likely that Southgate's Royal Marine grandfather would have much time for them.

From the players' perspective, they were adopting a symbol of protest instituted by a fellow sports professional, one that was designed to be both thought-provoking yet conciliatory. This was a protest grounded in sport, not revolutionary Marxism. Given their experiences in Montenegro and Bulgaria, they were especially committed to demonstrating their solidarity with that cause. The anguish of what their teammate Danny Rose had suffered in Bulgaria was evident. 'I've had enough,' Rose said after that game. 'I just think: "I've got five or six more years left in football and I just can't wait to see the back of it." Seeing how things are done in the game at the minute . . . I just want to get out of it.' It was depressing stuff.

'The big question was are we going to continue doing it [taking the knee] through the Euros?,' said Sterling. 'When racism comes up we spend a lot of time in football and society to address it for that week and then normally brush it under the carpet and things are all fine now. And the next scenario happens and we go again. As players that have been in those scenarios and faced that racial abuse, we just wanted to keep highlighting that. There have been times that we've sat down and said: "Is the message still powerful?" And we've said: "Yes."'

The players had a powerful advocate in their manager. 'He has found a voice that nobody else has found in a post-Brexit UK world,' said Robert Sullivan, the former strategy director at the FA who had previously worked at the Conservative Party, so was no woke warrior. 'Who captures progressive values in a patriotic way? It's him. Nobody else. A lot of people wrap themselves in England and it makes you feel uneasy. When people go too far the other way, you think, "You're losing perspective." But he finds the sweet spot. It comes from authenticity. He tells you "my family have served, I'm a huge patriot," but he can also talk about who we are as a modern society and it works.'

Yet there had already been some hints that the idea of the footballer activist was not universally welcome. *The Mail on Sunday* had published Marcus Rashford's inspiring column about his pride in Britain back in June 2020 when he forced Prime Minister Boris Johnson into his first U-turn on school meal vouchers. Yet in November the same paper ran a story about how the 'campaigning football star' had bought 'five luxury homes worth more than £2 million'. *The Mail on Sunday*'s editor Ted Verity, Boris Johnson's most loyal media supporter, had been sufficiently annoyed by the outcry the story generated to write to *The Guardian* to deny that it was racist and insist it was simply of public interest and not intended to be negative.

There was a clue though that the England team might not get the reception they were anticipating. 'For the first time in my life I will not be watching my beloved England team whilst they are supporting a political movement whose core principles aim to undermine our very way of life,' wrote Lee Anderson, then a Conservative MP, on England's decision to take the knee.

Southgate is well used to bandwagoners like Anderson. 'We are totally united on it, we are totally committed to supporting each other,' he said. 'We feel, more than ever, determined to take the knee through this tournament. We accept that there might be an adverse reaction; we are just going to ignore that and move forward.'

The team's first pre-tournament friendly was against Austria at Southgate's old club, Middlesbrough, one of the more impoverished areas of the country that had voted for Brexit. Although its industrial roots meant it was once solidly Labour, the local Teesside mayor was now a Conservative and nearby Redcar had also fallen to the Conservatives for the first time in the landslide 2019 Boris Johnson victory of Popular Conservatism.

Southgate's England team were walking into a proverbial lion's den. Many of their hard-core fans were aligned with movements defending monuments from Black Lives Matter protesters, while Middlesbrough was the heartland of a new right-wing working-class movement that broadly rejected woke symbols.

As referee Lawrence Visser signalled kick-off, the England team knelt and boos rang out around the ground. Quickly cheers and applause supportive of the gesture rose up to drown them. Yet it was clear there was no consensus of support. The 1-0 victory was almost incidental in the post-match discussion which would eventually reach the House of Commons. 'I was pleased it was drowned out by the majority of the crowd, but I can't deny that it happened,' said Southgate afterwards. 'Some people seem to think it's a political stand and they don't agree with it. But that's not the reason the players are doing it.' A senior player like Sterling barely noticed the boos.

'You see reports on it but when it was coming to the game, I was so locked in [that] I wasn't even paying attention to it. If there were boos, I couldn't even pick up what they were booing for. Then you'd notice after the games from [the] reports.'

It was about to get even more political. Priti Patel, a hard-line, right winger, Brexiteer Home Secretary, was keen to have her say on taking the knee. 'I just don't support people participating in that type of gesture,' she said. Asked whether fans were wrong to boo, Patel equivocated: 'That's a choice for them,' she replied. The prime minister's spokesperson initially declined to condemn those who had booed. 'The PM fully respects the right of those who choose to peacefully protest and make their feelings known,' political journalists were told.

But appearing to support people booing their national team on the eve of a major tournament that would largely be hosted by England was a bold position for any politician, let alone a right-wing patriot. Perhaps sensing the potential political car crash, the prime minister's position was nuanced a few days later. Johnson was 'urging everyone to get behind the team and cheer'.

Southgate continued to take questions on the topic right up to the eve of the tournament as he felt it was his duty to do so, but he said that the team would no longer talk about the issue. They needed to focus on their football. Yet he was clearly exasperated. 'I was concerned what happened could affect young players in particular,' he said. 'In essence, people are booing their own team. That's a very strange response.' He had met with the players to discuss their position. 'I wanted to gauge that the players were happy to continue. There are elements of the crowd that may boo. If that happens, that will be hugely disappointing, but we're prepared to go through that. Whatever happens we're adamant that's the stance we're going to take through the tournament and if it [booing] happens, we won't be discussing it after because we don't want to give more oxygen to those people.'

Southgate's own optimistic take in his *Dear England* letter now seemed audacious. 'I feel like this generation of England players is closer to the supporters than they have been for decades,' he had written. 'Despite the polarisation we see in society, these lads are on the same wavelength as you on many issues.'

* * *

When Owen Eastwood had set about researching England culture to attempt to build a sense of identity for the team, as well as trawling through the National Archives in Kew for the original Three Lions crest, the Maori-New Zealander had also interviewed former players to understand what that felt like to play for the national team. A thought from Michael Owen, the former Liverpool, Real Madrid and Manchester United striker struck him as significant. 'Over the whole of my England career, within the dressing room there was never any mention of the team's history, nor what it was to be English,' said Owen. That struck him as wrong.

Eastwood, Reddin and Southgate worked on a way to connect the team to their story. Eastwood had written about the 'unbreakable chain of people going back and forward in time . . . arms interlocked . . . unbreakable, immortal' when pondering his Maori ancestors. England players, he felt, needed something tangible to connect with their past as a means to building a future. Which is why prior to the 2021 European Championships, the England players were gathered in St George's Park auditorium to watch another film about their history.

This one was more upbeat than the last, which had detailed England's failures in Southgate's first camp in 2017. It started with the story of Cuthbert Ottaway, England's captain in the first ever international football match against Scotland in 1872. It would take in Billy Bassett, Stanley Matthews, Bobby Charlton, Bobby Moore and Kevin Keegan. Also the first black player to represent the senior team, Viv Anderson, and special mention was made of Laurie Cunningham, who was the first black man to represent England playing for the Under-21s. It highlighted the roles of John Barnes and Paul Ince. Observers say the players absolutely bought into the emotion of the message.

At the end, a ceremony was convened in the reception area at St George's Park. 'We are part of England's history,' Southgate would say. 'There is a longer history than just us so [we must] have the humility to recognise where we are in that journey but make the most of the moment and leave the team in a better place after the tournament than we found it. We want to connect with the public and part of that is recognising that we are no more special than anybody who has been before or anybody that will come after us.'

There followed a presentation which many say had a profound effect. England players have always received beautiful embroidered blue velvet Victorian-style caps when they play for their country. Kevin Keegan wrote in the 1980s how he once showed his Hamburger SV teammates one of his and it 'made my German teammates quite envious. They are paid nearly four times as much as England players for international appearances but money goes, whereas a caps lasts as an heirloom.'

However, Andy Walker, part of the FA communications teams, wanted to do something more. It was he who came up with the idea of legacy numbers. More than a thousand men had represented their country since 1872, an elite club. Walker suggested giving each a number – from number one for Robert Baker, the goalkeeper in that 1872 inaugural game, to the present day, an unbroken legacy chain. Initially the players were assigned a number before the Euro qualifiers in 2019, which took the chain up to James Maddison, the 1,245th player ever to play for England, making his debut in the game against Montenegro in which the players wore their legacy numbers on their shirt collars. The significance was that Montenegro was the 1,000th England game, but the FA almost missed it: it was only in conducting the research project into their history that alerted them to the fact that the anniversary was approaching.

Already the FA had tried to make more of the players receiving their actual England caps. Either Southgate or a former player will now present the first cap to a new player. 'Players would start on their England journey, play for their country, a huge moment in their career . . . and then get a cap through the post,' said Reddin. 'So that special moment was brought to them by Royal Mail. Matt Crocker [the FA's head of development teams] replaced that with a cap presentation evening and it became the big deal it should be.'

Now the England management team came up with an amplification of the England cap to seal a player's sense of himself in the national team's story. A new red velvet legacy cap was introduced, with their legacy number embroidered on the front. So after the history film and Southgate's speech, the new red legacy caps were presented to the squad. The whole FA team was involved, as a member of the backroom staff would hand a cap to a player, such as Jordan Henderson. He would then present the cap to a colleague and in Henderson's case, that was Jude Bellingham: the significance of passing the baton from one generation to another was deliberate, another emphasis of the unbreakable chain. And then Southgate and his assistant Chris Powell presented each other their own legacy caps. It quickly became an important marker for players. That day most players proudly posted their caps on social media. Declan Rice, James Maddison and John Stones would eventually get tattoos of their numbers. Former pros who later received theirs, such as Alan Shearer and Stan Collymore, spoke of their own pride. Cynicism had been banished from a camp which, back in 2016, players were reluctant to join.

Amidst the history, there were more contemporary touches to England's training camp for the Euros. They would be based at St George's Park, as most of their games were scheduled to be at Wembley and because Covid restrictions around Europe were still extreme. Mason Mount and Ben Chilwell would end up missing games simply for spending too long chatting to Scotland's Billy Gilmour, their Chelsea teammate after a group game. The England bubble had been potentially contaminated, according to the rules, so they had to quarantine. Players would not be allowed off site except for games and no family visits were permitted.

As such, Southgate had probably worked even harder than in Russia to make St George's a home from home and it was the foliage that made the initial impression, 'It's like a forest in here!' said Mount on arrival to St George's. Trees and plants had transformed the normally business-like areas of the centre. A juice bar, bean bags and sofas now occupied where once there were meeting rooms. The Hilton hotel reception was a basketball court, where you would have seen Harry Kane and Kieran Trippier beating Mason Mount and Phil Foden in a two-v-two match.

Rooms had again been decorated with photos of family members and given that there were no downtime days off site, the England team worked hard to break up the day. Text message alerts would beep on the players' phones to tell them the ice-cream van was in town and apparently the rush from the rooms to the outdoor space at St George's Park resembled a stampede. Fabio Capello, who famously banned butter and ketchup from his austere England training camps, would not have approved. A food van would turn up with barbecued meat. Ed Sheeran came to deliver an evening singalong concert. The unicorns, made famous in Russia, returned, the players mucking around in the swimming pool on recovery days. The image of Bukayo Saka sat grinning astride one became an iconic summer photo. In the gym, players contended in strength competitions for the boxing-style 'world title' belts, which Bryce Cavendish would then award them, to make training fun and competitive.

On mindset, Pippa Grange had been replaced by psychologist Ian Mitchell, who had also been a journeyman pro with Hereford United and Merthyr Tydfil. His approach was different to Grange's in that he used his footballing strengths to create openings. 'I definitely think there were players who felt more comfortable opening up because I am female,' said Rebecca Levett (née Symes), who worked with the Under-21s as a psychologist. 'But Ian has skills from a football perspective. When he's out on the training pitch, he's kicking balls.

I'm absolutely not going to be doing that!' By now anyway psychology was totally integrated into all the work the team did and had long since ceased to be a mere bolt-on extra activity.

Perhaps the most relaxed the players ever felt though would be for their evening massage. In front of the massage table were giant TV screens and Luke Shaw revealed why the late evening slot was so popular. 'You book your treatment times so you're on your bed when *Love Island* comes on,' said Shaw.

When they had a film night, it wasn't just any old movie: they had a sneak preview of Tom Cruise's *Top Gun Maverick*, not due out until 2022. Not only that but Cruise, friends with David Beckham, joined them in a Zoom call to chat and wish them luck. No wonder Shaw would say: 'We love St George's. It's unbelievable. It's felt like home.' Certainly it was a world isolated not just from Covid and the pressure of the games but the politics that had engulfed them prior to the Euros.

* * *

Raheem Sterling's nimblest piece of footwork was to evade the legs of goalkeeper Manuel Neuer, skipping over him as he plotted his celebration. Having cleared Neuer's outstretched arms, he was able to embark on that distinctive short-stepped skip-like run he does, kissing the badge before Harry Maguire and John Stones grabbed him. In the Royal Box, HRH Prince William undiplomatically also celebrated with gusto, punching the air with both arms aloft. Sterling had travelled a long way since being the self-proclaimed #HatedOne in Euro 2016.

'Being locked away at St George's Park, you don't really have the realisation of how humongous the tournament is,' he recalled. 'The build-up to the [Germany] game, travelling to London and seeing the fans in numbers, that's you when you realise: "It's here now." It was a lovely day. Especially with the people in the stadium, each game the stadium was getting more and more packed.'

Indeed, Covid restrictions had been eased for the last 16 Euro game against Germany at Wembley in June 2021 so that 41,000 were permitted rather than the 20,000 of the group games. Even before kick-off there was an air of anticipation from a nation that had been locked down for more than a year. The crowd noise seemed louder than when the stadium was full. 'When the lads go out to warm up, sometimes I'll just stay in the changing room, but [that day] you could hear the crowd in the changing room,' said Southgate. 'You can't always hear that. But you could hear them singing when the players were warming up. So it had the sense of a different sort of occasion.'

There would be more to come, however. Sterling's goal from three yards out after a lovely slick move he had initiated with Harry Kane, Mason Mount and Luke Shaw had opened the scoring in the 75th minute. The jeopardy of that slender lead was never more apparent than when Thomas Müller was put through on England's goal minutes later. With time to compose himself, he scuffed his shot wide. Five minutes later, Harry Kane scored the second and England fans could relax into their 2-0 victory. Not only had they won another knockout game – only their third since 2006 – but this was their first win over Germany in a major tournament since 1966.

What might have happened had Müller scored and Germany gone on to win that game is an intriguing counter-factual. As it was, something shifted in the summer's dynamic that evening. It is true that even prior to the Germany game, against Croatia, Scotland and the Czech Republic, fans were largely behind the team taking the knee, applause greeting the gesture. Southgate's calculation that the majority were with them proved correct. That said, the uninspiring

0-0 draw against Scotland had allowed doubters and haters alike to turn on Southgate. England weren't setting the tournament alight with 1-0 wins over Croatia and the Czech Republic, tricky though that first assignment had been.

Now though there was momentum and the Germany game had also seen a further embrace of a civil rights movement or, as their critics might put it, another virtue signal. Harry Kane had joined Germany captain Manuel Neuer in wearing a rainbow armband 'in support of LGBTQ+ rights' to mark Pride month. Germany had started the trend – England aren't the only national team to realise they have agency beyond football – provoking a UEFA investigation into whether it was a banned political symbol. They ruled that it wasn't but even so, some fans complained that they were told not to display rainbow flags in UEFA fan zones in Budapest, where Hungary Prime Minister Viktor Orbán has complained about the European Union's 'LGBT offensive', vowing to return Hungary to its Christian roots. No one embraced this cause more enthusiastically than Jordan Henderson. When a queer, non-binary fan tweeted about how much they had enjoyed the Germany game and felt no threat from fans, Henderson tweeted them back: 'Great to hear you enjoyed the game, as you should,' said Henderson. 'No one should be afraid because football is for everyone.' He added the strong arm and rainbow emojis and received 68,000 likes. It really did look like a new England.

There was the odd throwback to the old tropes. Southgate may not have gone the full Piers Morgan in goading the Germans. (The tabloid newspaper editor turned TV interviewer was lambasted in 1996 for his Second World War-themed 'Achtung Surrender!' front page.) But he ventured to go there. 'People have tried to invade us and we've had the courage to hold that back,' Southgate said. 'You can't hide that some of the energy in the stadium against Germany was because of that.'

In the quarter-final against Ukraine that Saturday, the only match England would play away from home at the Euros, travelling to Rome, England were 4-0 up within 63 minutes. Tension evaporated and semi-finals now seemed par for the course for England. Admittedly, against Denmark at Wembley, familiar nerves returned. They fell behind for the first and what would turn out to be the only time in the tournament, when Mikkel Damsgaard scored a spectacular free kick. But Denmark's lead lasted only nine minutes before Simon Kjaer scored an own goal in a desperate attempt to prevent Sterling from scoring. Penalties loomed in extra time until Sterling's clever footwork induced Joakim Maehle to hang out a lazy leg. It is fair to say Sterling maximised the opportunity presented to him, collapsing to the ground. It was very much at the softer end of the penalty scale. And few remember now that Harry Kane missed his spot kick, only scoring on the rebound.

With 64,000 fans permitted for the game, the volume and intensity of the celebrations exceeded even the Germany game, though keener-eyed observers noted that there seemed very few empty seats given the stadium was only meant to be two-thirds full. No matter, this time when Perry played 'Sweet Caroline', Southgate was doing his lap of honour and fist-pumping with the crowd. Harry Kane led the singing before joining the players, who were lined up in front of the stand reserved for their families. As they bounced up and down, arms round each other, grins as broad as the Wembley Arch, they all yelled 'So Good! So Good! So Good!' at the appropriate moment when the DJ required. It was both cheesy and profound. You might argue team spirit is an illusion forged in the aftermath of victory, as Scotland and Barcelona striker Steve Archibald once said. Yet this seemed something more. Like the culmination of what Southgate had been working towards since 2016, a team together and a nation united in support.

* * *

Bukayo Saka looked even younger than his callow 19 years as he prepared. The sheer innocence of his youth struck you given the momentous task with which he was entrusted. He puffed his cheeks and scratched his nose. A few seconds before he had bumped fists with Jordan Pickford, as he had been taught to: the FA penalty study showed that making a connection with a teammate before the penalty strike increased the likelihood of success. Yet now he was alone, just him against the giant Gianluigi Donnarumma. And he had to score to keep England in with a chance of winning the Euros.

In truth, he rushed. Not as much as Jadon Sancho, who took just three seconds from referee's whistle to strike. Saka took four, while Rashford was the most unfortunate of all the penalty failures, calmly waiting his time, hesitating before Donnarumma made his move, before striking the opposite way but hitting the post.

Saka's quick take was a sure sign of the stress he was under. He tried to place the ball, striking left-footed across his body to his right. It's a safe penalty for a player under pressure: that's a more natural movement than opening the body up. Petr Čech's summary in a similar situation was: 'Left-footed, under pressure in his own stadium: easier to hit across the ball so a goalkeeper has to go to his left side.' That's how Čech worked out how to save Ivica Olić's penalty in Munich to allow Chelsea to win the 2012 Champions League final.

Donnarumma clearly had received the memo from the goalkeepers' union, diving to his left to push away Saka's effort, a comfortable save. From thereon in, the player who has missed the last penalty in a shoot-out is left stranded. Saka looked lost as he pulled up his shirt to cover part of his face. Winning players always get to the scene quicker, meaning Saka was swamped by Italians darting this way and that around him to celebrate with Donnarumma.

One England player saw and quickened his pace to reach Saka first, who by now had his hands on his knees. 'Kalvin Phillips covered 83km over Euro 2020, more than anyone except Jorginho,' wrote Oliver Kay in *The Athletic*. 'He had a superb tournament but I think finding the energy and compassion to run to console Bukayo Saka was his best contribution of all.' Once Phillips had him in his arms, five more players formed a phalanx around him before Southgate – been there, done that – spoke to him and almost grabbed him in a protective head lock. 'I decided on the penalty takers based on what we had done in training and nobody is on their own,' Southgate would say. 'We have won together as a team and it is absolutely on all of us in terms of not being able to win the game tonight. In terms of the penalties, that is my call and totally rests with me.'

A few miles away in Feltham, a 52-year-old forklift driver decided to livestream on Facebook in the wake of the defeat. What followed was a racially charged invective directed at Saka, Sancho and Rashford. He would be sentenced to ten weeks in prison.

A 50-year-old plasterer from Kent also turned to Facebook Live: 'Where do I start? Where do I start?' he said seemingly anguished. 'So gutted like all of us. Proper deflated, big proud of the boys, big proud, but anyone and everyone that knows me well will understand what I am talking about . . .' At which point he used a racist term to describe Rashford, Sancho and Saka. He had signed off with 'England 'til I die' on the comments section. He was sentenced to 50 days' imprisonment suspended for 12 months.

In Cheshire, a 43-year-old father posted racist comments about the players 'to make people laugh', he would later tell police. He was sentenced to 14 weeks' imprisonment suspended for 18 months. In Worcester, a 19-year-old sent Rashford racial abuse on Twitter and would spend six weeks in a Young Offenders' Institute. In Withington, south Manchester, a mural depicting Rashford was defaced. Saka would say: 'I knew instantly the kind of hate I was about to receive.'

It was left to a young man who had only just turned 18 a few days before the final to best summarise all of the above. 'It felt like the country had united and we were heading on the same path. We had black players in the team, players of all different backgrounds in the team. And then as soon as they missed the penalty, they're not English, they're just black,' said Jude Bellingham.

The football almost seemed incidental. Outside, rogue ticketless fans, who had been waiting to storm the stadium, melted away into a rainy evening. FA staff who had spent their entire life building to this moment were relieved England had lost, fearing fatal consequences had they won. An official from the Sports Grounds Safety Authority said: 'Thank God they lost. If they had won you would have had to open the doors to let people out and the stadium would have been stormed.' The Casey review would describe the game as a 'near miss' that almost led to deaths.

And yet the football happened. Southgate had switched from a back four to 3-4-3 for the final, a move that spooked Italy, who were utterly baffled for 20 minutes. England were 1-0 up within two minutes through Luke Shaw and Italy's full-backs couldn't cope with Kieran Trippier and Shaw's aggressive runs as wing-backs. England were exceptional in spreading the ball wide quickly and Harry Kane was dropping deep, which had led to the first goal. Italy were chasing shadows.

But if Southgate won the opening exchanges, Italy manager

Roberto Mancini emphatically won the rest of the tactical battle. Already by the end of the first half, Italy were getting more possession. You began to see Emerson Palmieri and Giovanni Di Lorenzo attacking from full-back positions and Federico Chiesa and Lorenzo Insigne were making darting runs with Giorgio Chiellini beginning to play those searching long balls. That said, they couldn't get in behind England.

But as against Croatia in the World Cup semi-final, England were retreating into a back five rather than an offensive back three. Jorginho stepped into the vacant space to dominate midfield, just as Luka Modrić had in 2018. Mancini made a double substitution on 55 minutes, the key change being Domenico Berardi for Ciro Immobile, which allowed Insigne to go central. Suddenly Italy were getting runs in behind. The pressure mounted until on 67 minutes the Leonardo Bonucci equaliser came. In the 2018 semi-final against Croatia it had come on 68 minutes.

Against Croatia, Southgate seemed frozen. Here at least he made a quick change, bringing on Saka and reverting to 4-3-3. It made a difference, but didn't wrest the game back from Italy. Mancini was bold with his substitutes, changing the entire front five, allowing them to maintain their pressing game. England tired and passing became sloppy; too many long balls were hit to nowhere in particular.

One sporting director of a leading Premier League club thought Southgate's set-up was instinctively negative. 'If our manager set up like that for a final we would part company,' he said. This fuelled those who saw Southgate as over-negative and cautious. 'I just feel that Gareth Southgate's team are playing with the handbrake on,' Cesc Fabregas, World Cup winner and Euro winner with Spain, had written during the tournament. 'I think going forward England have to find a way of being more attack-minded,' tweeted Gary Lineker immediately after the final. 'Braver in possession and throwing more people forward. We have the forward talent to scare teams; at present we seem scared ourselves to release that talent.' The set-up seemed to owe much to Southgate's assistant Steve Holland, who was schooled at Chelsea by José Mourinho, a man not averse to use of the handbrake.

Overall, England had 38 per cent possession, almost a reversion to the bad old days of being out-passed and out-thought. That said, by extra time we were witnessing two extremely tired teams, not just at the end of a long tournament but also negotiating the extraordinary strain of playing football almost non-stop from June 2020.

* * *

By the end of the week, Rashford's mural in Withington had again been altered. Not defaced this time though. By now crowds were congregating to leave flowers, as the wall around Rashford's face was covered with hearts, Post-it notes and England flags. 'We're proud of you' they read and 'role model'. 'You stepped up'. Rashford said he was on the verge of tears.

Government ministers were now keen to align themselves with the England team again. Patel, the Home Secretary who didn't want players to take the knee, nor condemn those who booed them, tweeted: 'I am disgusted that England players who have given so much for our country have been subject to vile racist abuse on social media. It has no place in our country and I back the police to hold those responsible accountable.' Though her support wasn't welcomed by many players and Tyrone Mings, part of the Euro squad, took to social media to point out why. 'You don't get to stoke the fire at the beginning of the tournament by labelling our anti-racism message as "Gesture Politics" and then pretend to be disgusted when the very thing we're campaigning against happens.'

But just five weeks after that trauma, Saka would take to an English football pitch again. He would do so at Tottenham, Arsenal's hated rivals. He would come on as a 63rd-minute substitute in a pre-season friendly. Phil Neville's wife once came home to a burning England shirt after the full-back was blamed for the Euro 2000 exit. David Beckham was hung in effigy after the 1998 World Cup. Both were booed that season by opposing fans, taunted that they had 'let their country down'. If Saka was going to get it anywhere, it would be now, Spurs fans having never previously missed the opportunity to exploit an Arsenal player's vulnerability.

And yet something extraordinary happened at Spurs as Saka entered the pitch. A ripple of supportive applause spread through the stadium. Admittedly, he can never expect to be greeted that way there ever again. Yet it represented a moment. Saka, realising what was happening, acknowledged the Spurs fans. The same would happen when he played at Brentford a week later; he was warmly applauded by opposition fans. It was as though a line had been drawn.

'I think what hurt me was that this was a group of players that had brought everybody together for 30 days on a brilliant journey and then the first time we have a setback and defeat, now all of a sudden we're going to allow this division to happen,' said Southgate. 'I wasn't happy about that at all. What I was really pleased [about] was that although there was a horrible reaction that night from too many people but still a minority, I thought there was a brilliant counter-reaction where the majority of fans and public were saying: "Actually, we're not having this. We're with Bukayo, Marcus and Jadon."'

Southgate had written about racists in his *Dear England* letter. 'I have some bad news. You're on the losing side.'

And his overall goal for the tournament had been clearly set out in his letter. 'It's about how we conduct ourselves on and off the pitch, how we bring people together, how we inspire and unite, how we create memories that last beyond the 90 minutes. That last beyond the summer. That last forever. If we can do that, it will be a summer to be proud of.'

Amidst a night of carnage of a summer evening, perhaps some seeds of hope had been planted.

CHAPTER 8

LONG, DARK NIGHT OF THE SOUL

What a team, what a coach, what fun in the sunshine.

There were England, playing with abandon and joy, to win when nobody expected them to. This was an England who did things differently, whose confidence coursed from a breath-of-fresh-air leader. The country was in love with them. 'A victory for the ages' enthused *The Times*. The headline on *The Sun*'s match report was about kebabs but 'Power & the Glory' was the *Daily Star*'s.

But this was not *our* England. Not the footballers. These were the cricketers, Ben Stokes, Jonny Bairstow, Joe Root and co. who, inspired by the ultra-positive coaching of Brendon McCullum, blitzed an impossible triumph against New Zealand at a giddy Trent Bridge.

It was 14 June 2022 – one of those days when sport, with its uncanny sense of storylines, throws up a dramatic juxtaposition. In Nottingham, English cricket enjoyed one of its greatest afternoons. And then in Wolverhampton, English football endured one of its bleakest evenings.

A little more than two hours after Stokes bludgeoned the winning runs at Trent Bridge, 60 miles away, at Molineux, Zsolt Nagy took the kick-off in a Nations League encounter between England and Hungary. Over the next 90 minutes of football, the Hungarians would break all sorts of records, inflicting on England their biggest home defeat since 1928, and the first defeat by four goals or more without scoring in 64 years. Muddled, inhibited, the crowd on their backs, the coach getting stick – England's football side seemed all the bad things England's cricket side were not.

England 0 Hungary 4: a stupefying, grimly iconic final score. Full-time brought a cascade of boos and then a chant that would cut straight to any manager's core. The words rang in Gareth Southgate's ears: *You don't know what you're doing. You don't know what you're doing.*

YOU DON'T KNOW WHAT YOU'RE DOING.

Southgate entered the post-match press conference knowing it was going to be brutal and the first three questions, asked by the man from Sky for live TV, set the tone:

Are you embarrassed by that?

How damaging will that be?

How much has this damaged your relationship with fans?

'Tonight was a difficult night,' Southgate said. 'My predecessors have had nights like this. I've watched from the sofa as a kid and I've watched as a player and I recognise those difficult times. But you can't just be at the front when things are going well and not stand up when you have difficult experiences. That's part of football and part of life.'

He said he understood supporters' frustrations and added with typical sense of duty, 'The responsibility lies with me.'

On a personal level, Southgate would be okay. But would his team? Leaving Molineux that evening he could not see a way for his relationship with England to last beyond the World Cup in Qatar. So much of his early work had been about freeing players, lightening the shirt, making England enjoyable, making England new and fresh. Not so long ago *he* was Brendon McCullum. Not so long ago the chant was 'Southgate, you're the one!' But now he wondered if his presence had become a burden upon his team.

Southgate turned it over in his mind. He just could not see how the pressure on him would do anything other than affect his players. And this weighed heavily on him.

At home in Harrogate, where on the oak-panelled wall of his office is a picture of Muhammad Ali hugging Pele, he was surrounded by his family, Alison, his wife, and Mia and Flynn, his children – young adults now. Their support was incredible. They could see the effect the past fortnight had had on him. And, as a family, they talked things over. What emerged was a decision. Southgate would continue as England manager until the World Cup, and however bad the scrutiny got, there would be no walking away.

The clarity was helpful to everyone. But doubts persisted in Southgate's mind and two weeks after Molineux, he had a long conversation with Steve Holland. 'Look, I might have to tell people I'm going,' he told Holland. He wondered if the best course might be to announce publicly he would leave after the tournament, to take the sting out of the campaign to force him out and liberate his players. Maybe that would give England the best chance of a proper crack at the World Cup.

What did Holland think? Should he say he was going to quit?

About one thing, Southgate had always been clear. He even spelled it out to journalists a few days before the Hungary debacle: 'I won't outstay my welcome.'

* * *

Southgate did not agree with the criticism that had followed him since Euro 2020. He and Holland met at St George's Park two days after the final to review the tournament and since then there had been a lot of analysis and self-reflection. The notions that he had been out-thought by Mancini and had the 'handbrake on' seemed very unfair. In his and Holland's analysis, England won the early tactical skirmishes by outflanking Italy with their 3-4-3, exploiting the benefits of their formation when one wing-back crossed for the other to score. And Italy had regained ground by flooding midfield. So, if anything, the strategic battle between Southgate and Mancini had been a draw – and Italy's goal came from bad England defending at a corner, not some great coaching manoeuvre.

Handbrake? No matter the system, as *The Telegraph*'s Jason Burt observed, his England always defended with five and attacked with six, and swapping between a back three and back four had been good enough for Terry Venables. Southgate resolved to continue being flexible with his formations and ignore noise about negativity and those post Euro 2020 games suggested that, as 2021 ended, he had done a good job in shaking any tournament hangover from his players. They appeared to have taken up a challenge he laid down for them when, in the squad's first meet-up after Euro 2020, Southgate asked: 'Is that us? Are we done now? Semi-final and final losers? Is that our pinnacle and are we going to drop away now – or does this make you even stronger and determined to win?'

The New Year brought March friendlies against Switzerland and Ivory Coast. They were bland games but, hampered by a considerable injury list, 2-1 and 3-1 victories were a decent outcome, and Southgate was able to try out new players, giving debuts to Tyrick Mitchell, Marc Guéhi and Kyle Walker-Peters and a first start to Conor Gallagher. But a change in the vibe at Wembley concerned him. There was Maguire, the fan favourite of 2018, suddenly being booed by England supporters before and during the Ivory Coast game. 'An absolute joke,' Southgate said.

Kane was similarly despairing. 'We've worked hard to rebuild our connection with England fans in the last few years, so to hear Harry Maguire booed at Wembley before kick-off was just not right. The fact he's been brilliant on the pitch and given us all so many great memories makes it even harder to understand,' he said. Jordan Henderson took to Twitter. 'I can't get my head around what happened to Wembley tonight,' he wrote. 'Harry Maguire has been a colossus for England. Without him, the progress made at the last two tournaments would not have been possible.

'To be booed in his home stadium, for no reason? What have we become?'

* * *

How to convey the horror of Hungary? Let's begin near the touchline on England's left flank.

Marc Guéhi goes to control a high ball but his touch is untidy. Pressed by Dániel Gazdag, he passes back to Aaron Ramsdale, playing safe. Ramsdale gives the ball to Stones, who attempts to come forward but is so exasperated by the lack of options he throws his hands wide in a gesture which says: 'What am I supposed to do?' He is forced to pass square to Walker, who sends the ball back to Ramsdale again.

From there the sequence goes: Ramsdale to Guéhi, Guéhi to Bellingham, Bellingham to Phillips, Phillips back to Guéhi.

Then: Guéhi to Stones, Stones to Walker, Walker back to Stones.

Then: Stones to Guéhi, Guéhi to Bellingham, Bellingham to Bukayo Saka, Saka back to Guéhi

Finally, England try something different, with Guéhi gathering his courage and hitting a long diagonal towards Reece James. But James gives the ball away. Very soon, it's back in England's half yet again.

This was not England trying to be measured at 0-0 but *chasing the game*, with 58 minutes gone and Hungary already leading 1-0. Their country's worst result in 94 years was beginning to seem a possibility, but all the team could manage was this timid dance of back, forward, sideways, back again. The sequence described was a 60-second spell of unbroken possession, involving 16 passes that did not get England one single inch further up the pitch. Over the whole 90 minutes, Southgate's team had 789 touches, yet 522 were shared by their defenders, defensive midfielder and goalkeeper. The heat maps showed almost zero England touches in either Hungary's goalmouth or 'Zone 14' – that central strip of pitch on the edge of the penalty area which, in classic analysis, is regarded as the prime zone for creating chances.

And yet, despite hanging back, England still conceded four goals for the first time in a decade. They pulled off that rare trick of being at the same time conservative and reckless, with Stones sent off and the defence parting for the Hungarians to go through on Ramsdale for their second, third and fourth goals. For the first and only time in Southgate's reign, his England looked like the England who met Iceland on that day of epochal humiliation in 2016. The boos and howls were pitiless. *You don't know what you're doing.*

YOU DON'T KNOW WHAT YOU'RE DOING.

In his main press conference, in his mild way, Southgate tried to point out that the only bad times of his reign had come in the Nations League whereas 'in the [traditional tournament] matches where every other England managers have been judged we've had the best performances for 50 years.'

But were a great many listening? Afterwards, Southgate went to the Molineux boardroom to give the national newspaper number ones a briefing (he never ducked them, whatever the result). The atmosphere was hostile. The questioning from a particular journalist shocked others present in its personal nature. The next day's headlines would not be kind.

'It took longer than I thought, but Gareth Southgate and his sidekick, Steve Holland, have finally been well and truly found out. Although I entirely agree with Southgate that the 4-0 Hungary mauling at Molineux was not the players' fault, but his alone,' said a letter to *The Times* and the newspaper's chief football writer, Henry Winter, backed the terracing rebellion.

'It is pretty arrogant to claim, as some do, that those disgruntled England supporters mutinying at Molineux should really know their place, bite their tongue and meekly accept a wretched performance from a collection of ill-prepared talents. That they should acquiesce to the debacle against Hungary and absorb uncomplainingly England's heaviest home loss since Evelyn Waugh published *Decline and Fall*,' Winter wrote.

'Because those following England closely will know that their Molineux mauling was not a blip, as some believe, but a trend. It was a continuation of Gareth Southgate's failure to respond decisively in the second half of the Euro 2020 final against Italy, amid excruciating echoes of losing the 2018 World Cup semi-final against Croatia . . . Southgate is a great man, but not a great manager. Even his cheerleaders must admit that.'

* * *

A long-time friend of Southgate, who could tell you a hundred stories about his decency but also a few about his hidden steel, says Molineux changed the man he knows. Southgate emerged, harder, wiser and in some ways freer. As the friend puts it, 'Gareth lost his virginity that night.'

The FA never even thought about asking him to quit. Its chair, Debbie Hewitt, offered Southgate both private and public backing in the week after the 4-0 defeat to Hungary. A stellar businesswoman who has chaired major brands like Visa and White Stuff, Hewitt said, 'I've worked with a lot of chief executives and Gareth's skills – his high IQ and high EQ [emotional quotient] would make him a chief exec in any sphere.

'That resilience and accountability are the two qualities I admire most about him. There's no slopey shoulders, he doesn't huff, he's resilient, and that's what you want in an England manager.'

But there are stages on the journey when the 'Impossible Job' feels a little less possible than it does at others. And the destination can be cruel. Think of Sir Alf Ramsey. One Wednesday afternoon in May 1974, the only man to win England a major tournament boarded the 5.30 p.m. train from London Liverpool Street to Ipswich and met Ted Phillips, a striker he had managed at Ipswich Town. Ramsey fetched two beers. They chatted and Ramsey bought another round of drinks. He did not mention that earlier in the day he had been fired as England manager. Said his widow, Lady Victoria Ramsey, 'I really do think it broke him.'

Ron Greenwood? Once, this kind, understated man and underrated coach was asked to whom an England manager is answerable. His reply was pithy: 'Nobody, except the nation. It is a one-in-fifty-million job. I was my own boss but everyone's Aunt Sally.'

Graham Taylor . . . Keegan . . . Sven . . . Capello . . . Steve McClaren . . . Don Revie. Sir Bobby Robson – who ended a hero and everyone's favourite uncle, but only after taking a pasting first. Southgate knows his history. All get tested and most get broken, doing the role he is in.

He has known about the realities of management since being sacked at Middlesbrough, in October 2009. That happened on the same evening his young team beat Derby to move to within one point of top spot in the Championship. The chairman, Steve Gibson, told him it was time for a change and that 'after a few days, you'll feel relieved'.

'Sacked in the morning,' was another of the refrains on that stifling June evening at Molineux. But there Southgate was, at St George's Park on a crisp November day, naming his World Cup squad. He was upbeat. He had toughed it out. If this really was going to be the last dance, he was damn sure he was going to enjoy it.

* * *

Harry Kane pulled up his England shirt over his chin and bit the top, holding it between his teeth. For a moment, the archetypal English lionheart looked like a little boy, chewing on his T-shirt to gain comfort during a stressful day at nursery. It does that to you, penalties, strips you down to the inner child. 'There is no one I would rather have taking it and if we had one tomorrow I would say the same,' Gareth Southgate would say later, dissecting England's exit.

In that moment, immediately after the miss, he stood alone as France's players rushed to congratulate Hugo Lloris, coincidentally a close friend and Spurs teammate. The goalkeeper had, of course, done nothing, Kane striking the ball over the bar. But instinctively a team needs a celebration focal point.

The England players seemed to have forgotten the Jordan Henderson moment against Colombia: that body language after a penalty miss matters. They all stood rooted to the spot, like hope had been sucked from their lungs. It was understandable as there were 84 minutes on the clock and traditionally that is the last chance saloon for teams. Yet this was the World Cup of ten-plus minutes of injury time, thanks to the new FIFA directive cracking down on time-wasting.

There were actually still 14 minutes to play, which is plenty of time to fashion another chance to equalise, especially as England had momentum in the game.

Only one player reacted, the 19-year-old Jude Bellingham, who sprinted to Kane and whispered in his ear, cradling his neck. It was a scene that would near enough be repeated in May 2024 when Kane stood over a penalty for Bayern Munich. On that occasion, Bellingham's intentions were not benign. 'I know you're going left,' he would tell his England teammate in a vain attempt to spook him: all's fair in love, war and Champions League semi-finals. But that night in Qatar, Bellingham demonstrated maturity beyond his years and confirmed his status as England captain in waiting. It was Bellingham who also first ran to the penalty spot to protect it when the kick was awarded. (It is standard practice for the team conceding the penalty to scuff up the spot nowadays; the attacking teams needs a minder to defend it.) Bellingham also found time, along with the fouled Mason Mount, to suggest a red card for Theo Hernandez, which was unforthcoming but was a further demonstration of keeping his head when all about were losing theirs.

Kane isn't one to be haunted by demons, even though, as he has conceded, that miss will be with him for life. 'I have a routine for penalties,' he said. 'The same steps, the same breathing, the same mindset. Before every game I choose where I'm going to go, what I'll do if we get two penalties. I had it all clear in my head, but sometimes you just don't execute. It's not like I underprepared, which maybe would have been the worst feeling. I've never let anything like that knock me. When you have disappointing moments it just makes me ready for another challenge.'

Which is the exemplary mindset of a world-class striker, very stiff upper lip and to be expected from Kane, who would make a plausible

Second World War RAF pilot in terms of emotional temperament. And yet, at the end of it all, England were out of the World Cup at the quarter-final stage, again. And it was a penalty, again. Stop all clocks at St George's Park, especially Greg Dyke's countdown one. The vision had not been realised. There would be no World Cup win.

* * *

Qatar 2022 was always going to be a 'noisy' World Cup. That was the verdict within the FA and as such, their goal was noise management rather than radio silence. The circumstances in which the tournament had been awarded to Qatar were in themselves inauspicious: as his last significant act as FIFA president, Sepp Blatter had organised a double-header vote for both the 2018 and 2022 World Cups. The FA, still in calamity phase, embarrassingly flew out Prince William, then the Duke of Cambridge, and Prime Minister David Cameron to Zurich to garner the two votes they received for their 2018 World Cup bid, won by Russia, one of which came from their own chairman. They had persuaded just one of the 22 committee members of their merits despite having spent £21 million. Russian President Vladimir Putin by contrast didn't even bother to stay for voting in November 2010, leaving the night before. 'All the fish have sold in this market,' said the leader of a rival Spain/Portugal bid. Putin knew.

The dual award had descended into an orgy of corruption for many of the elderly 22 voters on the FIFA executive committee, seemingly anxious this would be the last vote for years and their final payday. Their collective comeuppance came in May 2015 at a memorable dawn raid on the five-star Baur au Lac hotel, Zurich, when several executives there for a FIFA Congress were escorted from the premises by plain-clothed police officers. Many would later be charged with corruption. Of the 22 voters who awarded the World Cup to Russia and Qatar, ten would eventually be banned from FIFA with 14 accused of corruption and money laundering. That said, the case in the US still rumbles on and in 2023, two convictions of TV and marketing executives connected to the FIFA case were overturned.

But Phaedra Almajid, a media officer turned whistle-blower on the Qatar bid, had told a UK reporter one month before the vote: 'I don't think Qatar will win 2022, I *know* they will.' She said she had witnessed bribes being offered. Even FIFA, in its subsequent inquiry, inadvertently revealed on its official website that executives had received money to vote for Qatar although officially it never confirmed this. The Qatar bid have always strenuously denied any corruption which, if true, makes their shock victory all the more astonishing given so many of the electorate have been shown to be corrupt.

Even so, few could imagine the furore that would engulf Qatar over the coming decade. Social media was in its infancy in 2010 so a world where random Arab and European citizens would be regularly exchanging insults about the *kafala* system, gay rights, and British and American imperialism was unimaginable, but by 2022 a reality.

Yet many times over that decade the Qatari bid team and their advisers must have pondered the maxim, 'There's no such thing as bad publicity'. For Qatar, there was plenty of that. The inequitable *kafala* system, which meant migrant workers relied on a local sponsor, leaving them with almost non-existent rights, suddenly became the focus of worldwide attention and was officially abolished in 2019. Most major infrastructure projects prior to major games have some construction worker deaths: Qatar 2022 would insist there had been just three for those working on the stadia. (Seven new stadia had been constructed specially for the tournament. The insane environmental cost of Qatar 2022 was often lost in the analysis, a secondary issue, less important than having to break the European football season to play in winter and not having Budweiser on sale at stadia.) Yet the best independent estimate of migrant worker deaths working on World Cup infrastructure came from journalist Nick Harris, who put the figure at around 2,800 since 2011. During the tournament, even Hassan Al-Thawadi, the Secretary General of the Qatar organising committee, admitted to Piers Morgan that 'about 400–500' had died. And that was before you started detailing those who had been ill-treated, injured or simply not paid for work. Qatar would protest that enormous strides were made between 2010 and 2022 to improve workers' rights with *kafala* abolished. Many younger Qatari leaders absolutely understood the need to change. But human rights organisations had discovered that persuading Qatari courts to enforce workers' rights was another challenge altogether.

Gareth Southgate was perhaps more across the topic than some of the journalists interrogating him. He read extensively and even met with migrant workers in an independent, non-official meeting which has never been made public before now, because of the political sensitivities. It was not an officially sanctioned Qatari photo-op, of which there were many and which invariably produced happy workers delighted with their lot. It was independently arranged with the help of a human rights organisation so that workers could speak freely about their conditions.

'The area of human rights is so broad that I've found it quite overwhelming to piece together,' said Southgate, shortly before travelling to Qatar for the World Cup draw in April 2022. 'I'm quite clear about the areas of concern: the building of stadiums was obviously the first and unfortunately there is nothing we can do about that now. They're built. There are ongoing concerns about the rights of workers and the conditions they live in. It seems universally accepted that it is better than it was, but not in the position where people feel it could be. And maybe policies that have been put in place are not always enforced as they might be.'

An additional challenge was that England had embraced the LGBTQ+ community with their rainbow armband at Euro 2020, to great applause, with Jordan Henderson's enthusiastic endorsement particularly lauded. In a country where homosexuality was illegal, as it is in almost every country with a Muslim majority, and punishable with imprisonment, it was hardly an inviting prospect for gay fans. The Qatar organisers' insistence that there would be no issues as long as there weren't over-demonstrative shows of affection hardly reassured.

'Sadly, from discussions I've had, I don't think those [LGBTQ+] fans will go,' said Southgate. 'And that's a great shame. We stand for inclusivity as a team; that's been a big driver in a lot of the stances we've taken in the last couple of years and it would be horrible to think that some of our fans feel they can't go. We'll be highlighting the key areas to the players. We have to prepare them as best we can to make the best possible decisions. There will be different narratives depending on whom you speak to and both sides of those arguments are very strong and inconsistent if you listen to the two stories.

'We're not going to be able to come out with a statement that will satisfy everything. It's different to where we were on taking the knee and the importance we felt on that. We're not saying this is any less important. We feel the World Cup is an opportunity to highlight some of those issues and we have a platform to do that. But we have to do that in a responsible way. I'm taking it very seriously; we want to make sure players are protected. I want them to make sure they're able to use their voice in the right way, but I also don't want them to be used with broader agenda at play. It's going to be complicated and I think we're going to get criticism whatever we do.'

He was certainly correct in the latter assessment. Having spoken out on some non-football-related issues, they had opened a Pandora's box. Which human rights should you prefer? In highlighting some, people would inevitably demand you support their preferred cause. And if you didn't – or didn't do so with sufficient enthusiasm – there was an assumption you didn't care. You could understand why in the past, footballers had steered well clear of such issues, their stance summed up by Michael Jordan, the multimillionaire, Nike-sponsored, African-American basketball player. Asked why he didn't campaign against a Republican electoral candidate accused of racism, he replied: 'Republicans buy sneakers too.'

Eventually, the FA would happen upon what seemed like a neat solution. Several of their fellow northern European football federations were coming under similar pressure from media and campaigners. They would band together in what became known as the Seven Nation Army, with Wales, Belgium, Netherlands, Denmark, Germany and Switzerland to wear a multi-coloured One Love armband. It was not exactly the rainbow symbol of the LGBTQ+ movement, but was deemed to be against 'discrimination', which in itself seemed somewhat nebulous. It looked like a corporate decision rather than a Southgate-inspired or player-led one. Southgate had previously said: 'I'm not sure just wearing a T-shirt makes a difference,' and seemed to have little truck with the superficial.

To the credit of the Seven Nation Army, though the media focus and fury was on the armband, their statement also said there should be compensation for the families of migrant workers killed during construction, which could make a tangible difference to impoverished families and was the principal concern of human rights campaigners. And they also called for the establishment of a migrant workers' centre, an independent presence in Qatar where workers could get legal advice on their disputes when in trouble. In response, FIFA announced a vague legacy fund, which promised to help support education projects and create a 'labour excellence hub', whatever that was.

The armband was probably the worst of all worlds: it angered LGBTQ+ activists as being insufficient and upset the hosts, who considered it evangelical colonial moralising. Essentially the armband said West is Best, or that Western European values trumped those of Islamic countries. The fact that homosexuality had been illegal in England when they last won a trophy was frequently cited, including by Southgate, as evidence that the West was in no real position to preach. Yet presenting this as a progressive issue, one that would be righted in time once Qatar became enlightened like the UK, was a philosophical cul-de-sac, which left you in the position that Western Europe had the last word on morality. And if inclusion was a big enough tent to bring every minority under the canopy, from gay activist to devout Muslim, then there were clearly going to be profound disagreements around the proverbial campfire. As such, an armband always seemed an unlikely answer to complex issues. The way to hell, it is said, is paved with good intentions and it is a route well-trodden by the FA over the years.

* * *

'Today I feel Qatari,' FIFA president Gianni Infantino declared. 'Today I feel Arabic. Today I feel African. Today I feel gay. Today I feel disabled. Today I feel a migrant worker.' Later, after his 57-minute monologue to the international press on the opening day of Qatar 2022, it was pointed out he had not mentioned women. 'I feel like a woman too!' was Infantino's response. There really is no way to embarrass the shameless.

'I know what it means to be discriminated [against], to be

bullied, as a foreigner in a foreign country,' he added. 'As a child I was bullied because I had red hair and freckles, plus I was Italian, so imagine.' Re-casting Qatar 2022 as a celebration of minorities was such a brazen move it threw his critics completely off guard. It was an unimaginable take. Yet the section of the speech in which the Swiss lawyer aligned himself with Global South, criticising the moralising of former imperial powers, went down very well outside of Western Europe, North America and Australasia. 'We have been told many, many lessons from some Europeans, from the Western world,' said Infantino. 'I think for what we Europeans have been doing the last 3,000 years, we should be apologising for the next 3,000 years before starting to give moral lessons to people.'

As such, the FA and their Seven Nation Army should have been forewarned. England were due to play their opening game two days later, the first of the One Love teams to take the field in Qatar. Having been led to believe by FIFA that the armband gesture would result in a fine for displaying a political slogan, which the FA could then nobly pay, they shouldn't really have been surprised when a five-person delegation arrived at their hotel on match day against Iran to tell them otherwise.

It was a 'punchy meeting' according to some, but ultimately, if you want to play politics with FIFA, you had best arm yourself appropriately: the FA had taken an armband to a knife fight. FIFA, so closely aligned to Qatar, was never going to allow their hosts to be embarrassed. The day before England played Iran, Infantino had sat next to The Emir of Qatar, Sheikh Tamim bin Hamad Al Thani, at the tournament's opening game. Next to them was Saudi Crown Prince, Mohammed bin Salman, the de facto ruler of Saudi Arabia accused by US intelligence of 'approving an operation in Istanbul to capture or kill Saudi journalist Jamal Khashoggi'. In the aftermath of

FIFA's decision there was some talk among the Seven Nation Army of 'never again' allowing the World Cup to be hosted by a country where homosexuality was illegal. In 2023, it was announced by Infantino that Saudi Arabia would host the 2034 World Cup. There was no contest nor a vote: they were the sole bidder.

Former England striker Ian Wright had expressed the disillusion of many England fans when he said: 'There's no protest without risk. It would have been such a powerful protest. The LGBTQ community [would] see they've actually put something on the line like they do every day of their lives.' Bullingham's response was: 'We couldn't put the players in a position where they might be facing a ban.'

The players had taken the knee because it felt personal to their experience and, other than boos and criticism, there was minimal cost. Although members of the FA staff and goalkeeper Aaron Ramsdale had family who were part of the LGBTQ+ community, this issue wasn't as visceral. And they weren't prepared for the kind of sacrifice Colin Kaepernick made when he took the knee, which led to him being effectively blacklisted by NFL clubs, for which he eventually received a settlement thought to be worth several million dollars. Nor were they Tommie Smith and John Carlos, the most famous sports protesters of all, who faced the threat of losing their Olympic medals for making the black power salute at the 1968 Olympics. Captain Kane ended up wearing FIFA's official #NoDiscrimination armband.

Southgate himself looked completely nonplussed by the furore. 'I do understand FIFA's situation in that you can set a precedent and it's difficult to know where to draw the line,' he said. 'I think in an ideal world there would have been a much clearer situation earlier. [But] it has not been a distraction for us. We had to focus on the football, we can't be involved in that now. There's nothing I won't speak about, but the predominant part of my energy has to be on preparing the team.'

It was understandable. In the run-up to the World Cup, the average Southgate press conference would start on migrant workers' rights, move to LGBTQ+ issues, before taking in Black Lives Matter and the Russia–Ukraine War. Occasionally, football was discussed. This was the logical conclusion of an open media policy, which Southgate embraced. 'But he can't be a spokesperson for the world,' said one member of the FA staff. After a tumultuous couple of years, the limits of player protest seemed to have been found.

* * *

The scene at the Souq Al Wakra, a few miles south of Doha city centre, was the one Qatar organisers wanted you to see, away from the migrant workers' camps. On a Thursday night, before Friday's Islamic congregational prayers, the seafront was bustling with families searching for seats at beachside restaurants. A young mum in a hijab kicked a football to her toddler while the mini train ferrying kids up and down had the vibe of a British seaside resort; the camels honking noisily on the beach where men in flowing Arab robes offered rides, less so. Posters in English carried evangelical Muslim messages. 'Smiling is a form of charity – Prophet Muhammad.' Morocco, the poster boys for the extended Arab nation, were beating Canada that night, to the delight of locals enjoying grilled lamb at the restaurants, which had large screen TVs erected to ensure no one missed a moment of the tournament.

The Souq is a modern recreation of what a fishing village might have looked like there 100 years ago. Away from the brash high rises of downtown Doha, where the serious business was now done, the Qatari authorities had constructed a reminder of a simpler time. For that month though there were visitors in town at Souq Al Wakra Hotel and the number of police stationed outside gave an indication of their importance.

England had come a long way from Stalag Capello in Rustenburg and not just in the preparation that went into their training camp. Their narrative was different now too. All around the hotel were photos fashioned artistically from Arabic script of key moments of the new England story: Saka on his unicorn was one, the chorus line of players belting out 'Sweet Caroline' at the Euros was another, while Eric Dier scoring the penalty that knocked out Colombia in Russia was also immortalised. Everything was designed to lighten the load, emphasise the opportunity, extenuate fun over fear.

In those long, warm evenings, Conor Coady took centre stage. The England players had moved on from card game Uno to an even more interactive role play pastime, Werewolf. Not unlike Claudia Winkleman's TV show *Traitors,* which coincidentally was proving an unlikely hit back home amidst the dark, frozen nights in England, it was a card game in which you drew lots secretly to decide who would be werewolves among villagers. Coady played the Winkleman role as the moderator. 'He was there in the middle, running it like a TV game show host!' said one observer. Often up to 12 or 15 of the squad were sitting around playing late into the evening.

'The villagers have to search out the wolves and it's who the best liar is,' said Declan Rice. 'Conor is the narrator and the lads have a big discussion [over who are the wolves]. There's a lot of teamwork, a lot of ganging up! You vote every round on who the wolves are and when the wolves win, they do the wolf sound.' The howling coming from the England camp was no longer the anguished cries of imprisoned players but something altogether lighter.

'The spirit within the group is a huge aspect of international football,' said Eric Dier, who having instigated Uno with England had introduced Werewolf at Spurs and now here. 'You never have enough time to be as good tactically as you would at your club. It's just not possible to achieve a lot of things that you can in a club set-up where you are each and every day of your lives. There's lot of things you can't get. But one thing you can is that spirit. It's definitely something that we've had in the last major tournaments.' Kyle Walker had recalled that when he first joined up, players disappeared to their rooms with their PCs and PlayStations.

Certainly it seemed to be having the desired effect in resetting the culture. 'The first encounter I had in the squad, I came down for lunch and I'm playing for the Blues [Birmingham City] and Jack [Grealish] was with Aston Villa at the time and I was thinking: "Will it be awkward?"' said Jude Bellingham, recalling his first ever call-up with England. 'So I came to the lunch line and he just gave me a massive hug straight away. And I just felt: "This is going to be sound."'

On the pitch in Qatar, England were also in a familiar zone. Iran had been dispatched 6-2 and the new generation were making their mark, Bellingham, Bukayo Saka, Marcus Rashford and Jack Grealish all scoring, along with a veteran of the scene in Raheem Sterling. Saka, who was outstanding, scored twice.

A 0-0 draw against the US did slightly scare the horses back home. 'Yawn in the USA' was *The Sun*'s front page, picturing Ramsdale's fiancée Georgina Irwin, unfortunately caught mid-yawn in what was a turgid match, which ended with England fans booing. Those kinds of photos make it much harder for the England media team to keep the peace between players and press. Although that kind of front-page decision is well above the pay grade of the average sports journalist, that is not always understood by an aggrieved player whose family has been upset.

More worryingly, the dark mood of the Molineux summer appeared to be re-emerging. 'Too defensive and too boring was the snap reaction of fans filtering out of the stadium,' wrote Sky's Rob Harris. 'England turned the clock back to the dismal days of summer,' wrote the BBC's Phil McNulty.

Southgate knew what was coming. 'People are going to react how they're going to react. I can't let that affect how I feel. This is the tournament of external noise, and we'll have another layer of that, I'm sure. But we're still on track.' He really didn't seem to care any more, having seemingly genuinely freed himself of worry about the things he couldn't control. He still reckoned at this stage this was his swansong, but he would go out on his terms.

* * *

Initially the team meeting seemed to have gone off without incident, according to Sam Wallace in the *Daily Telegraph*. Steve Holland, Southgate's assistant, was quizzing Walker about an aspect of Manchester City's performance. Holland then asked the same question of Ben White regarding his club Arsenal, but the defender said he didn't know the answer. It is said that Holland responded by saying that was probably because he wasn't sufficiently interested in football. For White, that accusation had hung around him, like an albatross, ever since he was candid enough to concede early on in his career that he didn't watch much football. Very unusually, for a generation raised under the mantra that you could never make it unless you had played 10,000 hours of sport, White hadn't played much football as a young boy and came from a family with almost zero interest in the game. His first World Cup memory was watching Dier score the penalty that took England through against Colombia in 2018. The angst of 2008, when he was ten, 2010, 2012, 2014 and

2016 had passed him by entirely. In some ways this was Southgate's prototype player, completely unaffected by history. Maybe too much so. Most coaches are instinctively suspicious of players who don't watch the game because they come from the weird breed of people absolutely immersed in every detail.

White, who had been a late call-up to the squad, had met with journalists in Qatar and seemed somewhat detached, but had expanded on his lack of curiosity about the wider game. 'Sitting down and watching a 90-minute game after I trained all day and had four or five meetings about football . . . the last thing I would do is watch more football!' he said. Put like that it seemed entirely reasonable. In Southgate's softer, emotionally open camp, with psychologist Ian Mitchell still prominent, you might have thought there could be space for all sorts. One journalist remarked privately after the meeting that White didn't seem quite right. But it was more a hunch than a story.

The day after England had secured their last-16 game against Senegal, the FA announced that White would be returning home, that he was not expected to return and asked for his privacy to be respected. It didn't take long for the *Daily Star*'s Jeremy Cross to be the first to unearth the exchange with Holland but mental health privacy is a genuine consideration these days for reporters and little more was made of it. The issue only resurfaced when White, in superb form for Arsenal, declined to accept his invitation to join England in March 2024, prompting Southgate to express his disappointment but also exonerate Holland as the cause of White's self-imposed exile.

Sources suggest that the fallout from the exchange wasn't angry and there was more than a week between the meeting and White's departure. White is said not to have appreciated the comment being made publicly but the pair had spoken afterwards and all seemed well.

No one can truly know why a player does not wish to be involved in playing for England, a dream for almost everyone who's watching. Yet Paul Scholes, as passionate about football as anyone and a committed player, stayed away for years for his own reasons. The unique demands of concentrated living in a team camp, especially for a fringe player, are now well recognised as mental health triggers in a way that would have been scorned 20 years ago, when representing your country was akin to a national duty among a post-war generation. But it seemed curious that this England set-up, where so much emphasis was placed on emotional wellbeing, left White feeling an outsider. Even Southgate couldn't keep all of the players happy all of the time.

Not that it seemed to affect the overall performance output. England's game against Senegal, a step up in opposition, was among their more impressive demolition jobs in knockout stages, which by now were routine. With Bellingham emphatic, they were 2–0 up at half-time, courtesy of Henderson and Kane, with Saka adding a third, set up by Foden. England knew this meant a quarter-final meeting with world champions France, yet for once, they had no fear nor sense of inevitability. The mood remained incredibly positive even though one more snag threatened to upset the external messaging. On the eve of the Senegal game, Sterling had come to see Southgate: there had been a break-in at his family home and his partner and children were distressed. He requested a brief leave of absence. It is a genuine fear for all players, their homes often targeted by criminal gangs who know their families are vulnerable when the players are away. It was an awful situation for the player to be in, pulled one way to his ultimate duty to family but also with a commitment to England and facing perhaps the biggest week in his professional life. His relationship with Southgate had come through the Joe Gomez incident and seemed stronger than ever. It was unfortunate it coincided with Sterling being dropped for the last-16 game, with Saka and Foden preferred. You wondered how Sterling, a mainstay of any England team since 2014, would react emotionally to such a blow. But scepticism that the robbery had been overstated in significance dissipated when a 23-year-old was charged in 2023 with burglary. The trial was waiting to be heard at the time of going to press.

Yet it was hard to deduce that this was a camp riven with splits when the overwhelming evidence was that most were happy. Winning matches is the ultimate fuel for team spirit. When England returned to the Souq Al Wakra Hotel after their 3-0 win over Senegal, the staff had dressed in England shirts and waved St George's crosses, cheering wildly and dancing as the squad returned. Some England players looked surprised but Jack Grealish immediately embraced the party, swaying and dancing with the best of them, wearing his baseball cap in regulation back-to-front style. Soon Mason Mount and Declan Rice were in the midst of the dancing, with Walker also enthusiastic. The shirt that seemed to hang heavy on White sat lightly on these players.

* * *

John McDermott is the FA's current technical director and in the small hours of that morning in Qatar's Al Bayt Stadium, a venue literally stuck at the end of a road in the middle of a desert, he sought some solace after England's defeat. It was then that he alighted on a France national team player he knows well. 'I was sitting on the steps with one of the French players and he was saying: "Wow, we were on the rocks there."'

McDermott is too discreet to reveal who that Frenchman was, yet he was previously academy director at Tottenham and Lloris was the France and Spurs captain at the time. And speaking a year later,

Lloris addressed the Kane miss. 'I have to say I was glad he put it over the bar because I think if he'd scored, the game would have changed completely,' said Lloris. 'Going into extra time, I think England would have won it. They finished the game stronger and to be honest, physically, we were done. We were saying it was a big relief to not have to go to extra time.'

Meanwhile, in the post-match press conference, France manager Didier Deschamps grew gradually more irritated with a persistent line of questioning from French journalists which suggested France hadn't hit the heights expected of them. 'Maybe it was because England were very good,' he said. 'They have quality in all areas. Certain things we could have done better but maybe it was because England didn't let us do those well.'

It was a very odd England exit. No scapegoat could be identified, unless you wanted to heap abuse on all-round England hero Kane, and even the lunatic fringe of social media seemed to recognise that was a bridge too far. Some would stoke as much fury as they could muster around Southgate: Walker was proving himself perhaps the best right-back in the world in his shackling of Kylian Mbappé but had Southgate stifled him? His instructions were not to risk crossing the halfway line in this game but, when playing the second best player in the world, that might seem wise to some. The one time Walker did cross the halfway line in the first half saw Mbappé break and contribute to the opening goal from Aurélien Tchouaméni. But there really wasn't sufficient energy to get behind this particular gripe. The reality was that there was no tactical silver bullet that would have won England the game.

The big difference between the Croatia semi-final in 2018 and the Italy final in 2021 was that England were in charge of the midfield for long periods. Bellingham and Rice were both outstanding and Saka gave Hernandez the kind of night that may still cause him to wake in a cold sweat in the middle of the night well into old age. Saka's mercurial skills had won the first penalty, inducing Tchouaméni to foul him. Kane had dispatched that one as normal for 1-1.

Jamie Carragher made a valid point, that maybe Southgate should have introduced Rashford, who did make an impact, earlier, when England were in the ascendancy in the second half. The game was more open then and he would have had space into which to run. It was while England were doing well that Olivier Giroud headed in for 2-1 on 78 minutes and by the time Rashford did come on, after Kane's penalty miss, France inevitably sat much deeper, making it harder for a player of pace. But then again, Southgate's first sub Mount had won the penalty which Kane missed.

England had better chances and 57 per cent possession, though the possession stat is a tricky customer: France make a habit of making teams they beat look good. They won the 2018 World Cup final with 36 per cent possession. The irony was that had Southgate played that way, he would have been castigated. And a further irony was that Southgate and Holland had been hugely influenced by Deschamps' 2018 win, which informed their more cautious approach at Euro 2020 and which almost worked. Southgate believes correctly that winning national teams build off solid defensive bases, but even he seemed to have evolved in Qatar. England were one of the best sides there. Just as they had been at Euro 2020.

England were back at the Souq Al Wakra Hotel at 3 a.m., where food was waiting prepared and they were flying out a few hours later. The turnaround time from tournament exit to departure is brutal. Yet even on the flight home to Birmingham there was an indication Southgate would be staying. Several players approached him asking him to remain. He joked with Walker that it took playing against

Mbappé for the world to acknowledge what Southgate had been saying since 2019: that Walker was the best in the world. Walker appreciated the exchange. This didn't feel like a team giving up on him. Some of them had been through a lot together with him. The bonds ran deep.

CHAPTER 9

THE ROAD TO GERMANY

After a divorce, Martin Glenn moved to a rented house in Twickenham. His next-door neighbour happened to be Greg Dyke. They got to know each other, chatting over the garden fence about football. Glenn had time on his hands and was going up and down the country at weekends to watch his beloved Wolves. Dyke was a season ticket holder and former chairman of Brentford.

'We were chattering and nattering over whatever else, and he said one day, "We're doing a search for the FA job." He knew I'd just left a business and been involved in football. "Would you be interested?"' Glenn recalled. And that was that. Glenn applied to be FA chief executive and landed the post in March 2015, the same month Harry Kane came bouncing off the bench at Wembley to score 79 seconds into his debut against Lithuania.

England football needed fresh starts. Roy Hodgson's senior team were 17th in the world, sandwiched between the Czech Republic and Algeria, and the FA was crippled by years of servicing high interest loans taken out to pay for Wembley's £757 million rebuilding. The organisation remained bloated and archaic. Dyke's attempts to shake things up were foundering, with the most headline-grabbing proposal of his commission – a B league of Premier League junior teams – already roundly rejected by the game.

As FA chairman he needed a refocusing. On the football side, the FA would concentrate on its core mission, the England team and the grassroots game, and empower Dan Ashworth to drive change via St George's Park. On the corporate side, he needed someone who could at last cut through the problems holding his organisation back – the debt, the politics, the impossibility of trying to be a modern, dynamic body while still carrying a Victorian structure that left power in the hands of the sprawling and secretive FA Council. Its 122 members, in newspaper shorthand 'the blazers', included a large number of county association reps, delegates from Oxford and Cambridge Universities, and representatives from the Army FA, Royal Navy FA, Royal Air Force FA, Amateur Football Alliance and Independent Schools FA.

'Male, stale and pale' did not even begin to describe it. Three-quarters of the membership was over 60, a tiny fraction were women and as late as February 2017, only 3 per cent were from an ethnic minority background. 'Worse still there are some 25 life vice-presidents on the FA Council – all elderly white men – who do not represent anyone but block even the most minor of changes,' said a letter to MPs that month. The remarkable thing was the signatories, not a pressure group but five former executives and chairmen of the FA itself (including Dyke, who had quit by then), writing to a select committee to try and hasten reform.

Glenn, the former CEO of United Biscuits, Walkers Crisps and Birds Eye – which saw him dubbed the 'Codfather' because of the brand's famous fish fingers – was also a qualified FA coach and former director of Leicester City. There, he helped a consortium including Gary Lineker and Lineker's agent, John Holmes, reboot the club after administration. Now he was tasked with transforming the FA. The first steps were a major round of redundancies that involved cutting 120 jobs from a swollen workforce of 890 largely office-based staff, and a refinancing of the Wembley loans. Then came hiring a new commercial director, Mark Bullingham, who oversaw the reselling of FA Cup rights.

'The initial phase was trying to restructure the organisation to free money up to get different/better things, but that meant ugly stuff like making people redundant. The FA Cup rights was an absolute game-changer and suddenly we could spend money in the right places.'

For Glenn, that meant the football. The only area exempt in the round of job cuts was Ashworth's technical department and now there were huge increases in the funding of the grassroots and women's games and a doubling of the budget at St George's Park. 'It was recognising that the supreme importance of England winning teams would set a positive shadow over the rest of what the FA does,' Glenn said. 'Because frankly if anyone ever stopped me on the Tube and said, "What do you do?" [If I say], "Work for the FA," the first question is about the England men's team.' Befitting his marketing background, Glenn's rallying cry was a slogan: 'Unite the game to inspire the nation'.

Often, the Codfather found himself swimming against the current. When presenting his plan to the FA Council he said, 'One of the reasons we're putting more money into St George's Park is because in the German team that won the 2014 World Cup, eight of the eleven came through the ranks and big camps and that's expensive, so we're gonna go and do that.' This was met by silence and at coffee time Glenn got a tap on the shoulder. A 'blazer' was most dischuffed.

'You're the new CEO, aren't you?'

'Yeah,' Glenn replied.

'Well, I tell you, I think it's disgraceful that you cite Germany, our biggest rival, as a role model.'

There was similar resistance when Owen Eastwood came in to overhaul England culture. 'Why are we spending money on a Kiwi?' And when Glenn talked about making the FA a 'world-class organisation' not even a blazer but a member of the actual FA board sneered, 'But we've *never* been a world-class organisation.'

'Looking back, in that mad first year we learned a lot of things. It was a bit like being the chief executive of a dysfunctional city council. Ringing in my ears was that brilliant line Ian Watmore [one of his predecessors] said: "[As FA CEO] I'm neither chief nor executive."'

The organisation's lack of purpose and oomph never seemed more obvious than when Glenn first started dealing with the Premier League. 'The FA were like *Dad's Army*, kind of well meaning but a bit useless. The Premier League were like Genghis Khan, red in tooth and claw. Efficient, conquered everything but people didn't much like them.' However, he struck up a good working relationship with the Premier League's then chief executive, Richard Scudamore, helping align the two bodies at executive level, as well as at football level, over EPPP.

The tanker began to turn. Extra investment allowed Ashworth and Dave Reddin to make their multitude of hires on the performance and specialist coaching side, and bring in Lane4 for sports psychology. 'It always used to be the clubs didn't like to release players for England games because they'd be getting an injection in a hotel bedroom from someone. Everything was peripatetic. It would be this masseur from this club . . . you hadn't got the consistency of experience that comes from having a proper staff. That costs money.'

However, until the FA found the right men's senior manager, the goal 'England winning teams' would remain far away. The first time

Glenn and Ashworth approached Southgate about taking over was during Euro 2016 in Paris when Roy Hodgson was still in charge, 'and he was just very unsure. I think his confidence built when he saw Sam [Allardyce] at work at St George's Park and was thinking, "There's nothing so special here that I couldn't do."' Glenn rejects the idea that the FA took Southgate for granted in the period before his permanent appointment.

'He was asked to do the job albeit on an interim basis [initially] and the interim basis cuts both ways. It also meant we could just offer him the job. We had a group and Howard Wilkinson was really good on that. We knew we wanted him but there were a couple of people that said, "He can't be the manager." I can see why [Southgate might have thought], "Give me three or four months and I'm at the mercy of performance," but I quite like the grip of performance. We had our first big falling-out with Roy before the Euros, not extending his contract.

'[Southgate being taken for granted] is in the play [*Dear England*]. I suppose objectively you'd say yes, it wasn't an unalloyed "you're our man, go do it". It was actually "you are our man, you don't have to qualify for the World Cup". That was the instruction. This was a building job,' Glenn said.

Wait. When Southgate was appointed, expectations were so low in the short term that it would have been *okay* if England had missed out on Russia 2018? It is quite a revelation and makes the run to the semi-finals there all the more remarkable. 'This is absolutely the case,' said Glenn. 'This is not post-reaction or hype. It was a rebuilding project so if we had limped over the line to qualify with a team that wasn't going anywhere, it would have felt like a false move and Dan [Ashworth]had done the work on DNA. We were starting to see success from the development teams, and it was a sense of "look, there's a good crop coming through, it's not all about qualifying" – and I think we could have explained it away.

'If we had not qualified but were seen to be playing a different kind of football with a different kind of players, we'd have got away with it. That was discussed at the FA board.'

Glenn remembers the presentation that, before being appointed permanently, Southgate made it to an interview panel at St George's Park that included himself, Ashworth, Wilkinson and Dyke's successor, Greg Clarke. It was old-school. Not a PowerPoint but clear ideas explained on a paper handout. Southgate was particularly strong on how he would use the limited contact time with players to instil tactical and culture principles, and build morale; also on his own learning journey as a coach, and what external links he hoped to build. There was no 'eureka moment' when the FA knew they had appointed the right man, but it was quickly clear England were playing better football, experimenting more and using the development pathways better with Southgate in charge. The dropping of Rooney 'was a big moment because I think that set the stall out to the world, to that new generation'.

'One of the things I laugh about is the idea of Gareth not being tough enough. I mean, if you look at his World Cup squad in 2018 and who was in the Euro 2020 squad, I mean he's pretty ruthless.'

Glenn is used to the world getting Southgate wrong. 'His humility can sometimes be seen as softness and [the difference] is something you have to grasp. When Gareth was appointed there were people saying, "He's just too nice." He hadn't been a major success for the Under-21s – not many people are – and it was, "FA man. Too nice."

'I said, "Well, hang on . . . based on what I've seen he's been a captain at every club he's been at." Which you don't tend to get – certainly in the era he grew up – without toughness. And there was a sense that tub-thumping management in any field was just going out, because it wasn't delivering results. It wasn't enough.

'When a hundred little things happen, if you're always looking at the sidelines saying, "What should we do now?", you're pretty much screwed. That's also true in business. In fast-changing worlds you need people who take accountability, care a bit more. So the management archetype goes from being "big, strong man" to someone with a clear vision, but trying to get there more by appealing through emotion than just telling. It was getting comfortable with that type of manager, which of course Gareth's actually very good at. I don't think Gareth ever doubted that what he does is effective and strong. But he's rarely a shouter. He will shout, we all do at times, but it's not his modus operandi.'

Southgate has helped not just change the conversation around management but around Englishness, in Glenn's view. 'There's a great *The Rest Is History* [podcast] on George Orwell and towards the end they talked about Gareth and the England set-up and how Orwell was a great patriot, obviously left-leaning, etc. I don't know what Gareth's politics are, but you don't have to be National Front to represent your country and I think they used a phrase about how he helped define a new kind of English identity which comes from a multicultural [base], and I think that's the unique thing that he was able to bring because he's thoughtful . . . It's certainly not about chest-thumping, but I think it's definitely about ambition, wanting to do well and I think there's something around teamwork. There's a kindness to it probably that hadn't existed before.'

* * *

During life BG – Before Gareth – Glenn went around seeking insights on what other countries did better than England, and had breakfast with Raphael Honigstein, the German writer. Honigstein's 2015 book, *Das Reboot: How German Football Reinvented Itself and Conquered the World*, sets out the story of his country's journey back from the international wilderness to becoming world champions in 2014. Glenn and Honigstein talked vibes.

'I said to Raphi, "What is it about team spirit that you understand?" He said, "A lot of the players don't really like some of the shitty parts of being at tournaments. It's like a bad school trip – so have fun on the bus." Which I thought was a great line.'

Just as Germany went from being a riven camp to becoming the happiest of travellers during the first half of the Joachim Löw era, so tournaments went from being the worst to the best of times for England players on Southgate's watch. It was not just the football his team played in Qatar that enticed Southgate to continue on to Euro 2024. It was the palpable feeling, packing up in Al Wakrah and sitting on the plane home, that he, the staff, the group could not wait to be together once more.

The first trip after the World Cup was quite the demonstration of a 'let's-go-again' spirit. England went to the intimidating Diego Armando Maradona Stadium in Naples and swept Italy away, more superior than suggested by a 2-1 winning scoreline. It was their first away victory against Italy since 1961 and in midfield, against the very same trio who were their masters in the Euro 2020 final, England were outstanding. Jude Bellingham and Declan Rice commanded the area, with Rice starting the scoring from close range after 13 minutes.

But it was not the goal history will remember. That came just before half-time when Kane banished any hangover from his World Cup miss against France by converting a penalty to move clear of Wayne Rooney, with 54 goals, as England's all-time leading scorer. The least surprised person on the planet was Rooney himself. When he broke the scoring record, in September 2015, the former captain mentioned Kane in the speech he made in the dressing room. Kane only had four caps and three England goals at the time, but Rooney had seen enough in training, and the few games they had played together, to sense that here was an extraordinary striking talent. 'I knew he could become England's greatest scorer if he kept going the way he was and I wanted to give him encouragement.'

A rich seam of form continued with a 2-0 win over Ukraine at Wembley, a routine 4-0 at the parched Ta' Qali stadium in Malta and one of the great England performances in a qualifier, a 7-0 annihilation of North Macedonia at Old Trafford, featuring a sublime Bukayo Saka hat-trick, yet two more goals for Harry Kane, and close-range strikes by Marcus Rashford and Kalvin Phillips. This was the same North Macedonia team that had won away against Germany and Italy in qualification for the 2022 World Cup. And it was a year to the week since Southgate's nadir at Molineux. Now he was the author of 'Gazball'.

A draw away to Ukraine, played out in Wroclaw, Poland, because of Russia's invasion of the home team's country, involved more prosaic football but still impressive resilience after going a goal behind in a hostile atmosphere. Inspired by Bellingham, England then beat Italy at Wembley to qualify for the Euros with two group games to spare. Before that was a friendly against Scotland to commemorate 150 years of the world's oldest fixture. Bellingham was out of this world, bestriding Hampden Park like his Real Madrid forebear, Di Stéfano, once did. 'The best England team I've seen in a lifetime,' said Joe Cole. With gritted teeth, Scots had to acknowledge that sadly, perhaps he was right.

* * *

Jordan Henderson sat with *The Athletic*'s Adam Crafton and David Ornstein and said all he had ever tried to do was help. 'And when I've been asked for help, I've gone above and beyond to help. I've worn the laces. I've worn the armband. I've spoken to people in that community to try and use my profile to help them.'

Um, noble stuff. Except the problem was Henderson was trying to justify, via a high-profile interview, his transfer from Liverpool to Saudi Arabian Pro League side Al-Ettifaq. It was earning him a fortune (though considerably less, he claimed, than the £700,000 per week reported) but it was also earning him the furious opprobrium of many who felt let down. Not least in the LGBTQ+ community. This was the Henderson who in November 2021 used his matchday programme notes as Liverpool captain to back the Rainbow Laces campaign in powerful terms. 'I do believe when you see something that is clearly wrong and makes another human being feel excluded you should stand shoulder to shoulder with them,' he wrote. 'You also have a responsibility to educate yourself better around the challenges they experience.

'That's where my own position on homophobia in football is rooted. Before I'm a footballer, I'm a parent, a husband, a son, a brother and a friend to the people in my life who matter so much to me. The idea that any of them would feel excluded from playing or attending a football match, simply for being and identifying as who they are, blows my mind.'

In Saudi Arabia, the LGBTQ+ community are excluded from considerably more than football. The country criminalises homosexuality. With Ornstein and Crafton – who is gay – holding him strongly to account, some of Henderson's answers were excruciating. Crafton asked about a video that went out on social media from Al-Ettifaq while announcing his signing, where it looked like a rainbow armband Henderson wore was greyed out. Henderson said, 'I didn't know anything about it until [the video] was out. And it's hard for me to know and understand everything because it is part of the religion. So if I wear the rainbow armband, if that disrespects their religion, then that's not right either. Everybody should be respectful of religion and culture. That's what I think we're all trying to fight for here in terms of inclusion and everything.'

Henderson went on to suggest his presence in the Saudi Pro League could drive change and that he 'strongly believed' his transfer was 'a positive thing'. He said it 'really, really hurt me' to be accused of turning his back on the LGBTQ+ community.

The interview came out four days after Southgate included Henderson in his squad for the away game with Ukraine and friendly with Scotland. If the hope was it would temper the controversy of that decision, it was unfounded. Three Lions Pride, an LGBT+ supporters group for England, pushed on with plans for a protest against the midfielder, having released a statement after Southgate picked him that concluded, 'Jordan Henderson's bank balance may be burgeoning but our respect and his off-field legacy is lost – and can never be won back.'

However, Southgate stood robustly by his decision. At the squad announcement he had said, 'I don't really know what the morality argument is because so many of our industries are wrapped up with Saudi investment . . . but I don't hear any noises about that. It's only the football that's highlighted.'

To the ears of some, though, this sounded like a depressing emission of whataboutery from a figure whose stances on anti-discrimination were previously clear. 'That was the moment Gareth lost me,' said a vastly respected journalist who was once among the manager's most staunch supporters in the press. Henderson played against

Ukraine and was selected again for the October internationals with Australia and Italy at Wembley, where on both occasions he was booed by home fans. By January he had quit Saudi and moved to Ajax in the Netherlands. 'It was very much a football decision,' he said.

Southgate, increasingly, wanted to talk only about football decisions. Stretching back to the build-up to Qatar, his diminished enthusiasm, in press conferences, for straying into other areas was notable. Had he become just another narrow, pragmatic manager – or was this simply experience? The coach of another European nation congratulated him, at the World Cup, for keeping England's players focused on the pitch, admitting that his team had made the mistake of getting distracted by the politics around being there.

The FA itself were finding how difficult it can be for sport to satisfy the world at large. Following the 7 October Hamas attacks on Israel, it came under pressure to light up the Wembley arch in the colours of the Israeli flag and faced heavy criticism, including from Downing Street, for declining to do so. Bullingham said he 'recognised the hurt' caused to the Jewish community, but, in the context of mounting casualties following Israeli reprisals in Gaza, said, 'We all feel now that football should stand for peace and humanity and that we should show compassion for all innocent victims of this terrible conflict.'

The following month, the FA announced the arch would only be lit for sport and entertainment purposes from thereon, having reviewed policy after the arch was previously illuminated in solidarity with such as the plight of Ukraine and International Women's Day. In all, it had been lit 18 times in that way, starting when it was illuminated in the red, white and blue of the French tricolour after terrorist attacks in Paris, in 2015. These illuminations had been well intentioned but it can be hard to see around corners, reflected FA execs. Adding to the complexity was that England's immediate opponents, following the 7 October attacks, were Australia – whose next game was against Palestine and would have found it very difficult to join in any major gesture beyond the minute's silence and black armbands used to acknowledge events.

The launch, in March, of new kit England would wear for the Euros was a triumph – if the goal was that modern one of hits on social media. However, if the objective was to join the nation together in excitement, it was less so. Things started harmoniously enough. On a Monday the manufacturers, Nike, released the first pictures from a photoshoot involving players from England's men's, women's and para teams. Kane and Foden wore white home jerseys and Saka and Declan Rice the new away top, which was described in the FA's blurb as 'a bold purple colour [that] mixes reds and blues from the past'. The style was retro and aimed at the leisure market. Saka wore cargo pants, Kane chinos and Rice jeans.

The players seemed bowled over. 'It is unbelievable. I think this is the best kit we are going to wear and that I will have worn. It has a classic look and the collar is top. It is ten out of ten,' was Saka's quote.

'This shirt is cold, it's sick,' Rice said.

The Sun seemed enthusiastic too. 'IT'S COMING HOME. Fans say "we're winning it all" as England release "some of the greatest EVER" kits ahead of Euro 2024' gushed the headline. 'Purple Reign' said the *Daily Star*. Nike also released a set of tweets about their designs and one drew attention to the back of the collar where instead of the plain red cross of a St George's flag was a cross comprising three different reds, and blue, lilac and purple. 'A playful update to the + of St. George appears on the collar to unite and inspire,' it said.

Until the Wednesday, that was about it. Aside from a letter to the *Daily Express* complaining about the price (£124.99 for adult shirts) and noting that the collar 'looks a bit odd', there was little blowback. Then, rather suddenly, the Nike collar tweet gained traction with a rush of furious responses about the 'playful update' to England's national flag. Now *The Sun* thundered about the 'woke cross' and the *Daily Mail* wheeled out England's most-capped men's player, Peter Shilton, to brand the design 'wrong on every level'. In the *Daily Star*, they had adult content creator, Astrid Wett, calling on fans to 'stand against' the new shirt. 'We should show that we are not woke and we are proud to be English. Don't change our flag! Leave it alone! I will be protesting against this until they change it. Nike, I await your response,' she said in a video posted on TikTok. Albeit that her anger had not actually stopped her buying it.

With the Labour leader, Sir Keir Starmer, condemning Nike and the FA on *The Sun*'s YouTube channel and Rishi Sunak, the prime minister, weighing in by telling reporters, 'When it comes to our national flags, we shouldn't mess with them because they're a source of pride, identity, who we are, and they're perfect as they are,' the temperature of England's build-up to a friendly against Brazil abruptly rose. Scottish Twitter was in hysterics, carrying posts of the many occasions, on various sports kits, the Saltire had been modified without the slightest peep of protest. South of the border, Scots felt, a little perspective was needed – and when Southgate sat down for his pre-match press conference, he provided it.

'I don't know if the debate is about the St George Flag needing to be on the England shirt because it hasn't always been,' he said. 'The most important thing that has to be on an England shirt are the Three Lions. It's our iconic symbol. It is what distinguishes us not only from other football teams around the world but England rugby and cricket.

'What you're really asking is, "Should we be tampering with the cross of St George?" In my head, if it's not a red cross on a white background then it isn't the cross of St George anyway. It's presumably some artistic take which I'm not creative enough to understand.'

His take was unscripted and uninfluenced by his employer and in the FA's minds, 'brilliant'. Immediately, the flames of 'Flaggate' subsided. 'It was so deft,' said Sullivan. 'Though strictly speaking, they're not lions but heraldic leopards.'

* * *

England did not play well against Brazil, who won 1-0 courtesy of a goal from their latest prodigy, Endrick. Three days later, another defeat loomed after a Jordan Pickford error – his first to cost a goal in 60 internationals – helped Belgium to a 2-1 lead going into the final seconds. Yet with the last kick and with typical competitive spirit, Bellingham equalised. 'I liked it,' the 20-year-old said. 'Because I know the rubbish we would have got if we had lost two games on the bounce.'

March internationals are historically nightmares for England coaches – at all age levels – because of call-offs and tiredness caused by it being deep into the club season, and Southgate was sanguine about the results. He was more interested in how the games had helped prepare his squad for the summer tournament. They were another example of him arranging tough friendlies against top opponents rather than easy outings to boost morale, and he felt it valuable to have tested new and fringe players against the world's third-and fifth-ranked teams. The 'finds' were Ivan Toney, who proved comfortable in the elite company, and Manchester United's teenage midfielder, Kobbie Mainoo. Jarrod Bowen and Anthony Gordon also advanced their claims.

It would not be easy picking the party of 26 to represent England at the Euros but, as Glenn noted, Southgate is never 'too nice' to make tough decisions. Jesse Lingard, whom Southgate championed from his Under-21 days before making him a key player at a World Cup, was not given an explanation when Southgate left him out of England's Euro 2020 squad. 'With the form I was in at West Ham, I thought I deserved to go to the Euros, I'm not going to lie. If it was now – now I've matured and grown up a little bit – I would have definitely questioned why. Now, I'd have said "based on form, I have to go, it's impossible". But I just took it on the chin. That's my only regret with England, not asking Gareth why,' Lingard said.

The Southgate who leads his lions (slash heraldic leopards) to Germany has never seemed more coldly focused on the business of succeeding on the pitch, and less interested in veering into issues off it, than during the period since Qatar. There is a stripped-back feel to his set-up. Gone are the in-house psychologists, the specialists like Allan Russell, and key performance drivers of the past such as Bryce Cavanagh, Ben Rosenblatt and Dave Reddin. Gone is the national coaches' room at St George's Park – meetings are held peripatetically now. But there, stronger than ever, is Southgate's ambition to succeed.

In a team meeting before the first of the 2023–24 internationals, against Ukraine, he told his players that winning Euro 2024 was unequivocally the target. 'I think now they need that challenge,' he explained. 'The players don't want us to come in and be talking differently, and we've got evidence over a long period of time that we should have that belief. Of course, you've got to go and deliver it and a lot can happen in terms of availability of players and everything, but for us that has to be the longer-term aim.'

No less than Pep Guardiola believes England can achieve it. 'I have the feeling, everyone has the feeling, that the England national team, in the last events, the World Cup and European Championships, they made steps. They are on the verge, they are really close. Just believe it. If they believe it, they can do it,' he said six weeks out from the start of Euro 2024. The FA's evidence is that an end to the years of hurt is nigh. Speaking to the authors in May 2023, John McDermott, FA technical director since 2020 (replacing Ashworth's successor, Les Reed) said, 'There is tangible data in what this team is doing and how they are accumulating evidence that we can win and that we are going to win. There is that inner belief but also something I sense when I am with the players and in the camp that it is not faux. There is genuine, authentic belief that this group of lads are going to do it.'

The Southgate who, at St James' Park at the end of April 2024, told fans of his excitement about the Euros was the late-period version. A Southgate a little slimmer in his mission, a little narrower in his influences, but also a Southgate more experienced, canny and bent on winning than when he started out. His players were less at the front of cultural debates – councils had even quietly abolished the free school holiday meal vouchers Rashford campaigned for so famously – and the big question around them was no more, and no less, than a football one. Can they win? Will they win?

There had been stronger England squads in terms of defence and midfield but never one with such attacking riches. In it, there was Foden, the newly crowned Footballer of the Year, and there was Saka, the Arsenal 'star boy' who had accrued more goal involvements than all but three players in Europe since his club debut in 2018.

In it, there was the prodigious, imperious Bellingham – already a Real Madrid legend and Spanish league winner. In it, there was the £100 million Rice, with his ever-expanding, increasingly marauding game. And its captain and symbol remained Kane, the goal king of German club football ready for a finals on his new 'home' soil; a Kane who was not shy about setting himself the lofty ambition of the Ballon d'Or, but who was grounded enough to know that achieving it depended on leading Bayern Munich or his country to silverware. 'The Bundesliga, the Champions League and with the Euros being here – only by winning them as a team are you going to win those individual awards,' he said on that wild day in Kirchweidach. 'You know me: I don't like to think about those. I'm just trying to push my team to win and will do the same in the summer with England.'

Like Kane, Southgate was trying to learn German. He had a language app on his phone and was using it for Deutsch practice as he prepared for the tournament. He was still to see the National Theatre play in his honour, despite it becoming such a phenomenon it was being adapted as a four-part television series by the BBC.

The West End? The sheep dip? The long walk? Gareth had conquered them all. Dear England, what a journey! And so on to the summer, where an open-top bus or the Tower of London awaits.

CHAPTER 10

THE END OF THE DAY

At the end of the day, it was a pile of dog vomit that came to epitomise Euro 2024 for Gareth Southgate. Though only minutes away from taking his team into extra time and the chance to win that historic trophy, it was, by many measures, the least successful and most torturous of all the four tournaments Southgate had navigated with the England team. The sense of dusk falling and an era ending was hard to ignore throughout England's laboured progress in Germany. And for Southgate, all was crystallised in a single moment as he returned to his Harrogate home the Monday after the night before.

Southgate was alone, the slickness of private jets and personal chauffeurs meaning that the England squad were home well before their spouses and children, labouring on scheduled flights. So it was an amost-empty house the England manager opened up after six weeks away. There was at least someone pleased to see him and greet him joyfully: Teddy, the family cockapoo.

'Teddy didn't care about the result; had no questions about who should have been playing on the left wing,' said Southgate. 'We had our little moment and I took my cases upstairs to the bedroom. I think I'm going to start unpacking but there's an enormous pile of dog sick. Bear in mind at this point, the Spanish coach [Luis de la Fuente] is in the middle of Madrid with the trophy and thousands of people, and here I am. And if you ever want a stark reminder of the difference between winning and losing, that's probably as good as it gets.'

Within 24 hours of cleaning up his dog's sick, Southgate's resignation statement would be shared, and quickly he adopted the life of a middle-aged man managing a career break: embracing padel, afternoons in Bettys Tea Room, becoming an enthusiastic member of a book club over beer and curry, as well as earnestly updating his LinkedIn profile. 'For the first time in 25 years, it [was a case of] where do I go? I'm not in a changing room, I'm not at work, I'm unemployed for the first time, I don't have a routine and I'm in the wife's way.'

That said, there was a book to write, a speaking tour to conduct, occasional lectures on leadership, podcasts to launch. None of it suggested he was desperate to be back in the fray. It was almost as if eight years with England and particularly the last five weeks of the job had depleted his reserves of vision and enthusiasm. 'The role chews you up,' he wrote. 'I had reached the point where it was a real challenge not to sit there and peer out at the faces, many of which hadn't changed in all that time, and just remember all the criticisms and the personal comments that had been made. I really wouldn't be missing this aspect of the job.'

* * *

It became so bad at Euro 2024 that there was a moment when you thought Gareth Southgate's endlessly polite, engaging persona might finally just crack and he would tell the world's assembled media to 'go f*** yourself!' He had spent eight years politely dealing with journalists' enquiries, no matter how obtuse, obscure or unrelated to football. Now, a barely concealed rage simmered below the surface.

'I'm just the type of guy you have to prod a lot to get a bark,' he would say later.

Euro 2024 would be the tournament at which the media target moved, perhaps forever. Once it was the red-top tabloid press who would bear the brunt of England players' fury for failing to get behind the team. Now the era of the celebrity podcast was upon us. And while journalists can be dismissed as embittered football failures who never played the game, when England legend Gary Lineker is dismissing your team as 'shit' and asking whether the coach is 'tactically inept', as he did on his hugely popular *The Rest is Football* podcast, it sticks.

It felt like the criticism came to a head after England reached the Euro semi-finals, beating Switzerland in an emphatic penalty shoot-out. When Southgate first achieved such a milestone in Russia 2018, the reception was jubilant and adoring. Now there was just scepticism and snark and it had become an international sport. England, perennial shoot-out flops, had just struck five of the best penalties you can imagine and the talk could have been of Bukayo Saka, redemption and three semi-finals in four tournaments. But then came the questions from foreign journalists, less emotionally invested in the Saka story and more concerned with the spectacle.

'Is there any thought of entertainment for neutrals?' asked one reporter from Scandinavia. Southgate bristled a little but remained in polite mode. 'Well, sorry for that. Our intention is always to play with the ball. These are not normal football matches but national events with young men under enormous pressure. None of this stuff is easy.'

Next up was a German reporter. 'People say England are the new Germans, winning somehow, scoring somehow, winning on penalties . . .' Southgate kept it together. 'Well, there's what we ideally want to be and how we've needed to find ways to win with all the obstacles we have had,' he said.

It was the representative from the *Westdeutsche Zeitung* that almost pushed him over the edge though. 'Congratulations for reaching the semi-final,' the questioner started. '[In 2021] the opponents you had to play were Croatia, Scotland, Czech Republic, a poor German team, Ukraine, Denmark . . .'

'A poor German team?' Southgate interrupted. 'It had about eight Champions League winners in it.'

'Yeah, but poor team,' his interrogator replied dismissively. Southgate couldn't win this argument. The 2021 German team, which had five of the same players that had started against Spain in 2024, and also Thomas Müller, Timo Werner and Mats Hummels, was now apparently terrible. Even when Southgate's team won, there was always a reason why it didn't count.

The reporter hadn't finished twisting the knife.

'Serbia, Denmark, Slovenia, Slovakia, Switzerland. No Belgium, Netherlands, Spain, France, Portugal. Is it maybe better for you to play better football if the team on the other side is better?'

'Are you sure you're not English?' said Southgate, dripping with sarcasm.

It was an unusual look for him. The tension in the room was almost palpable. 'I'm not really sure what to say?' said Southgate. This was the point at which you wondered whether a profanity might be forthcoming from the previously angelic manager. 'It's the madness of this job. But we've had an enjoyable night and we're going to try to keep it enjoyable if that's okay.'

A few minutes later he would speak to English reporters. He looked flushed with rage, they said, on the point of being emotionally overwhelmed. 'This is a job where you get ridiculed and your professional capability is questioned beyond belief, and I don't think it's normal to have beer thrown at you either,' he told them. 'But I'm fortunate that my life's taken me through a lot of resilience-building. I'm just using it as fuel.'

This was not the angst-ridden self-reflection that had greeted the boos at Molineux after the awful Hungary defeat in 2022. He now looked like a man who didn't care any more, and had given up trying to be liked. It was almost a culture war. Southgate had supporters who would trot out statistics that seemed a slam dunk for nailing the argument in his favour. Those against, making legitimate tactical points, were not going to be swayed by mere facts which, in their eyes, lacked context. Positions had been taken, lines drawn, minds made up. It no longer mattered what happened on the pitch. The die was cast. Southgate was either saviour or simpleton. If he won, it would be in spite of him, not because of him.

Where did this rage come from?

'We live in what's been an angry country,' Southgate would later reflect. In truth it had been simmering since the disappointment and missed opportunity of losing the Euro 2020 final. Yet something crystallised after the Denmark game in the group stages at Euro 2024. Denmark were bad, everyone agreed. 'We can't be making any excuses for the level of the performance,' said Southgate. 'I know I had a poor game,' said Declan Rice. 'It wasn't up to my standards.'

'We're struggling both with the ball and without the ball,' said Harry Kane. 'Everyone is just dropping below their levels a little bit. Maybe when teams are dropping deeper, we're not quite sure how to get the pressure on and who's the one supposed to be going.' That was an alarming admission from England's captain, Southgate's most trusted player, seemingly unsure regarding the plan for pressing the opposition, which in simple terms meant England were a tactical shambles. They had experimented with playing Trent Alexander-Arnold in midfield, and he had now been withdrawn twice, a humiliation for him and a clear indication it was a half-baked plan. Southgate's tenure had all been about the process, planning and not making wild, uncalculated decisions. Now it looked as though he was making it up as he went along, chucking paint at the canvas and hoping for a masterpiece.

So Lineker's comments that night about a 'shit' performance did not alone create the fury that would be unleashed on Southgate. And yet the balance of sensible judgement possibly tipped over the edge that night. *The Rest is Football* episode in question was even more informal than usual, with Thomas Frank and David Moyes heckling in the background, and Micah Richards, a co-host with Lineker, jocularly sniping back. Podcasts invite the viewer to experience what the pundits really think in the bar once they're off air: polished and professional on the BBC, Lineker was loose-tongued and scatological for the commercial podcast produced by his media company. It was like comparing a classical music concert to a punk gig. As one observer commented, Lineker made a much bigger impression on Euro 2024 than any Euro he actually played in.

'We have to reflect the mood of the nation,' said Lineker. 'I can't imagine anybody that is English would have enjoyed England's performance, because it was lethargic. It was dour. I mean, you can think of all sorts of words and expletives, if you like, but it was shit.' Lineker would later try to shift that position, suggesting he was saying the game itself was shit. 'Was it tactically inept?' he asked before quickly qualifying. 'It's really hard to be critical of Gareth Southgate, because overall, in the England role, he's turned England's fortunes around in many ways. Having said that, he's kind of ended up adopting a really talented bunch of players.'

The damage had been done. All people heard was 'shit' and 'tactically inept'. No one could have blamed Lineker for using the profanity privately. He would have been one among millions. Yet as an England legend and a former record goalscorer, his public words carried huge weight. Did they legitimise in some fans' eyes another level of rage that would culminate in a very public humiliation for Southgate a few days later?

The fabled mood in the camp, usually somewhere between amazing and fabulous, was cracking. There was a suggestion now that fringe players were unhappy at their lack of game time. The clamour to play Anthony Gordon was led by several pundits such as Lineker, Wayne Rooney, Jamie Carragher and Alan Shearer. The decision to leave the likes of Jordan Henderson and Harry Maguire at home, experienced leaders, as well as ebullient characters Jack Grealish and James Maddison, now looked questionable. When one less experienced player suggested a team meeting to sort things out – a crisis meeting? – more experienced players were said to have explained to him that this was normal mid-tournament angst.

Yet twelve players in the squad had no tournament experience and it seemed to be showing. The unity looked fragile. From the beginning, the mantra was media duties must be shared; everyone had to step up. Now, Jude Bellingham's profile was so enormous that one member of the FA staff explained they had to manage the situation differently. Bellingham didn't even appear for planned interviews with ITV and BBC. The happy days of unicorns and Conor Coady leading games of Wolf seemed distant. 'There was a danger of it unravelling,' Southgate would say later. 'We weren't playing at the level we wanted. That became a coaching challenge. How do we fix it? That was an open honest conversation confronting the reality of the environment.' He would add: 'As a coach, you recognise what you're doing well.

Had we gone out in the first knockout round here [against Slovakia], I know I've managed this period better than I did in Russia [2018]. But that wouldn't be how it was viewed and would sound like nonsense to the man in the street.'

That suggested he had been keeping a lid on several issues. We knew about the lack of a left-sided player, the huge hole left by the absence of Kalvin Phillips, though in reality he should have been better prepared, as it had been obvious for some time the Manchester City player was no longer at the required standard. There had also been a suggestion prior to the tournament from those close to the camp that Bellingham's role at Real Madrid might create problems with England. The freedom accorded him by Carlo Ancelotti as a number ten would be hard to graft into Southgate's system.

And then there was his talisman, his captain, the man on whom he pinned his regime back at the Marines' Boot Camp in 2017. Kane never looked fit and yet laboured on as centre-forward all the way to the final. Back in the autumn, when he had scored back-to-back hat-tricks against Borussia Dortmund and Darmstadt, he looked like the best centre-forward in the world and ended the season with 36 goals in 34 Bundesliga games. But a Champions League semi-final defeat against Real Madrid in May was the first sign all was not well, when Thomas Tuchel took him off on 85 minutes with Bayern 1-0 up and progressing. They lost 2-1 and went out. It seemed obtuse until Tuchel revealed he was struggling with a back problem, which also caused him to miss the last two Bundesliga games. 'Just a precaution,' Kane insisted. 'Our prep camp troubled me in terms of the physical sharpness of a number of players,' Southgate would write later. 'We had numerous fitness issues, including Harry Kane and Anthony Gordon reporting with injuries. A long season had taken its toll. Declan Rice, Bukayo Saka and Jude Bellingham had each played more than fifty matches. Playing a high pressing game with these issues and in summer heat would have been suicide.'

What had really annoyed Southgate about the Denmark game though was the body language. 'We've just drawn against Denmark, they're on two points, we're on four; they're celebrating with their fans, and we're on our knees,' he said. 'I don't want to see that again,' he would tell the players. Yet even Southgate would also acknowledge the issues ran deeper. 'Our decision making began to suffer on the pitch, reminding me of the bad old days of playing for England when the shirt felt so heavy,' he wrote.

As for the outside noise, officially the line was that the players weren't listening. Kyle Walker told a group of writers he never read anything they wrote. 'Keep writing though,' he added cheerfully as he left. The truth was different. Two days after Lineker's podcast dropped, Kane met the media. It wasn't a coincidence that he and Declan Rice, the team's leaders, were sent out to confront the elephant dung in the room. When Lineker's comments were put to Kane, he bit back. 'I always feel like they have a responsibility. I know they have got to be honest and give their opinion, but they also have a responsibility as an ex-England player that a lot of players looked up to. People do care about what they say and people do listen to them.'

'They're getting caught up in the weeds,' said Gary Neville. He feared they were making the same mistake his generation had, focusing energy on criticism rather than playing better. Southgate as good as confirmed this later. 'Whatever you say, the outside noise always finds its way inside,' he would tell ITV. 'I've talked to a lot of psychologists over the years and one of the things human beings want to avoid is public embarrassment. And we had a bit of that mindset in the group stages. We weren't free.'

This was the first camp under Southgate's tenure that didn't have a psychologist. Where Jonny Zneimer, Pippa Grange and Ian Mitchell had been obvious points of reference for manager and players, this time the FA said they were outsourcing the psychological support and could call it in when necessary, which seemed odd for an organisation and manager who had previously placed so much emphasis on mind games. That said, many of the team psychologists had been axed when the FA made 124 positions redundant due to Covid losses. It was already a much-reduced department. Was that in itself a retreat from the vision laid out by Dan Ashworth in 2013?

There was another echo of a past when lurid tabloid stories would bedevil players. Kieran Trippier's wife had unfollowed him on social media the day before the Slovenia game and posted a cryptic message on Instagram: 'Sooner or later you get over the s*** you swore you'd never get over and it's the best feeling in the world.' The *Daily Mail* had accompanied Kyle Walker's estranged partner Lauryn Goodman, who took his son Kairo to the Denmark game. Walker also has a ten-month-old daughter with Goodman, which had caused a temporary marital breakdown with wife Annie Kilner, who was also at the game with three of Walker's four other children.

At times, it felt as though this camp was ready to implode. 'People don't understand; we're trying to do what the manager wants,' one player told a colleague. 'We're telling him it's not working.' Another was so frustrated at their lowest point that they spoke to an adviser about quitting international football, a passing moment spoken in emotion but an indication of the mood. 'When I heard him say during the tournament that it was an "unusual environment", I thought his time was up,' said Neville. 'I've been at 12 major tournaments as a player, coach and pundit. I've been around England long enough to smell when things aren't quite right. I was hearing things in press conferences that I know would have created levels of division.'

In such circumstances, Rice was the go-to man for lifting the mood and the day before the last group game against Slovenia, he addressed the press. 'We will be going out there to perform and show everyone that we can be the team we are trying to be,' he said. 'You'll see a team that has a different pressing style, that wants to be on the front foot and press high up the pitch.' The game finished 0-0.

Metrics told you that England were producing some of the slowest football in the tournament, though you didn't need a PhD in statistical analysis to see they were turgid. Still, thanks to Denmark's inability to score against Serbia – Group C had been nicknamed the Group of Dearth – England were top of the group and in what pundits like to call the easy side of the draw.

At the end of the game, the players walked over to acknowledge the England fans, who had vociferously supported the side through the second half.

Southgate joined them and it was then that a defining moment of his England career occurred. As he walked towards the fans, plastic beer glasses were hurled at him, some empty, some containing beer. 'I had a choice,' said Southgate. 'Keep walking towards them or stop and head for the tunnel. In my view, walking away would have looked cowardly, like I wasn't prepared to stand up to the abuse. So I deliberately kept walking towards the fans and kept applauding. These are the moments when the leader has to step up and absorb the pressure to protect the group.' The campaign was beginning to look like a personal Calvary for Southgate, each game another Station of the Cross. 'That night was probably the final confirmation in my mind that this would be my last tournament as England manager.' The connection he had spoken of in his *Dear England* letter between fans, manager, nation and team seemed utterly broken.

It was about to get worse.

* * *

The game might have been the worst ever. The only fair comparison was with Iceland in Euro 2016, the point at which Southgate had entered this dysfunctional relationship, though objectively this was worse, as Slovakia were ranked lower. England were 1-0 down after Ivan Schranz's 25th-minute goal, which was well deserved and a consequence of another tactical malfunction, which allowed space in midfield. England offered little by response. Roy Keane, Gary Neville and Ian Wright, doing the ITV analysis, called for immediate half-time substitutions, but there were none forthcoming. Even the good patterns of play went bad. So when Trippier finally delivered a cross in from the left, in his anxiety Phil Foden rushed on to it and was flagged offside, the goal disallowed. When John Stones didn't realise that Jude Bellingham was playing a short free kick to him and David Strelec almost caught Jordan Pickford off his line from the halfway line, the sense of chaos and lack of control was off the scale. Kyle Walker had his worst game ever in an England shirt.

There were ironic cheers when Southgate finally reached for his subs on 66 minutes. The sense that he was always late to the party on in-game changes was hard to shake. Cole Palmer made a difference. Kane missed a header from Foden's free kick. Rice hit the post. But still Southgate waited. There were still twenty minutes to go, but if you have watched enough football matches, the patterns become familiar. And like Iceland, this was a calamity. 'They look resigned to their fate,' said Martin Keown, before being informed England had not created a single shot on goal. 'It's a scandal.' Eberechi Eze arrived only on 84 minutes. Southgate looked like a man who had frozen under pressure. 'I am looking at Gareth Southgate,' said Matthew Upson. 'Hands in pockets and looking at the floor. I think he feels what is coming.' Southgate would later argue it was quite the reverse, that he was the only thinking person amidst a nation of emotionally incontinent fans.

'My job on the sideline is to make good decisions, not to be a cheerleader,' said Southgate. 'I didn't see Terry Venables work that way. I have to be in a clear headspace.. I'm less worried now if people do or don't like that.' Ivan Toney didn't. He barely tried to hide his anger when he was sent on with the clock about to tick over into 95 minutes. And yet in a game that everyone thought was about the changes that should be made, it was the players Southgate left on that saved him.

Bellingham, 21 the day before, had looked weighed down with the self-imposed responsibility of carrying England up to this point. Yet it takes a special type of audacity to eye up the last chance of the game and decide to contort the body into an impossible shape, to attempt a highly improbable overhead kick, when failure would mean inevitable shame. From where Bellingham stood in the six-yard box, taking into account where the ball and the goal were, the expected goal potential would have been somewhere around zero. To have not just the ability but chutzpah to try that overhead kick with the last touch of the game and then to execute it was evidence of something approaching genius. He actually stole the chance off Harry Kane, who was in a better position.

'Who else?' shouted Bellingham to the world, having jumped to his feet from the floor, where he had collapsed in a heap. No one had time to dwell on that question. Harry Kane's header to make it 2-1 from Toney's flick came 52 seconds after the extra time restart. Ultimately, England's tournament and Southgate's reputation pivoted on a passage of football over two minutes and 19 seconds.

It might have been the moment when all tensions dissipated

and the campaign took off. For reporters in the camp, it felt far from that. An innocuous story that England had been training in a back three the next week prompted a short-lived but significant breakdown in relationship between the FA media team and writers. As the story broke, a heated series of phone calls between FA media representatives and senior writers took place. A senior member of the FA coaching staff had exploded with fury that their plans had been leaked and Southgate was still carping about it the following weekend, which seemed odd given that he had worked in the media and knew the drill. At the start of this journey, in Russia 2018, he patiently explained to the public, who had been abusing journalists on social media, that it was part of a reporter's job to get the team and he entirely understood them doing so. Four-letter expletives were uttered in the conversations by those who were usually perfectly aimable. It all indicated that the tension in the camp was huge as they prepared to play Switzerland in the quarter-finals.

* * *

'Under Pressure' by Queen rang out around the Düsseldorf Arena. On the pitch, players were preparing to take penalties in a shoot-out. When you boil it all down, tournament football is just a bit of fun so why not crank up the emotions with some appropriate music? And yet in England we know where this can end, and the ugliness that can be unleashed in the aftermath. Observers would note something interesting about England before the shoot-out against Switzerland in the quarter-finals. There was much less discussion than in 2018 or 2021.

Southgate was simply telling players the order. He would then have a quiet moment with the takers individually. There was no tub-thumping speech. The players had told him they preferred one calm voice rather than a multitude of pep talks. It had also applied to practice. There was less focus on quantity, more on quality of delivery, with Jimmy Floyd Hasselbaink, an assistant coach, taking the lead. 'We've refined the process since [Euro 2020],' said Southgate. 'We have more regular penalty-takers in the squad than we had then. And more that have been in shoot-outs. We had a calm process but the players had to show the composure that they did.'

The contrast with Switzerland was stark. In their corner, coach Murat Yakin appeared to have been superseded by goalkeeper Yann Sommer, the one man not under the same pressure as the outfield players, who was animatedly leading the team talk. Fortune favoured England, who won the toss to choose the end, in front of their fans, and the right to take first. They sent up Cole Palmer, who had scored nine penalties in nine attempts for Chelsea. Everyone knows the importance of scoring the first, the psychological boost it provides, and yet Switzerland sent up Manuel Akanji, who had missed against Spain in Euro 2020 and who had never taken the first penalty before. In fact, he had never taken a penalty in a club game and hadn't even taken one in a shoot-out for Manchester City or Borussia Dortmund. He was, however, their biggest personality, a treble winner at Manchester City, which is the kind of muddled thinking England used to deploy. His penalty, weakly struck and to Pickford's left, was well saved.

For England, all the rehearsed routines applied: Pickford collected the ball to deliver it to the taker; they exchanged a moment, bumping fists; the takers took their time, other than Cole Palmer, who plays by his own rules and waited less than three seconds before striking. Pickford had picked up some tips from the Emiliano Martínez school of gamesmanship, doing his best to delay the Swiss takers. It resulted in five of the best penalties ever seen by an England team.

Lucky? Bukayo Saka is a case in point. When he missed the decisive kick in the Euro 2021 final, he took four seconds from the ref's whistle to his penalty strike. This time he waited, composed himself and took 11 seconds, which, Palmer notwithstanding, is statistically more likely to result in success. And in the aftermath of that penalty miss against Italy, he had become Arsenal's penalty taker. Southgate has encouraged his players to volunteer for penalty-taking duties at their clubs for this reason. Palmer and Ivan Toney, whose 'no look' penalty became one of the memes of the summer, are both phenomenal club penalty-takers and Bellingham has taken them for Real Madrid and Borussia Dortmund. Only Trent Alexander-Arnold, who only came on with five minutes remaining for Foden and who confidently smashed the final penalty home, wasn't an experienced taker. England were a long way from David Batty's 1998 confession: 'I'd never taken one before.' Inadvertently, Alexander-Arnold would seem to reveal that he was only on duty because a regular taker hadn't fancied it. Filmed chatting to his family, he revealed that a mystery player 'didn't want to take one'.

Then there was Pickford's bottle, not a euphemism for his courage but his actual water bottle. In 2018, Pickford's cheat sheet of which way to go for each penalty take was sellotaped on to the side of a bottle and scribbled in pen. Here, the habits of eighteen of the Swiss players had been printed up on to a sheet that fitted around the water bottle. The key advice was 'Akanji – dive left'. He did and saved. And it might have been even better. Pickford's instructions said to 'Fake right, dive left' against Fabian Schär, but for some reason he did the opposite and Schär swept his penalty home to Pickford's left, just as Ignacio Palacios-Huerta had said he would. Still, back in Spain, Palacios-Huerta smiled with quiet satisfaction. You couldn't help but take some pride in his years of research, the hours of study and careful application of Game Theory being distilled into a crib sheet that made sense to Pickford. It's an academic's dream to be relevant. Prior to taking his assignment with England, Palacios-Huerta had been told that the players froze in extra time because they feared the prospect of penalties. In 2006, one England player privately told a reporter that when the extra time against Portugal finished, his overriding thought was: 'Oh no, it's penalties again!' But the curse was losing its hold with each significant victory.

Pickford had tried to cover the summary of Palacios-Huerta's work on his water bottle with a towel, but a sharp photographer caught it. Afterwards, Pickford smirked as he said, 'I thought I'd hidden it but obviously not well enough.' An FA media representative intervened when he was pressed further to insist they weren't talking about it. This was a trade secret they wished to protect. What was clear was that where England teams had failed in tight moments in the past, this team was succeeding.

The mood was euphoric even if foreign journalists introduced that cold dose of reality to the press conference with their observations on an England team still failing to create goalscoring chances. Having fallen behind, again, it was Saka, cutting inside and finding the far corner from outside the box in the 80th minute, who brought England level. It was a brilliant goal. England had failed to initiate much attacking football, but when they did, it was superb. Their highlights reel was going to look excellent. But that only compounded the frustration. If they could do it in moments or when they fell behind, why couldn't they start games like that and do it more consistently? The Netherlands now awaited them in a semi-final.

***

Ollie Watkins wheeled away to salute the fans after scoring the dramatic late winner. 'I scored and ran off, pulling my shirt up and there was one fan in the away end,' he recalled. It was his second ever goal in senior competitive football and was scored for Weston-super-Mare in the Conference South, the sixth tier of English football. He was 19 at the time, three years older than Lamine Yamal was at Euro 24, the same age as when Bellingham was negotiating his move to Real Madrid.

Even when he came back to Exeter that summer, in 2015, it wasn't exactly to a hero's welcome. Manager Paul Tisdale remembered they had a pre-season tour to Scotland. He had 24 places and Watkins only went because someone dropped out and played left-back to fill in at times. Yet he and Steve Perryman, the legendary Spurs captain who was director of football, knew they had something. It just wasn't evident what it was. It was while away at Swindon reserves that season that Tisdale took time to reconstruct his game, and help him to understand what type of goalscorer he was: the type who needs to make runs, however seemingly futile, to create something out of nothing. Rather like he did in Dortmund that night against the Netherlands.

England had conceded early, now a regular occurrence, to Xavi Simons, but thereafter were a revelation, playing their best football of the tournament. Phil Foden and Kobbie Mainoo were running the game, Stockport's finest footballing hour. The penalty, when it came for the foul on Kane, was at the softest end of even UEFA-endorsed VAR fouls, but it was struck nervelessly by Kane. And Foden, with his wriggle through the Dutch defence and shot through the keeper's legs which was cleared off the line, and with his shot from outside the box with devilish swerve on it that struck the post, suddenly looked free. Netherlands manager Ronald Koeman knew he had to switch at half-time and changed to a more compact midfield. Southgate responded. England retreated, again, though continued to dominate possession. And then came a bold switch. In retrospect, many would say Kane shouldn't have started the final two games of Euro 2024 and that Southgate could have been quicker to replace him. Yet whether any coach would have had the nerve to drop Kane in such important games is debatable.

Southgate took his captain off on 81 minutes, as well as Foden. On came Cole Palmer and Watkins. 'Look for me!' said Watkins to Bellingham. England would have a striker running in behind the Netherlands' back four, something Kane couldn't do. Watkins had spoken to Palmer before the match. 'We're going to come on and you're going to assist me for the winner,' he said. As such, he shouldn't have looked quite so surprised as he ran away, jaw gaping, mouth wide open with shock, to celebrate the winner. It came satisfyingly on 89 minutes and 58 seconds, Palmer's lovely slide pass, Watkins' little touch with the right, his turn and shot through Stefan de Vrij's legs, right in the far corner, off the post, to give keeper Bart Verbruggen no chance. Something out of nothing, just like Tisdale used to tell him at Exeter reserves.

Watkins grinned as he walked in for the player of the match press conference, still seemingly unable to take it all in. He relayed how Trippier had given an important team talk to the squad after the Denmark game. He reminded them of his experience in Euro 2020, where he had started the first game against Croatia, was dropped for the next two, started the last 16 against Germany, came on the next two games and then started the final. 'You have to be ready, you have your part to play,' said Trippier. 'It was a good speech,' said Watkins.

It could equally have applied to Toney, for his flick-on against Slovakia for Kane and his penalty against Switzerland. Or to

Alexander-Arnold, who scored the winning penalty against Switzerland; or Palmer with his assist here, his penalty against Switzerland and a goal in the final. Southgate will go to his grave with fans debating his substitutions, but the reality was that all his substitutes made impacts.

There was a lovely moment for him that night as the manager walked over to euphoric England fans in Dortmund. Nothing diminishes anger and tension like a last-minute winner in a semi-final. Not since David Platt scored a goal of similar quality in the last minute of extra time against Belgium in 1990 had there been something quite like this. Maybe among the fans there were some who threw beer at him after Slovenia, yet this time, 'Sweet Caroline' was pounding over the PA at the Westfalenstadion. And 'So Good! So Good! So Good!' was the fans' refrain. Southgate punched the air. The fans responded back, this time with acclaim rather than beer. 'One more!' shouted Southgate to the fans. 'One more!' In a draining tactical battle of constantly changing shapes, Southgate had come out on top. Having connected with the fans, he had a raft of TV interviews to conduct and then his press conference. There were no chippy questions, though one journalist who told the Netherlands' manager Ronald Koeman that he was hoping that he would save football by beating boring England was put in his place. 'England played some great football tonight,' said Koeman. He knows the madness of this dance, the hot takes that belittle a serious profession.

Southgate took his turn, addressing the assembled press for around 15 minutes. He was much calmer than he had been on Saturday after Switzerland, seemingly freed from the angst that bedevilled him there. The last question came, a reference to that reconnection with the fans he had at the end and how sweet it must have been after the beer-chucking point of disconnection against Slovenia.

'When you're doing something for your country, you're a proud Englishman and you don't feel that back, when all you read is criticism, it's hard,' he said. 'So to be able to celebrate a second final [in three years] is very, very special. To be able to give our fans nights like these, there have been a few over the last six years, it means a lot. If I hadn't been on the grass, I'd have been watching somewhere like they were. So we're kindred spirits in many ways.'

Southgate had dropped his guard for a second. 'I mean, we all want to be loved, right?'

* * *

Pickford was superb, the speed at which he delivered the ball from hand to Bellingham's feet halfway up the pitch unnerving Spain, who were flustered, their structure undone. Bellingham controlled brilliantly and touched the ball to Palmer, who played it first time, direct up the pitch. It was Premier League football at its best, Saka now in full flight up against Aymeric Laporte, out of position because left-back Marc Cucurella was caught high up the pitch and struggling to get back. England were toying with Spain. Saka cut back and passed to Bellingham, who stuck out a leg to divert it back to Palmer, and because England had attacked so incisively and Spain's players were flummoxed, the Chelsea player had space aplenty in which to line up his shot. Even so, it was a wonderful finish from the edge of the box. Here was the England team everyone had waited for. Bellingham bossing midfield, Saka running at defenders, Palmer bursting through: quick, incisive, possession-based football.

It was a superb sequence of play. 'England teams aim to dominate possession intelligently, selecting the right moments to progress the play and penetrate the opposition,' Dan Ashworth's much-derided

England's DNA document had read. Like this, he had meant. And it had come after one of Southgate's substitutions, 142 seconds after Palmer had come on for Mainoo. 'It was the fastest-ever goal by an England substitute,' Southgate reflected. 'More importantly, we were level with Spain and our fans banked in the stadium's west stand could start to believe again. And why not? Weren't resurrections a bit of a theme for England in these Euros?'

Yet there was little life left in this team. That was pretty much the only time England managed to play like that in the final against Spain. A trope Southgate had vowed to eliminate returned. 'We weren't good enough on the ball,' he said afterwards. 'That should be the title of England's Euro 24 performance review,' said Neville. England scored and retreated rather than advanced. They failed to keep possession. Southgate didn't name names but mentioned one incident that was emblematic of the final and, for his critics, of his era in charge. Just after scoring, England had a chance to launch a long throw into the Spain penalty area. Spain were rattled, the crowd, the majority of whom were English, were up and vociferous in their support. Saka gestured to encourage more noise.

England were on the advance. Spain looked vulnerable. The clock read 74 minutes and 49 seconds. Kyle Walker spent 31 seconds contemplating the throw. The noise died down a bit. He considered his options again and then threw the ball backwards, to John Stones, who, under pressure, passed to Jordan Pickford. Attack to defence in a few seconds, momentum lost, optimism tempered. Pickford's long kick went out for a goal kick and Spain were back in possession. They barely conceded it again until Mikel Oyarzabal scored on 85 minutes and 56 seconds. In fact, if you break down the 11 minutes of play between that throw-in and Spain's winner, England were abysmal. With a final to win and history within grasp, they consistently conceded possession, could only string together two or three passes and often hoofed the ball long, with Pickford sending his kicks directly back to Spanish players.

'England teams aim to regain possession intelligently and as early and as efficiently as possible,' said Ashworth's DNA document, launched with Southgate alongside him in 2014. But this England team were incapable of pressing the ball efficiently and sat back, having just 37 per cent of possession in the final, the lowest of Southgate's tenure. In fact, the biggest three games of his England reign were those in which he had least possession: this final, the Italy final (39 per cent) and the Croatia semi-final (46 per cent). They were passed off the park in all of them.

It was hard to avoid the conclusion that both manager and players, on the cusp of greatness, had frozen after that Palmer goal. It was an echo of the Croatia semi-final. The final step over the line though looked as though it remained a terrifying prospect for the players. 'Like a punch in the gut,' was Southgate's line about Oyarzabal's 86th-minute winner. 'I'm not sure I've ever known disappointment so visceral – so much like an actual physical blow. Was this really how it was going to end?'

It was. Kane would give the Henri Delaunay trophy a plaintive glance as he walked past it for a second time in his career. A bewildered group of England players congregating at the side of the pitch as Spain celebrated wildly. Sir Trevor Brooking used the vision of Spain 2010 to reboot England, but they remained some way ahead. Bellingham kicked an advertising hoarding, Pickford cried. Everyone dealt with it in their own way. 'It's time for change, and for a new chapter,' was Southgate's succinct summary two days later. 'As a proud Englishman, it has been the honour of my life to play for England and to manage England. It has meant everything to me, and I have given it my all.'

Assessments of his impact varied. 'He had a great group of players and failed,' said talkSPORT's Andy Goldstein. 'Eight years in charge, won nothing.'

'His legacy will be a generation of young people who have learned from him that leadership is primarily about decency, integrity and bringing honour to others. That is worth more to our country than any trophy. The crown of a good name supersedes all,' said the Chief Rabbi, Sir Ephraim Mirvis. Amidst it all, your mind went back to the extraordinary moment against Slovakia where Southgate stared into the abyss and confronted the ghosts of England past, all the failures and subsequent indignities. And to Bellingham's response after his extraordinary goal. 'It will only really be important if we win,' said Bellingham.

Yet he was only partially right. As Southgate wrote in that letter to fans back in 2021, you don't forget where you were when England have those special moments. That said, the trophy remained elusive and the final chapter was still unwritten.

CHAPTER 11

FROM DOUBT TO THOMAS

The heavy shirt. The backpack. By the end of Euro 2024, England were in a curious place.

They had won penalty shoot-outs, prevailed in stoppage time and extra time, and ground their way to a final while ignoring critics. All those psychological burdens Southgate made it his cause to address – they had been overcome.

But that left an uncomfortable truth. Mentality was no longer England's problem. The football was.

And if anyone was carrying a backpack it was Southgate. The weariness, the emotion, his petty touchiness when newspapers revealed three at the back – here was a very different man to the smiling agent of glasnost of his first tournament in Russia, 2018. Once, he had worn it lightly as a waistcoat; now the role of England manager weighed on him.

Southgate's path since suggested pain remains. He has retreated from football to safer spaces like LinkedIn and discussed the England job only in settings that are benign and controlled, like a Harvard Business School Q&A or a Barbican stage show to launch his book, *Dear England: Lessons in Leadership*.

It is less a sports book than an attempt to climb to higher

ground and to draw wider meaning from coaching a football team. 'Right until the end, on that pitch in Berlin, and in the moments afterwards when we were finally able to retreat to the dressing room, I was learning lessons in leadership . . .' Southgate writes with a certain drama.

'I was learning them in what I think most people will agree is, however you look at it, an extraordinary role. Actually, I think there might be no job quite like managing England.'

* * *

What if the England job went back to being something less lofty though? More 'ordinary'. What if the incumbent was not looking for lessons in leadership or to heal society but merely to coach and manage? What if it went back to being foursquare about the football?

For the FA it was the moment to find out. Four days after announcing Southgate's resignation, they advertised the vacancy and the first thing notable was the job ad's headline: 'England Men's Senior Team Head Coach'. Southgate was 'England manager' but his successor would be 'head coach'. No major statement was intended, but it did imply a narrower focus.

The ad outlined three core duties which were all sporting/technical:

- lead and develop the England senior men's team to win a major tournament and be consistently ranked as one of the top teams in the world
- provide inspiring leadership to a world-class, multi-disciplinary technical team based at St George's Park
- develop and maintain strong relationships with clubs who employ English qualified players.

Only in the subsection listing candidates' desired qualities was there mention of 'personal values' and 'inspiring the nation' and it was the very last bullet point. The rest of the ad was about work on the grass, football leadership and results, results, results.

In charge of the recruitment process were Mark Bullingham and John McDermott, who were of one mind. England had such talent, had come so close and the next objective was clear. To win. Any appointment had to reflect this.

The World Cup was less than two years away, so what they were looking for was a winner – not a development hire, but a hire for here and now. It was also telling the job ad did not mention nationality: from the start, Bullingham and McDermott agreed that if the best candidate was a foreigner, that should not matter – so long as that coach had a connection to English players and English football.

They did not want to compromise by rushing the process, but England had a programme of six autumn Nations League matches beginning in seven weeks' time. A solution was under their noses. McDermott's background as a leading academy director made him experienced in not only overseeing player development but the pathways of coaches, and since becoming technical director in 2020 he had immersed himself in all the FA's teams, senior and junior, men's and women's. He had become a mentor figure to a number of the FA's coaches including Lee Carsley, and was in camp with the England Under-21s in 2023 when Carsley guided them to a first European Under-21 Championship in 39 years.

McDermott felt Carsley was more than capable of stepping in to lead England through the Nations League campaign as an interim head coach. Southgate himself arrived into the senior role from coaching the '21s' and Luis de la Fuente, Spain's victorious manager at Euro 2024, had served a long apprenticeship in international age group football. Lionel Scaloni, Argentina's World Cup-winning head coach (note the title) got his job after six games in charge of Argentina's Under-20s.

Other attractions of Carsley included his reputation for playing in an innovative, attractive style, and his number two was Ashley Cole, one of England's most capped players, with a wealth of senior international wisdom to lend him. Carsley had been at Euro 2024, as an FA scout tasked with monitoring Group F in case any of its sides (Portugal, Turkey, Georgia and Czech Republic) became England's opponents, but they were all knocked out by the quarter-finals and Carsley went home. He watched England's semi-final and final on his sofa in Kenilworth.

'It didn't even cross my mind,' he says, that he might be asked to step into Southgate's shoes and McDermott broached it gently, meeting him a few days after the Euros to say, 'Just something to put on your radar – start having a look at England's Nations League group.'

'At that point I was focused on the next Under-21 matches and working with a new group of 21s players, but then talks developed and it became a firm possibility [the seniors] would need me,' Carsley says. The interim role was agreed in a call with Bullingham and had clear boundaries. 'Mark said we're doing three camps and that was it.'

When Carsley was announced as interim on 9 August, the FA only confirmed he was in charge for the first two fixtures, in September, away to Ireland and at home to Finland, 'but with a view to remaining in the position throughout the autumn while the recruitment process for a new permanent head coach continues'.

The ambiguity was perhaps necessary – for what if the FA found a brilliant candidate who wanted to take over immediately – but wouldn't help Carsley as he tried to navigate what he sensed would be the hardest part of the job ahead? The press conferences. The messaging.

The dance began on the second question of his first press conference: 'You've got the job on an interim basis. Do you want it? Long term?' Carsley replied that his own situation was not important but – and it certainly would not be the last time – that did not satisfy reporters.

He had been an interim manager before, several times in fact, at Coventry, Birmingham and Brentford. From experience he knew it was a difficult question to answer. 'At Brentford, in my very first press conference as caretaker, I said, "I don't want the job; I didn't ask for it." I was thinking about the guy (Marinus Dijkhuizen) who had just been sacked. We were working in Portakabins next to each other and I'd watched him clear his office. I didn't want him looking on Sky, going, "Ah, been waiting for me to get sacked, have you?"

'But I hadn't appreciated the impact my words would have on the players. They're like, "Oh this guy doesn't even want the job; who's in charge then?" So with England I just tried to say, "I'm going to do my best, and see how it goes." But of course that answer doesn't help the journalists and maybe it didn't help me.'

He was disarmingly honest when he sat down with newspaper writers, admitting having to overcome doubts he could step into the senior role.

'You always doubt yourself,' he says, looking back. 'Sometimes I had to remind myself I was a European champion. I'd won the same amount of [Under-21] trophies as the Spain coach and one more [at junior level] than Argentina's. At the back of my mind I knew I was capable, but you doubt because you know managing any team is always more difficult than it looks.'

Those doubts were nothing to do with coaching, though. 'One

hundred per cent not.' In that sphere he felt very confident of making a difference. With good reason. In a playing career spanning nearly 600 games for Everton, Coventry, Blackburn, Birmingham, Derby and Ireland, Carsley was a shrewd and selfless midfielder, always on the team sheet and almost never in the press.

His coaching career had been one of similar steadiness and under-the-radar excellence. Much of it had been spent as an assistant or age group coach and he had turned down numerous senior number one posts, including managing Ireland, the country he represented through grandparents from Dunmanway in County Cork.

He was encouraged to take his badges while playing for Everton by David Moyes and a formative experience was working under Pep Guardiola at Manchester City, where Carsley coached an exceptional City Under-18 side featuring Phil Foden, Jadon Sancho, Brahim Díaz,, Jeremie Frimpong and Lukas Nmecha.

He imbibed classic Guardiolan ideas around dominating possession, playing in the opposition half, placing ball mastery over athleticism, and tactical invention. His Under-21s had played in such a bold, distinctive style that an epithet – half-jokey but half in worship – had sprung up among journalists who covered the team: 'Carsball'.

Taking over the seniors, he saw an opportunity. 'I was focused on the players and the style we played in,' Carsley says. 'The big thing I talk about as a coach is control and I wanted to prove to the players they were capable of it. The Nations League group wasn't the strongest, but [establishing a new style] could be important for moving things forward.

'Because at some point in the biggest games, in the most crucial moments, England are going to have to play with control so I wanted to leave that stamp on the team. I had sensed with the 21s that if we're going to develop the next generation of England players, in the biggest moments they have to believe they can win.'

There was a line in the FA's job ad – '[the candidate] will have a strong track record of delivering results in the Premier League and/ or *leading international competitions*' – which many read as putting Carsley in the frame, but 'it was quite clear to me I wasn't going to apply for the job,' he says.

Why? 'Well, I think if it was tomorrow, it would be different, being a back-to-back European champion [Carsley retained the Under-21 Euros title in 2025] is different to the experience I had behind me at that point. I think I'm an all-round better coach now and have a better understanding of how [the senior job] looks.'

But Carsley's thoughts were not on his own progression when he sat down to choose his first squad, they were on England's. His Under-21s beat Germany, Portugal and Spain to become European champions, wowing with their emphasis on possession and attack, even when facing the very best teams. He felt the seniors were waiting to be unshackled and to do the same.

His squad was a statement. Recalled was that symbol of flair and expression, Jack Grealish, and called up for the first time were talents he had worked with at junior level: Noni Madueke, Tino Livramento, Morgan Gibbs-White and Angel Gomes.

The selection of Gomes was striking. At five foot six and nine and a half stone, on the pitch he almost looked like one of the other players had brought their son along. He was a million miles (and at least three stone and six inches) away from the traditional English ideal of the muscular, running-machine midfielder. But he kept passes ticking like a metronome and that's what Carsley wanted at the centre of his team.

'My thought was, "Let's not do what we've done in the past."

I wanted to try something different. I understand that ultimately you've got to win and the human instinct is to do something safe, make sure you don't mess up, but I didn't see the value to England of me approaching it like that,' Carsley says.

'After the defeat to Greece [which, oh yes, we will come to] when people were like, "That's it now, he won't get the job," I remember thinking, *I was never getting the job! I know I'm doing it for six games and handing it over. So it's important we took this opportunity to try something.*'

Carsley enacts humility and transparency in his way of working. In camp, he and his staff sit among the players doing their game prep out in the open rather than retire to the coaches' room; before training sessions he is the one who goes and puts out the cones. He admits getting so engrossed in 'the football' he sometimes loses awareness and there was a funny moment, at his first game at the Aviva Stadium in Dublin, when he came out for the kick-off and went the wrong way, going and sitting in the Ireland dugout rather than England's. He explained he was so busy thinking about the game he went on autopilot – having sat on that Irish bench so many times during his international playing career.

His line-up was a statement too: Grealish at number ten, Anthony Gordon on the left, Trent Alexander-Arnold at right-back. Gordon and Alexander-Arnold had fallen from Southgate's favour during Euro 2024, but were now central to an England game plan, with Gordon trusted to provide penetration in behind and Alexander-Arnold cast as main creator.

The first half was breathtaking. England's centre-backs pushed high, Grealish roamed, and with sauntering elegance Alexander-Arnold probed. All over the pitch, England players were connecting, making triangles, rotating. Liquid football compared to the leaden stuff of Euro 2024.

After just 26 minutes, Carsley's side had accrued a higher xG than England managed in any whole match during the Euros, and by the interval had 86 per cent possession and a 2-0 lead. After 11 minutes, Alexander-Arnold spotted a gap down Ireland's centre and flighted a pass to Gordon of such delicious insouciance he could have been wearing a smoking jacket rather than a football kit. Caoimhin Kelleher saved Gordon's shot but Gordon retrieved and after Nathan Collins blocked Harry Kane's attempt to steer home Gordon's cut back, Declan Rice arrived to hammer the loose ball home.

Carsley had empowered Rice too, licensing him to maraud forward like he does for Arsenal rather than sitting in the holding role he fulfilled for Southgate. Working his way into Ireland's area via sweet passing exchanges with Kobbie Mainoo and Bukayo Saka, he picked out Grealish, who rattled in England's second goal from 20 yards. The second half was notable for Gomes's assured cameo when he came on for his debut. Carsley watched, lost in his football, the first England manager to wear a tracksuit since Kevin Keegan, and at the end ambled to the tunnel, iPad in hand.

Carsball 2 Stuck Thinking 0? Well, not unanimously. Some were not happy. On the eve of the game, a controversy was confected out of Carsley saying he was not going to sing 'God Save the King'. He explained it was simply because he liked to get 'in the zone' before kick-off, and that he had never sung during the anthems whether playing for Ireland or coaching the '21s'. Birmingham born and raised – and proud of it – he was not making a political point or an Irish statement, yet the *Telegraph*'s leading sports article, penned by one of the country's best and biggest football writers, was headlined: 'If Lee Carsley does not sing the national anthem, he cannot expect to manage England'.

And a *Daily Mail* column invoked Winston Churchill, thundering,

'Where England used to have Sir Alf Ramsey, we now have Little Lee.' Carsley should be sacked, said the columnist, even if he won 10-0 in Dublin for his 'true is green'. Southgate had his faults but at least 'dressed like an English gentleman'.

Welcome to the England job, where even in the 2020s nonsense is never far away. At the time, Carsley, who tends to ignore social and mainstream media, was not fully aware of what continued to reverberate despite England's fine performance. Later, he went back through the coverage and digested 'anthem-gate'.

'We [he and the FA staff] have spoken a lot about it since. My feelings would have been, if someone had said to me it's going to really affect the team, then obviously I'd sing the anthem because anything that harms the players – I would definitely not want that.'

It did not affect performance though. 'No.'

Did the fallout affect his family? 'Not at all. Because of the circle I'm in. But I wouldn't want to just palm it off. It upset a lot of people and I can sort of see that other side, how if I'd done it to be political then [outrage would have been justified].'

The whole thing was a lesson in how managing the senior England team is different. 'Sometimes people are going to get offended and you just can't win.

'I think that's what Gareth was so good at. In terms of current affairs, having a real understanding of what's going on and where, and I think I'm the other way, I'm just pure football. I suppose there is a responsibility but, you know, we still haven't won since 1966 so . . . I wouldn't spend a lot of time watching news, you know.'

* * *

Included in the FA's job advert was a line that sounded no more than PR. 'Our succession planning has already identified a number of candidates,' it said. However, it was genuine. Bullingham and McDermott already had a clear idea where to start their search: at the very top. With the help of two external data companies, they profiled the top 50 coaches in the world and ended up with three categories, the uppermost of which was 'super-elite'.

There were five coaches on this list and they were the best of the best, in terms of candidates with an English football connection. But one candidate in particular was emerging. Flashback to London, the summer of 2021, when the manager who had just won the club version found himself wowed by the European championship at national team level.

Thomas Tuchel.

'I was Chelsea coach at the time the Euros [the delayed Euro 2020] were played . . . I felt the excitement of the country, it felt so different. I called my manager and said, "Wow, this is my dream. I want to win as many titles as possible with Chelsea and then let's try to become England coach,"' Tuchel would recall.

'And he answered along the lines of, "Yeah, that's nice. I know how much you love it; this will not happen."'

After Chelsea dismissed him in September 2022, Tuchel discreetly signalled interest in managing England, amidst speculation Southgate would step down after that winter's World Cup. In the event, Southgate stayed and Tuchel went to Bayern Munich, where his star signing was Harry Kane.

Tactically, he was super-elite. Trophies-wise, he had won at national, European and world level. As for his record with English players, he had not only developed such as Reece James and Mason Mount at Chelsea, but helped Kane reach even greater heights at

Bayern. He scored just as highly as Guardiola and having been hard to get a hold of initially was – as soon as contact was established – very receptive to the FA's approach.

In the end, according to a source close to the process, the FA spoke to 'eight to ten' candidates. 'Some were more formal conversations and a couple were more informal soundings out.' This included talking to a small number of English coaches whose work was admired, and who impressed, but were not seen as being quite yet on the level as those on the 'super-elite' list, all of whom were foreign-born.

By mid-September, Bullingham and McDermott were pressing forward with the Tuchel candidacy, McDermott having dined with the German in Munich and the pair having subsequently – and secretly – met Tuchel and his number two, Anthony Barry, for more formal talks. Bullingham and McDermott were determined to keep the process private and avoid the media circus of some previous FA recruitment drives. Like in 2006 when, with the World Cup approaching, the FA's then chief executive Brian Barwick blithely told reporters he had met Phil Scolari and considered the Brazilian the 'preferred candidate' to succeed Sven-Göran Eriksson. Humiliatingly, Scolari turned England down.

Almost nobody at the FA knew about the Tuchel approach. Even senior members of its communication team were unaware he was taking over until 20 minutes before the story broke on 15 October. But one person who was kept up to speed was Carsley and, by the time of England's next game against Greece at Wembley on 10 October, he found himself in a very, very difficult position.

Two days previously, Tuchel had signed his contract. Late that afternoon – on Tuesday 8 October – Bullingham told the FA board in a 30-minute conference call that Tuchel was the man and the FA's remuneration committee had been through the details of a deal that would begin on 1 January, last until after the 2026 World Cup, and net Tuchel around £5–6 million. Board members were not asked for their opinions but none objected and the hiring of Tuchel was rubber-stamped.

Why continue to keep things quiet? One reason was to give England space to play two important matches without hullaballoo. Another was so a proper unveiling for Tuchel could be planned and here, one of those quirks of football came into play. Included in Tuchel's appeal was the fact that as number two, he would bring an outstanding young English coach, a graduate of the FA's own Pro Licence programme, Anthony Barry.

However, Barry was still Portugal assistant manager and Portugal happened to be playing, on Monday 15 October. The game was against Scotland at Hampden Park. Out of courtesy to the Portuguese, and to spare Barry any local grief, it was better to get that match over with before any unveiling.

Carsley knew what was going on but what could he tell the press? When, the day before the Greece game, a reporter put it to him that the match was part of 'a six-game audition', Carsley replied, 'I definitely don't feel like it's an audition. I have really enjoyed the challenge. I'm seeing it for what it is: three camps, three windows. The next training session is the important one.' It would prove almost impossible to continue in 'take each day as it comes' mode after the match itself.

Release the handbrake! Play all the stars! Under Southgate, these had been regular refrains from the public and press. Now Carsley gave the romantics what they wanted. He chose a team with three natural number tens, two wingers and two full-backs who liked to step into midfield, lining up as follows: Pickford; Alexander-Arnold, Stones, Colwill, Lewis; Saka, Palmer, Rice, Gordon; Foden, Bellingham.

On paper it was a 4-4-2, but on the pitch it was far less orthodox.

Jude Bellingham was a false nine with Declan Rice screening the defence and between was a midfield diamond with Cole Palmer the deepest point and Phil Foden at the apex.

The result? Slow, stodgy, middle-heavy play where the build-up was unfocused and England moved the ball as slowly and laboriously as at the Euros. Greece, supercharged with emotion following the death of their player, George Baldock, played via electric counter-attacks and led before a brilliant late Bellingham equaliser. In stoppage time, the Greeks pushed again and got their winner when Vangelis Pavlidis converted after Rico Lewis and Levi Colwill got in such a tangle in England's box while trying to clear that both fell over. It was a tableau that symbolised England's messy night.

Fans booed as they made for Wembley's exits. A honeymoon was over. The post-match press conference was excruciating. The questions to Carsley had two subtexts. *What the hell were you thinking?* and *what the hell are the FA thinking?* Carsley remarked he would 'hopefully' soon be returning to his role as Under-21 boss and was pressed to clarify. Did he actually want the top job? His reply – that he was neither in nor out but simply focusing on the last three Nations League games – exasperated the room.

But how else could he have played it? 'What I sensed from the press conferences was frustration. They [journalists] didn't know what was going on. "Are you staying?" "Are you going?" "Who's coming in?" They wanted me to give them something, which wasn't my job. I was there to coach the team,' Carsley reflects.

'I think if we were doing it again, we'd probably do it a little differently. I understood the pressure on the press and get that I'm sitting there, as the figurehead, saying, "I don't know, I don't know, I don't know."

'And that "I'm only looking to take it game by game" doesn't sell newspapers, does it?'

Yet the FA's discretion was one of the factors that impressed Tuchel about his prospective employer. Had he felt the FA was the circus of old, he would not have taken the job.

'After one of the press conferences I said to Andy [Walker – the FA's senior communications manager], there's a lot of frustration and I'm not sure what we can do apart from telling them what's going on, which is going to put a lot of things up in the air,' Carsley says.

'I was pretty aware of everything [going on in the recruitment process]. I knew from the start I was doing six games and that never changed one bit.'

He felt on firmer ground solving football problems. England needed to win their three remaining fixtures, including a hazardous assignment in Athens, to have a chance of avoiding the ignominy of finishing second in a Nations League 'B' group, and the headache of a play-off in March. He got to work reviewing the video of the Greece game, for which talkSPORT's football anchor, Adrian Durham, had rated his coaching performance as '1 out of 10'.

Why had Carsley thought his smorgasbord of midfield ball-players would work? 'So, I remember trying it the day before in training. We'd done an 11 v 11, unreal. It was so good, honestly, it was so good,' Carsley says with a rueful grin.

'I was excited by it, I really was. I couldn't see [Greece] getting the ball off us. I thought we'd have too much possession. I thought we'd create too many chances.

'The worry was always that we'd have too many players coming towards the ball trying to get a touch, but I thought our wide players, Noni and Bukayo, would pin them back. I think what we underestimated was the emotion of the game. Greece lost a player the day before and played with incredible passion.

'They counter-attacked us very well and our build-up ended up being a bit slow and side to side and Wembley got edgy.' But the narrative did, he points out, hinge on a 94th- minute goal. No regrets. 'It might help England in the future,' he shrugs. 'I tried something. It's what I was there to do.'

The next day he took players individually on walks around the pitches of Tottenham's training ground (where England were based) to debrief one-to-one about what went wrong. When he next spoke to the press, before leaving for Helsinki, he talked about keeping balanced through football's highs – and lows.

He mentioned his son, Connor, who has Down's syndrome.

'I definitely don't want anyone in the room to make too much of it, but when Connor was born, it made a big difference to our lives and put things in perspective. So, it was a setback the other night and I felt bad for a couple of days, but it's a game of football,' he said. 'I tried my best. It didn't come off. I'm here to fight again.'

England had beaten Finland comfortably in September, in Carsley's first Wembley game. In Helsinki they were even more impressive. Carsley made six changes, fielding a much more conventional XI, and the 3-1 victory contained delicious morsels like Gomes's ingenious little through ball for Grealish's opener and Alexander-Arnold curling home a 25-yard free kick and winning a £500 bet with Grealish in the process.

But post-match, the comms position neared an untenable point. Pinned down by one of the best football interviewers in the business, ITV's Gabriel Clarke, Carsley said, 'This job deserves a world-class coach that's won trophies and been there and done it and I'm still on the path.' So he *was* ruling himself out, was he? His ensuing post-match press conference was even testier than the one after Greece, with reporters pressing him: *do you even want the job? what did you mean?*

The Clarke interview 'triggered an internal cascade' at the FA, a source conceded, causing the organisation to speed up plans for communicating Tuchel's arrival and an unveiling at Wembley for three days hence – on Wednesday 16 October – was tentatively scheduled.

Could the secret keep until then?

On the morning of Tuesday 15 October, the reporting team at *The Times* got to the bottom of things. Tuchel was the man. There would be a Wembley unveiling and photoshoot the following day. Tuchel would not start until 1 January.

It took a few hours to check the info from all angles and at 6 p.m., *The Times* were able to get most of it into a story, breaking news of Tuchel's appointment online.

* * *

Everyone who knows Carsley well says the same thing. He never changes. The only difference the England job made to him is that he now employs an agent – the experience left him with the sensible thought, that 'sometimes it's good to have a third party to bounce stuff off.'

His nature served him well in the hot seat. His obliviousness to the media meant he was not fully aware of the backlash that followed the home defeat to Greece. However, subsequently he has looked back at everything, read the articles, watched the TV coverage, debriefed with the FA's communications team.

'It was amazing how negative it got,' he smiles. 'By the way I also looked at the second Greece game – not the same! That we did well in Athens didn't quite get the same amount of coverage.'

All the way through his England stint, he continued coaching a group of youngsters at the Strachan Foundation at the University of

Warwick. He has been working with them for years, putting on a session every Friday. Were the kids excited that their coach was also training Jude Bellingham and Harry Kane? 'They weren't bothered because I'm there every week,' Carsley shrugs.

A colleague bumped into England's interim manager in a south Birmingham pub on a Sunday afternoon. He was a sipping a soft drink (Carsley is teetotal), minding his own business, with nobody around him batting an eyelid.

'Yeah, I'm sort of low-key,' says Carsley. 'I'm not stumbling out of The Ivy. Connor has his Downs group on Friday. I'll stand behind the goal, collect the balls, throw them back in. Go for a Nando's sometimes on a Wednesday. Other than that, and work, I'm at home.'

Though sometimes staying under the radar was impossible. Carsley grins as he remembers being accosted by a West Ham fan at a petrol station in Beaconsfield, demanding to know why Jarrod Bowen was not in his squad. Another time, 'I was in a queue in a Starbucks and a fella was talking about the false nine and the tactics after the Greece game. I just wanted a soy latte.'

After the first camp he allowed himself to watch *Mike Bassett: England Manager* ('hilarious') and after the second camp the seminal fly-on-the-wall documentary, *The Impossible Job*, which followed Graham Taylor at the height of Fleet Street cruelty towards England managers. 'James Ryder, our match analyst, had seen it and he said, "Don't watch it; wait for a bit." I thought it was so interesting. Quite sad.'

The press conferences were much easier after everyone knew Tuchel was taking over. And Carsley is right: Greece away was a triumph for which he was not given sufficient credit. England needed to win by two clear goals, nine players withdrew from the squad and he made the bravest of calls – to drop Harry Kane. A 3-0 romp where Kane's replacement, Ollie Watkins, starred, and Curtis Jones sealed victory with the most 'Carsball' of pass-and-move goals, ensued.

'Yeah [starting Watkins] was a big call,' he says, 'but I thought it was a really good opportunity to give ownership and trust, to give Ollie the experience of leading the attack in a must-win game. That might help England in a tournament sometime.'

When it was over, Carsley reported to St George's Park for a presentation to the FA's 'MDT' – the multi-disciplinary team comprising senior representatives of all the departments involved in England. It took place in the Noel Blake Room of the Football Centre.

'I described [being in charge of England seniors] as the Wizard of Oz. You know, we're on the way to the castle and it's all happening, but they go behind the curtain and you see it's just a fella on a bike puffing out smoke.

'I'd never been inside it but from the outside you're always thinking they must be doing something weird and wonderful. But actually, it's really good, talented people doing things really simply. It was important for me to acknowledge all the support an England manager gets from the staff and departments.

That was November 2024. Tuchel's start date was 1 January and so, ever conscientious, Carsley continued scouting and monitoring senior players right up until that point so he could give the German the most up-to-date handover. They met at St George's Park with John McDermott, Anthony Barry and new goalkeeper coach Hilario also present, 'and it was very informal. I had a presentation ready but it wasn't a presentation-type occasion, just 'this is what I think of the players, these are the changes we made, "this is how they reacted to playing or not playing".

'Thomas was really receptive, liked my thoughts and asked a lot of questions about the campaign and the cadence of the camp. International management was new to him so he was very keen to know those details: when do you train, where is there downtime and what do you do with downtime, all those kinds of things.'

After returning to the Under-21s, Carsley retained the European Championship in 2025 with a superb new side whose holding midfielder, Elliot Anderson, whom he converted from a number eight, particularly caught Tuchel's eye. He is proud of the number of players in Tuchel's squad who came through his Under-21s and/or he brought into the senior set-up during his interim stint.

Another of Carsley's legacies is helping 'reset' the comms expected from an England manager. Since his departure, press conferences and broadcast manager interviews have remained focused on football. The FA prefer it that way. As Chelsea boss, when the club's owner, Roman Abramovich, was sanctioned, Tuchel found himself discussing all manner of topics – like the invasion of Ukraine – and he is happy, too, to 'stick to the football' as England boss.

It all fits in with the FA's desire for a narrower 'head coach' role. 'I suppose the benefit Gareth had was having Steve [Holland] to take care of a lot of the coaching and football. Whereas we'd prep for a press conference: "Oh, and you could potentially get asked about this event that happened somewhere else in the world, or this thing that's happening in the UK, or this thing Pep has said."

'But I'm thinking, like, "How can we get Jack in the team? How can we get him coming off the line?"' Carsley says.

In the September, before his first and second camps, Carsley went with McDermott to a UEFA Coaches Conference at the Grand Hyatt in Berlin. 'I didn't get the feeling [England] were rated. It was just the way [delegates] spoke about the Spanish team and the Italian team and the German team whereas the England team were "very powerful and fast". There's a bit more to us than that,' Carsley says.

If Carsley's tenure proved one thing, it was this. There *is* more to England and English players than conventional thinking, down the years, has allowed. When he looks back, he marvels at the talent. 'Harry Kane? Goalscoring-wise, shooting practices, dedication, example set . . . unreal. The best I've ever seen. Jude, unreal, we're so lucky to have him. Declan, so lucky to have him. I mean you could go through a lot of players . . . John Stones, so supportive. It's a shame how the Greece home game ended, but one of the great things about the job was making John captain for that match.'

Carsley is a man of hidden layers. For several years, he has been working with the Royal Ballet, exchanging coaching knowledge. He comes up with a colourful simile when he describes the feeling he had at his final match, glancing around a rocking Wembley, with England 5 Ireland 0 gleaming on the electronic scoreboard. 'I'm sat there thinking, *I've really enjoyed this. It's been so good.*

'I suppose it's the equivalent of hiring a Ferrari for six weeks, absolutely ragging it, getting it valeted and then handing it back over. The players that we've got are so, so good. England have such a great opportunity to win. It's '66 since we did, but it's like the Tottenham motto. To dare is to do. Let's go for it.'

CHAPTER 12

THE COCKTAIL BAR COACH

The jeers and boos echoed around the City Ground. For those that could be bothered to stay to the end, Senegal's injury-time goal to make it 3-1 was the breaking point for an enthusiastic crowd, keen to enjoy a rare visit by the national team to Nottingham Forest's stadium. England were abysmal in defeat, even more lamentable than they had been a few days before against Andorra in Barcelona, where they were also lambasted by travelling fans as they laboured to a 1-0 win labelled the 'worst victory in England's history'.

It was June 2025 and less than a year since Thomas Tuchel had walked into a press conference in October 2024, looking immaculate in designer suit and crisp white shirt, flashing a friendly smile at the bank of potential press critics before boldly declaring that his mission was to put a second star on the England shirt. He did not put a foot wrong in that opening introduction to the English public, tiptoeing nimbly around the delicate issues such as singing the national anthem and the small fact of holding a German passport. He namechecked Pelé calling Wembley the cathedral of football and pronounced England the heartland of the game. 'This role brought the young me alive – my teenage days,' Tuchel enthused. 'I got excited for such a big task.'

Yet the confident Champions League winner who strode into Wembley and owned the room was some way removed from the angry young man working in a cocktail bar in Stuttgart during the 1998 World Cup. While Michael Owen was leaving Argentine defenders in his wake at France '98, Tuchel was washing up glasses and waiting tables at Radio Bar, one of Stuttgart's coolest nightlife venues, occupying a disused music shop where twenty-somethings got high on hedonism and hip hop. Knee cartilage damage had ended Tuchel's professional career in the German third tier with SSV Ulm. He had no qualifications to speak of. He was not a great footballer, though he had played for Germany's Under-18 team. He had given the best part of his life to football and discovered that it has nothing to give back in return to young hopefuls with bad knees. Tuchel was lost, possibly depressed and certainly a young man without purpose.

What undoubtedly made it worse was that SSV Ulm were undergoing an unprecedented transformation, rising through the divisions to reach the Bundesliga, a football fairy tale embraced by the national media. The club were coached by an idiosyncratic outsider with no significant football pedigree, Ralf Rangnick, and players Tuchel once shared a dressing room with were now national personalities, while he was the guy on washing-up duty occasionally bumping into an old friend, who would make the well-meaning yet harrowing enquiry: 'You not playing any more?'

'I saw my teammates getting better and better under Ralf and making it to the Bundesliga, which was always my dream,' Tuchel said. 'This was my team and these were my teammates. It was so close. When that happened, I was angry. I felt betrayed by the situation. All my life I dreamed of being a football player. Until that point, I had put all my energy and effort into this goal. When this was not a possibility any more, I needed to refocus, which is not always easy.

It wasn't the only minimum-wage job he did at the time. In Ulm, he was initially rising early to roll out pastry in a bakery, prompting the wonderful local newspaper headline, *'Vom Brötchensortierer zum Millionär'* ('From bread-roll sorter to millionaire') when he joined Paris Saint-Germain as coach.

'To overcome your pride and go to a bar and work for money, to meet people who know you and say, "Don't you play any more?" – you have to swallow your pride and overcome some difficult moments,' Tuchel recalled. In Stuttgart, he enrolled on a business and economics course at the university. 'I felt it was all over in football. I did not know what to do, so I studied economics because I thought my mother would sleep well if, for once, I finished something at university and didn't only start things. To make some extra money, I worked in the bar. It was actually a fantastic time in my life, but it did not feel right to be close to football or watch games at that moment because I was angry.'

Indeed, Radio Bar wasn't all bad. 'That's where I learned how to carry a tray over your head, bend your wrist back, lock your elbow and lift,' he told *Die Zeit Magazin*. 'I had to overcome the inhibition of asking strangers if they needed me. And suddenly I realised, "Your colleagues like you simply for you. They have no idea you used to be a professional footballer."'

Yet it must have felt somewhat akin to divine intervention when Rangnick, by then coach of Bundesliga side VfB Stuttgart, called him. 'Ralf knew I was in Stuttgart studying. He asked me if I could imagine trying coaching in the academy,' he said. Who can tell where Tuchel might have ended up but for that sliding-doors intervention? He really was working as a waiter in a cocktail bar when Rangnick picked him up and turned him around. 'I have no idea,' Tuchel says of what might have been. 'You never know.' He accepted an internship as a youth team coach. 'I still worked in the bar while I was coaching and I still finished my economics studies. Ralf opened the door. At some point, you have to go through the door and you are responsible for making the very best of your opportunities. That's why I'm a lucky and blessed person, happy and grateful for where I am.'

* * *

Tuchel, like Rangnick, Jürgen Klopp and Julian Nagelsmann, is typical of what has become known as the Stuttgart Schule of coaching, which will have a disproportionate influence on the World Cup, providing national team managers for Germany, Austria and England. All four were raised around the Swabian mountains of Bavaria and Baden-Württemberg and they all had steady, dependable family upbringings in comfortable circumstances in small German towns rather than the major football cities. Indeed, visitors make Tuchel's home town Krumbach in north-west Bavaria sound like the German version of the archetypal, idyllic Small Town, USA. Parents Rudolf, a water management engineer and also the coach of the town's football team, and Gabriele, a special needs teacher, are now retired and still live in the family home where Tuchel grew up with sister Sabrina. Tuchel was smart and was recommended to attend the Simpert-Kraemer Gymnasium, the German equivalent of a grammar school, where he led the Under-14 school football team to a German national title in Berlin but also excelled at tennis, volleyball and basketball.

The Gymnasium leavers' yearbook, compiled by students, refers to a 'playful arrogance' when it came to his football ability, and his classmates joked he 'must have an FC Bayern contract in his pocket'. His nickname, Don Alfredo El Tuchel, suggests that confident strut of the opening England press conference was an early feature of life. Tuchel's emotional impulse was also evident early on. He was a Borussia Mönchengladbach fan and when 'Gladbach's coach, the legendary Jupp Heynckes, left the club to join Bayern, a tearful 13-year-old Tuchel ripped his Heynckes posters off his bedroom wall in retribution.

His football trajectory was in the ascendant as he was training with Augsburg who, despite being a third-tier club at the time, won the German Under-19 Cup two years in succession. His selection for Germany's Under-18 team indicates that he was a better player than Klopp or Rangnick and earned him a contract from Stuttgarter Kickers, a respectable Bundesliga 2 team, though very much Stuttgart's second club. All seemed well, his career developing as it should. And yet it turned into a soul-sapping, confidence-crushing ordeal.

'Tuchel, why don't you learn to tackle?' Kickers coach Rolf Schafstall once snapped. 'What am I supposed to do with you?' Tuchel was being inducted into the true life of a hardened pro. Approaching his big break all fresh-faced and optimistic, he was about to receive a hard lesson in the needs-must approach of pro football. After making a terrible start to the season, Kickers had brought in an old-school, no-nonsense coach in Schafstall to buck up ideas and results. Young, idealistic defenders with a propensity to talk back and question tactics were not to Schafstall's taste, according to Alois Schwartz, a Kickers' contemporary of Tuchel's, who is quoted in *Rulebreaker*, the biography of Tuchel's life. 'He [Schafstall] was poison for a player like Thomas,' said Schwartz. 'The thing he [Tuchel] couldn't do at all was tackle. He was just a sweeper and in training they didn't put as much emphasis on tackling for this position.' In Schafstall's defence, Kickers stayed up but Tuchel was mainly confined to the bomb squad, doing pointless laps of the pitch as the first team did proper training, though it is unclear whether any veteran manager would have taken kindly to the precocious questions Tuchel would pose. 'I was certainly not an easy player to coach. I questioned a lot of things and was sometimes a bit too mature,' Tuchel told *Frankfurter Rundschau*. 'I also stood up for others with a very pronounced sense of justice, although that wasn't my department at all.' After eight substitute appearances over two seasons, Tuchel was let go and picked up by regional third-tier side Ulm.

It might have been a banal experience, seeing out a career in regional football, but it would prove life-changing. Initially Tuchel made little impression, not even making the starting eleven unless there were injuries. Despite seeming shy, he did make friends, and one story in *Rulebreaker* stands out. Tuchel was sharing a room on a training trip in Lanzarote with Oliver Wölki when his teammate received a phone call: Wölki's pregnant girlfriend had suffered a miscarriage. The club seemed unable to organise a flight home, but Tuchel took over. 'This is an emergency case!' he shouted down the phone and space was found on a flight. Tuchel then organised a whip-round among the players to cover the cost.

A season after Tuchel signed, Ulm appointed Rangnick, a former player, as head coach. Though Rangnick had pedigree as a successful youth coach – he had won the Under-19 Bundesliga with VfB Stuttgart – nothing could prepare the sleepy Swabian football club for what this iconoclastic coach was about to unleash, though Tuchel was not exactly in prime position to benefit. His contemporaries remember him as 'not the fastest . . . weaknesses on one-on-ones' and pointedly 'too smart for the dressing room'. The latter sobriquet, though, would commend him to fiercely intelligent Rangnick.

For Rangnick is a trailblazer, the overlooked innovator who spawned Klopp, Tuchel and Nagelsmann, yet never gets the adulation or wins the trophies his protégés have done. Indeed in England he is pretty much only remembered as a quixotic interim Manchester United manager. But if the national team are to win a World Cup, perhaps one of the most important days in English football will be when legendary Ukrainian coach Valeriy Lobanovskyi brought Dynamo Kyiv to the sleepy town of Backnang in February 1983 to play a mid-winter friendly. 'A few minutes in, I had to stop and count their players,' Rangnick recalled. 'Something was wrong. Did they have 13 or 14 men on the pitch? Kiev were the first team I had ever come up against who systematically pressed the ball. That was my football epiphany.' In a German game dominated by a back three and a sweeper, Rangnick was sold on Lobanovskyi's back four, pressing and systematic football, a belief only underscored by Arrigo Sacchi's success with AC Milan in the late 1980s and 1990s. Yet no major club would trust a wild visionary like Rangnick, which is how he was jobbing his way through the lower leagues at clubs like Ulm.

Tuchel was transfixed by Rangnick. 'He taught us the back four and ball-oriented play. That was completely new for us and, accordingly, we were initially sceptical about implementing it so consistently,' said Tuchel. It's fair to say not everyone was enamoured with the erudite, bespectacled Rangnick. Franz Beckenbauer, pretty much the high priest of German football, having won the World Cup as both player and manager, was a particularly vehement critic. 'All this talk about systems – it's a load of crap,' said Beckenbauer. 'Foreign players can do more with the ball. Ours can't. Back four, zonal marking, libero – it all doesn't matter a damn. The back four is a fatal mistake.' Rangnick though was about to revolutionise the German game. The problem was Tuchel would be left behind, serving vodka Red Bull at the Radio Bar as Ulm captivated the nation.

After his remarkable success at Ulm, guiding them up through the divisions, Rangnick was rewarded with a major opportunity as head coach of Bundesliga stalwarts VfB Stuttgart, where another gegenpressing visionary and mentor to Rangnick, Helmut Groß, was youth coordinator. So when Rangnick dragged Tuchel out of the Radio Bar to coach VfB Stuttgart's Under-14s, he was introducing him to a culture not unlike Liverpool's famous Boot Room, a university of football where great minds would create one of the most significant tactical revolutions of the 21st century. VfB Stuttgart's youth coaches' room was a Petri dish for new ideas that would transform German football and later the global game. Tuchel himself compared it to the Ajax school: 'When Ralf and Helmut Groß installed a new game system in Stuttgart at the end of the eighties and early 1990s, it was a model for the entire region. I was inspired,' he said. 'I found the passion again and instantly found the joy to be on the pitch out there. It was like a second chance, but I never thought about being a professional coach because when I started coaching, one hundred per cent of coaches [in the top division] had played in the Bundesliga. There was no example [of anyone] who made it through the academy and ended up in a professional coaching position.'

He was part of the coaching team that won the Under-19 title at VfB Stuttgart and moved to Augsburg in 2005, where he had trained as a youngster and who remained in the third tier of German football, playing regional games. Here he had responsibility for an entire youth structure, from Under-9s to Under-23s. Money was short. He had no car and commuted by train from his Munich home, which he shared with his girlfriend Sissi, whom he would marry in 2009. It was while at Augsburg that he encountered a promising young midfielder whose career was also ended by a serious knee injury at the age of just 20. Tuchel was uniquely qualified to sympathise and took the Augsburg II player, Julian Nagelsmann, under his wing, sent him on scouting missions and encouraged him to coach. And Tuchel was beginning to get noticed. Despite being a provincial club off the radar of the mainstream, Tuchel took Augsburg II to fourth in the Bayernliga Süd, the fourth tier of German football. As such he was offered a chance to coach the Under-19s at Mainz 05, no longer a Bundesliga team, having been relegated the previous summer in 2007, but still a step up from Augsburg.

Players such as future World Cup winner André Schürrle recall an intense young coach who pushed the Under-19s harder than usual. Indeed, they led a delegation to Tuchel after a few weeks to ask him to ease back. The players couldn't cope. Tuchel relented, but he remained a popular, inspirational figure. On the initial pre-season trip in Austria he had insisted on four-hour training sessions, something of a shock for teenagers. One day he insisted the whole squad hire mountain bikes and ride to the summit of the Simmering mountain, where they had lunch and admired the beautiful views before the head coach demonstrated his rhetorical powers, using the moment to tell the team that their goal was to win the league – something never achieved previously by Mainz's youngsters. Tuchel wanted a ceremony to mark the covenant between team and coach. He turned to his assistant Volker Kersting, who was wearing a Mainz 05 pin badge. Maintaining his earnest tone of orator, he solemnly wrapped the badge in a Snickers wrapper and buried it at the mountain top before reaching the climax of his speech. 'When we reach our final, we will return to dig up our treasure!' Tuchel told them.

But his methods were also paying off. The Under-19s were making their way through the national competition, which featured play-offs and a final. By June 2009, Mainz 05 had qualified for the Bundesliga Under-19 final. Tuchel decided for his final team talk he needed something inspirational, something to remind the squad of what they had been through. The pin badge he had buried was the obvious prop.

But rather than retrieve an identical one from the club shop, Tuchel insisted on authenticity. So Tuchel, Kersting and another club official drove the 300 miles south to Obsteig, Austria, climbed the mountain, dug up the pin and returned to Mainz, unbeknown to the players. He even filmed himself digging up the pin so the players knew it was real.

As they prepared for the final, against Borussia Dortmund's equivalent age-group team, Tuchel's team talk rose to a climax and he lifted the lid from a covered bell jar in the centre of the dressing room to reveal the pin. 'Here is our treasure!' he cried triumphantly. 'We have kept our promise, we retrieved our pin! Now complete our dream and win our treasure, the cup!'

'The boys were so pumped you can't even describe it,' Kersting recalled in *Rulebreaker*. 'They could have beaten anyone.' And Mainz 05 did beat Dortmund 2-1, with two future World Cup winners in Mario Götze, scorer of the winning goal in the 2014 final against Argentina, and Schürrle competing for Dortmund and Mainz 05 respectively. Also in the crowd was Dortmund's first-team coach, Jürgen Klopp, formerly of Mainz 05. 'Today the best team beat a team with the better players,' Klopp told his friend and former boss, Christian Heidel, then managing director of Mainz 05.

Tuchel's talent had been noted by Heidel, but that summer he was still a relative nobody in the wider football world. He travelled to Barcelona to watch Pep Guardiola's side and even asked a locally based German journalist if he could arrange a meeting with his coaching idol. He had about as much chance as any fanboy hoping to pick the brains of the world's most prominent coach. What he didn't know was that he was about to be plucked from the periphery of the game to centre stage and would soon be pitting his wits against Guardiola.

Mainz 05 had been promoted that same season Tuchel's Under-19s won the cup. Heidel, the man who had once promoted Klopp to player-manager, had already earmarked the young coach as a future first-team boss. And even though the senior side had returned to the Bundesliga for the first time since Klopp's departure, Heidel was already beginning to lose confidence in the coach who had taken them back up, Jørn Andersen. Reports were circulating during pre-season about unease among the players over his methods. When Mainz 05 lost a pre-season German Cup match to VfB Lübeck, Heidel made up his mind: Andersen would go, and Tuchel, just about to turn 36, would step up. It was an extraordinary gamble to take five days before the start of the 2009–10 Bundesliga season.

'Can I think about it?' Tuchel asked. For a young man who had just become a father – his eldest daughter Emma had only just been born – it was a seismic life change. But Heidel made it clear: football doesn't wait. Take it or leave it. The sliding-doors moment might never come again. 'Heidel had the courage to appoint me when I hadn't played a single Bundesliga game as a player,' Tuchel later recalled. 'And I hadn't managed a senior team either. My job began on a Tuesday and my first ever Bundesliga game was on Saturday against Bayer Leverkusen. And the team had just been knocked out of the cup by a fourth division side. So the ideal moment!'

It was the youthful 39-year-old Tuchel, dressed in a black T-shirt and looking more like a tech entrepreneur than a football manager, who would later reflect on the audacity of his appointment at an event for the Rulebreaker Society, an elite German industry club. The society's mantra was not unlike Elon Musk's 'move fast and break things'. Tuchel was invited to explain how Mainz 05 consistently punched above their weight in the Bundesliga, for, a small miracle unfolded on the Rhine. Tuchel outperformed even Klopp, finishing 9th, 5th, 13th, 13th and 7th across five seasons and qualifying for Europe. And it was during that period that his football caught the attention of the man he had once tried, unsuccessfully, to meet in Barcelona. Tuchel took a sabbatical year in 2014–15 and was taking time to meet with football figures, picking their brains and scouting out future job opportunities. As such, he was due to have dinner with Bayern Munich technical director Michael Reschke, who happened to mention the fact to Guardiola, who had joined Bayern as coach in 2013. The coach's interest was immediately piqued. 'Tuchel? I like him,' Guardiola said. He recalled how Mainz 05 had, unlike most teams, pressed his team high up the pitch and put Bayern under pressure the season before. 'Can I come too?' Finally Tuchel had the summit he desired with his tactical guru. The meeting of minds came to pass at Schumann's, the famed Munich cocktail bar. There is no record as to whether Tuchel drew on his Radio Bar experience to help prepare the margaritas, yet it was a deeply symbolic moment, the former waiter now dining at the top table of coaching. They met promptly at 7.30 p.m. and, according to Reschke, they were still going at 1.30 a.m., moving cocktail glasses around the table to discuss formations. 'It was like watching Plato come to meet Socrates, great philosophers of our time,' Reschke told the *Daily Mail*. 'The two of them swim in football like fish in an aquarium. It consumes their thinking.'

At the end of that year, Tuchel stepped into Klopp's shoes once again, taking over the Borussia Dortmund coaching job in the immediate aftermath of the departure of an iconic coach who had twice won the Bundesliga at the club. It was probably always going to be impossible to follow Klopp at Dortmund, even though he had done so at Mainz 05 and Tuchel's time at Dortmund was perceived as disappointing. Yet in retrospect, finishing second and third in the Bundesliga and winning the DFB-Pokal, the German FA Cup, seems a decent return. However, a 5-1 defeat to Guardiola's Bayern in the opening season was a watershed moment, when some of the team stopped believing in their new coach. Tuchel's relationship with Sven Mislintat, the chief scout credited with many of Dortmund's smarter transfer buys, including the capture of Robert Lewandowski, was also breaking down from January 2016, when Tuchel failed to back Mislintat's recommendation to signing Oliver Torres from Atlético Madrid.

There followed the extraordinary Europa League quarter-final game against Klopp's Liverpool, in which Dortmund led 3-1 but, wilting under the pressure of one of Anfield's great European nights, lost 4-3. Klopp's shadow stalked him throughout his early career. A few weeks later, Dortmund lost on penalties to Bayern in the German Cup final, with Mats Hummels' final game for the club in that stage of his career marred by a public fallout with Tuchel. With Ilkay Gündogan and Henrikh Mkhitaryan also leaving that summer, Dortmund were beginning to look like a pale imitation of the Klopp team. That said, though the first half of the second season started poorly, with Champions League qualification seemingly in doubt, it would end with Dortmund in third place and winning the DFB-Pokal in Berlin, having knocked Bayern out in the semi-finals.

Yet the die was already cast by then. What really did for Tuchel at Dortmund was the emotional fallout from a horrific evening in April 2017. Sergej Wenergold, a German citizen with Russian roots, who had shorted stock market options in Borussia Dortmund, detonated bombs close to the Dortmund team bus as they travelled to their stadium to play Monaco in a Champions League quarter-final match. Windows were shattered and defender Marc Bartra's arm was scarred by debris. It was a terrifying experience, but Dortmund president Hans-Joachim Watzke felt it important to play the following night, to show that the team would not be dictated to by terrorists. He thought he had Tuchel's backing. Unsurprisingly, Dortmund lost on the night

3-2 and the tie overall. Yet the following weekend, Tuchel told the press: 'We would have liked a few more days. The team felt they were pushed into the game. We had the feeling we were being treated as if the bus had been hit with a can of beer.' In retrospect it seems extraordinary that the game did go ahead 24 hours later, yet the key issue was that Watzke felt undermined by his coach, made to look bad when he thought they were on the same page. It meant Tuchel's departure was inevitable despite the famous cup win.

A sabbatical year followed before he joined Paris Saint-Germain in May 2018. Here was his evidence that bad culture can destroy even the best players. At PSG, a club very much playing catch-up as a major European power, the training ground at Camp des Loges was embarrassingly substandard, like something a League One club might tolerate in England. The physios' room was a bare, small antechamber, whereas a top training ground would have MRI scanning facilities and hydrotherapy pools. The training ground was dirty, with mould in the showers and clutter in the offices, including obsolete photocopiers (very 20th century), leftover files and old calendars. When owner Nasser Al-Khelaifi asked Tuchel what he could do to support him, the manager was typically practical and hands-on. 'Get me a skip,' he asked and then Tuchel himself organised a work party in which he and staff cleared the premises of junk.

That said, it was on the pitch that his real problems manifested. Peak Tuchel frustration perhaps came in the Champions League tie at Anfield in September 2018. Tuchel stood on the sidelines aghast as Liverpool raced into a two-goal lead, with his PSG players strolling about as though it were an average Ligue 1 fixture, where intensity and pressing were not huge features. When Tuchel exhorted them to sprint and track back more, he was met with a collection of Gallic shrugs and confused faces. 'Why?' they asked. 'Well, because we're playing Liverpool at Anfield.' They did at least get the game back to 2-2, but lost to a last-minute Roberto Firmino goal. Very early on in his tenure at PSG, goalkeeper Gianluigi Buffon would exchange knowing glances with Tuchel and share his own bewilderment. 'Juventus was nothing like this,' Buffon would comment. Another senior figure added: 'It is not a football club. There is no culture there. It's a vanity project.'

Egos threatened to derail the entire project. In the biggest domestic fixture against Olympique de Marseille, Tuchel dropped a key player to the bench, who subsequently sat in the dressing room refusing to change. The player's parent (also his agent) rang the sporting director Leonardo, who then had to call Tuchel to ask him to explain the decision to the player. Once that was done, the player did at least deign to join the substitutes. Despite the chaos, PSG won Ligue 1 twice, the Coupe de France once and, most significantly, made the Covid-affected Champions League final of 2020, losing 1-0 to Bayern Munich thanks to a goal from Kingsley Coman, a young Parisian who had once trained at PSG, in itself emblematic of the cultural issues PSG had back then. PSG dismissed Tuchel seven months later, classily on Christmas Eve, 2020. The biggest battles, it seems, had actually been with Leonardo and those above him in the hierarchy. As such, his ability to 'manage up', and his reputation as something of a troublemaker, shrouded his subsequent appointment as Chelsea manager. It presumably informed Roman Abramovich's decision, communicated by managing director Marina Granovskaia, to give him only an 18-month contract. Tuchel conceded on joining Chelsea that he didn't always say the things people want to hear. 'I am so far away from being a politician that you cannot imagine. I am as far away from being a politician as being a maths teacher, because I was horrible at maths at school. I am a coach, I am a football coach and I have absolutely the feeling, one hundred per cent, that they signed me as a football coach.'

Chelsea was pretty much an instant success. Though he lost the 2021 FA Cup final to Leicester, he pipped the same team to fourth place and made the Champions League. He also demonstrated his capacity to get into Pep Guardiola's head, beating him 1-0 in the FA Cup semi-final and 2-1 at the Etihad before the ultimate showdown: a Champions League final in Porto. It had the feeling of the apprentice versus master, the younger man hunting down his one-time mentor. On the eve of the game, as Chelsea trained at Estádio do Dragão, Tuchel wandered over to speak to Jan Åge Fjørtoft, the former Middlesbrough and Eintracht Frankfurt centre-forward, who is now a Norwegian TV presenter, and some other German media colleagues. He was supremely relaxed for a man on the brink of destiny, Fjørtoft recalled. He chatted, joked and then offered them a prediction. 'I know we will win,' he said. With that, he walked off. The onlookers were left in no doubt that he was serious. He felt he had the better of Guardiola. And Guardiola had one of his periodic brain freezes in Porto, starting neither Fernandinho nor Rodri, opting for a midfield so open that it would have been a challenge to beat a mediocre team, let alone one with Jorginho and N'Golo Kanté at its heart, backed up by wing-backs Ben Chilwell and Reece James, as well as assiduous backtracking from players such as Mason Mount and Kai Havertz.

The decisive goal was a lesson in how to unpick a Guardiola team of the era. A quick long pass from keeper Edouard Mendy exposed their lack of defensive midfielders, which was exacerbated by Ben Chilwell's first-time touch on to Mason Mount. His genius was to thread the ball through Rúben Dias and John Stones to allow Kai Havertz to run on and score. City were undone by a couple of seconds of incisive football. The UEFA Super Cup victory followed and then, in February 2022, the Club World Cup in Abu Dhabi. He had been warned by Granovskaia when he took over that he was expected to challenge for trophies. To his credit, he had now won three in 12 months, one of them the biggest in the game and another the last trophy eluding Chelsea.

His contract had been extended by two years after the Champions League final and in Abu Dhabi it felt almost like peak Chelsea under Abramovich, though Tuchel almost missed the crowning moment. It was still Covid times and he was confined to London for the semi-finals against Al-Hilal, having tested positive. Indeed, he kept failing the necessary test to travel and it was only at the last minute he was cleared to be in Abu Dhabi for the final. Though no one knew it, it was the end of the Abramovich era. Worsening Anglo-Russian relations after the Salisbury poisonings meant that his visa hadn't been renewed in the UK and the Putin-supporting oligarch had stopped attending at Stamford Bridge. But Abu Dhabi was a safe haven for Putin cronies and he flew in for a rare visit to watch the team he had transformed. It was the 21st trophy the club had won in the 19 years since he took it over in 2003 – the only one they hadn't secured in that time. He had completed the set. It was also his last.

There was talk of Russia potentially invading Ukraine at that Abu Dhabi tournament but still no one really anticipated the end of the Roman era. That came just four weeks after the Club World Cup win, on 12 March 2022, when the UK government sanctioned Abramovich following Russia's invasion. When the game was finally up for Roman Abramovich and questions needed to be answered, predictably Granovskaia and Bruce Buck, Abramovich's key lieutenants, kept themselves well behind the front line and allowed Thomas Tuchel to absorb all the media flak. It led to the somewhat farcical situation of Tuchel having to comment on his views of Russia's invasion and their war crimes while not completely alienating a man who, if not in theory then in practice, was still his boss, and while also being sensitive to the outrage felt across Western Europe at Vladimir Putin and his enablers.

Maintaining Chelsea's UEFA Champions League qualification and finishing third in the Premier League, amidst a backdrop of the club potentially going into administration, players seeking swift exits to better-placed clubs, the club's corporate credit card being blocked and sponsors terminating deals, remains a remarkable achievement. At one point, with the government allowing the club to spend only £20,000 on away travel, Tuchel even offered to drive the bus to Lille to fulfil a Champions League tie.

And yet Tuchel would not even last out the summer under the new owners – Todd Boehly, Behdad Eghbali and José E. Feliciano. It was an inauspicious sign when Boehly, with no experience in the game, made himself interim sporting director. But it was on the pre-season US tour that it became clear this would not be a long-term relationship. Tuchel was surprised to attend a breakfast meeting at the club's UCLA base in Los Angeles, where staff were ready to announce the signing of Raphinha from Leeds United. 'He's going to Barcelona,' said Tuchel, puzzled. 'His agent is there at the moment, negotiating his deal.' Having agreed a deal with the Leeds United board, Boehly had seemingly assumed it was a done deal, not realising that European footballers have considerably more agency over their transfers than US baseball players. Tuchel was tearing what was left of his receding hairline out when Boehly even proposed giving a player away to Newcastle United to remove him from the payroll. 'He's worth £20 million!' pleaded Tuchel, who could see his prospective transfer budget being rapidly torched. An indifferent start to the season was enough to see him sacked on 7 September, something some members of the Chelsea board now privately admit was a mistake.

That seemed pretty much to be Thomas Tuchel's hindsight assessment of his decision to take the Bayern Munich job in March 2023 following the dismissal of his one-time protégé Julian Nagelsmann. Though Tuchel somehow snatched the Bundesliga title, it came despite suffering meltdowns at 1. FSV Mainz 05 and at home to RB Leipzig in the penultimate game. Borussia Dortmund pretty much chucked the title away for Tuchel to pick it up. That summer, Bayern, famed for its stability, fired sporting director Hasan Salihamidžić and CEO Oliver Kahn in acrimonious circumstances. In some respects, though, the summer boded well: the new transfer committee – effectively the old guard of Uli Hoeneß and Karl-Heinz Rummenigge, alongside CEO Jan-Christian Dreesen – managed to sign Harry Kane, the biggest capture of a foreign star for the Bundesliga since Franck Ribéry joined Bayern in 2007. Tuchel couldn't contain his glee: 'It's a huge deal. We took the England captain out of England.'

Yet behind the scenes, familiar tensions were emerging. Tuchel was intolerant of Bayern's performance meltdowns and wanted a defensive midfielder. Declan Rice was Arsenal-bound and a deal for João Palhinha fell through. Having made it clear publicly that he didn't trust Leon Goretzka and Joshua Kimmich to fulfil those duties, he was then left trying to get the best out of two players who knew he had tried to sell them. 'He emasculated them,' wrote Raphael Honigstein in *The Athletic*, quoting a source close to the dressing room. Tuchel's familiar antics on the sideline, often resembling John Cleese whacking his broken car with a tree branch in *Fawlty Towers*, didn't endear him to the players. There was ambivalence towards him in the dressing room. 'Some liked the man and his ideas,' wrote Honigstein. 'Some liked one or the other. Some liked neither.'

The end was announced in February 2024, meaning he was a lame duck long before the end of the season. Bayern narrowly lost in the UEFA Champions League semi-final to Real Madrid, but more embarrassingly ceded the Bundesliga title for the first time in 12 years, losing out to Bayer 04 Leverkusen. He left with his reputation somewhat damaged. His tactical credentials remained intact, but it was unclear whether the balance between his demanding nature and emotional intelligence had tipped too far towards the former. The suspicion was that he had become too divisive a figure to bind a dressing room together.

* * *

It was supposed to be the week that bonded coach and team and to make England feel like a band of brothers again. Tuchel and his coaching staff had long looked forward to the summer training camp in Catalonia as their first real opportunity to make an emotional connection with the players. Tuchel's opening games against Albania and Latvia had been encouraging enough, winning 2-0 and 3-0. Before kick-off against Albania, the stadium DJ ratcheted up excitement with Teutonic techno over a chant of 'Thomas Tuchel's army'. But with the score locked at 1-0 until the 77th minute, paper aeroplanes wafted on to the pitch launched by a restless crowd. Having criticised Southgate's performances at Euro 2024 – 'The players were more afraid to drop out of the tournament than having the excitement and hunger to win it' – it was a stark reminder to Tuchel that it was easier to talk about dynamism and being on the front foot than to execute it. The biggest story from Tuchel's early selections was the return from exile of Jordan Henderson.' It was not my idea initially [to select him],' said Tuchel. '[But] I talked to players, I talked to staff, I talked to people in the federation and his name came up constantly.' Critics labelled Henderson the 'captain of vibes'. Yet it was clear that many in the squad felt he brought a synergy and balance to relationships that had been lacking during Euro 2024. Tuchel himself had been won over by the midfielder's infectious charisma during an early telephone call. 'After 20 minutes on the phone, I was pretty convinced that I needed this guy in camp.'

But it was the week at the Camiral resort near Girona, in preparation for their fixture against Andorra in June, that Tuchel and his assistant Anthony Barry had been anticipating as their chance to get to know the players and impose their style of play. The Camiral Golf and Wellness Club, which will host the 2031 Ryder Cup, seemed perfect, not least to satisfy some of the players' obsession with an 18-hole round. Yet, despite the spectacular Catalan sunshine, this didn't quite feel like the days of old. There was a trip to the Formula One Grand Prix at the Circuit de Barcelona and observers said that the players seemed aloof and awkward. It's hard to judge how it went from the outside, though Cole Palmer, who was at his charismatic best when quizzed by reporters, seemed a little underwhelmed. 'It was good,' he said, adding it was an improvement on his last Formula One experience. 'I went to one in Abu Dhabi not long ago. But I fell asleep at that one. This one I was awake.'

On the rest day, some players predictably chose golf in the afternoon. Henderson, restored to the squad, got his old gang back together again and was sunbathing with Trent Alexander-Arnold and Jude Bellingham by the pool. All seemed well on the surface, but somehow a little forced. Whatever critics thought of Gareth Southgate, all the players agreed that he made squad get-togethers very natural. Here, rather than crawling through tunnels on Woodbury Common and camping overnight, they were soothed by wind chimes, yoga brunch and Pilates. There was some method behind the meditation. Mornings were intense, players on exercise bikes in sweat tents designed to replicate conditions in North and Central America. The new marginal gains breakthrough exciting the media were the biometrics tablets England players were taking, which helped monitor their reaction to heat and dehydration and their recovery. It was very much intended to be a mix of specific training and R&R, Andorra hardly providing the stiffest of tests.

However, the Olympic Stadium in Barcelona has form as far as England are concerned. The venue for the 1992 Olympics, perched on top of Montjuïc, which overlooks Barcelona, has its own freezing microclimate in winter and is barely accessible at any time of year. It is the city's main cemetery and was once a metaphorical graveyard for England manager Steve McClaren. He was so roundly abused and harassed by the thousands of England fans who had made the trip to watch the team play Andorra in 2007 that it marked the end of his credibility as England manager. And that team won 3-0. Fabio Capello's England team also struggled to break down Andorra here in 2008 and were booed off at half-time, but won 2-0.

And now it was Tuchel's turn at a stadium that brings out the worst in England teams and fans. He started with Jude Bellingham, Cole Palmer, Harry Kane and Henderson, while Andorra had the usual mix of teachers, tradesmen and semi-pros. England did win the game 1-0, but it would surely rank as their worst ever victory. At times, Andorra looked their equal, with England's superstars plodding leaden-footed through the early evening heat, hardly boding well for the 2026 World Cup. The nadir was Andorra's 37-year-old left-back Marc Garcia nutmegging Noni Madueke in injury time as England hung on to their lead. By then, many of the 7,000 England fans had left for the bars of Barcelona. The standout chant of the afternoon, apart from abuse for Prime Minister Keir Starmer, was: 'We nearly scored, we're on the piss.' Tuchel was unimpressed. 'I didn't like the attitude, how we ended the game,' he said. 'We lacked the seriousness and the urgency that is needed in a World Cup qualifier and I didn't like the body language. It was not what the occasion needed.'

There was one fixture to go before the season finally finished: a friendly at home to Senegal at Nottingham Forest's City Ground. Against a decent side, as opposed to part-time triers with no incentive to engage, perhaps England might show their true colours? Yet it seemed the Andorra game would not in fact be their nadir. Tuchel, who had criticised Southgate's England at Euro 2024, had now contrived to produce significantly worse performances. The initial 4-4-2 formation was an incoherent mess by the end; Curtis Jones appeared to be required to run the midfield alone as teammates wandered hither and thither; Kyle Walker looked as though his England career had finally come to a close. Two-one down with injury time looming, it did appear that Bellingham had initiated another last-minute rescue act with a close-range prod across the line, but VAR intervened and disallowed it for an earlier handball. Immediately afterwards, Jones lost possession, Senegal's Lamine Camara stormed down the pitch unattended by any England players and centred for Cheikh Sabaly to side-foot home. The England fans who hadn't already left treated the team to a cacophony of boos, reminiscent of Southgate's Molineux meltdown. The spiritual vibes at the Camiral Wellness Resort had clearly not been altogether positive given the lack of cohesion on the pitch.

At least once the final whistle went, they could all pack up and start again in September. Except that Tuchel's frankness and eagerness to engage in a direct Germanic fashion did not even allow that respite. He had one last interview to do the morning after the Senegal debacle.

It was with talkSPORT's Adrian Durham and Stuart Pearce. Tuchel hadn't slept much after the post-match media round at the City Ground. Pearce and Durham quizzed him on a range of topics, from his favourite book – T. C. Boyle's *Water Music* – to his best ways to unwind, such as meeting friends for coffee. But Pearce had noted how he had to calm Bellingham down at the end of the game, so infuriated was England's talisman with the performance.

'The edge needs to be channelled towards the opponent, towards our goal and not to intimidate teammates or to be over-aggressive towards teammates or referees, but towards opponents,' agreed Tuchel. 'And always towards the solution, meaning towards winning. And we are on that, yes.'

Bellingham wasn't difficult to manage, insisted Tuchel, who was in most part enthused by his midfielder. In his fatigue, however, he started expanding on the point. 'I see that it can create mixed emotions. I see this with my parents, with my mum, that she sometimes cannot see the nice and well-educated and well-behaved guy that I see. And the smile – if he smiles, he wins everyone. But sometimes you see the rage, you see the hunger and the rage and the fire, and it comes out in a way that can be a bit repulsive. For example, for my mother when she sits in front of the TV. I see that.'

Only one adjective would make the headline from the lengthy and broadly complimentary discussion about Bellingham. Not only did Tuchel now have a woeful team, performing inadequately. He had just labelled their best player, the man who might win him the World Cup, repulsive.

CHAPTER 13

SHOOTING FOR THE SECOND STAR

Long before working together at the FA, Mark Bullingham and John McDermott were football colleagues of sorts. Fellow coaches. McDermott had a distinguished career in development, establishing Watford's grassroots programme in the early 1990s then heading Tottenham's academy, where he oversaw the emergence of players such as Harry Kane.

Bullingham's work was more modest; a sideline. While rising as a sports business exec, he took his FA Level One qualification and coached his son and daughter's boys' and girls' teams. Tika-taka or Mike Bassett style 4-4-fucking-2? 'Ha ha. Well, you start with five-a-side so the options are pretty limited. It's more about trying to persuade someone to go in goal, and some kids to play somewhere near the back.

'You obviously want to train them to play out, but the occasional ball over the top when the opposition is pushing up works too,' Bullingham says, chuckling.

In July 2024, when the pair were tasked with finding Gareth Southgate's successor, they had similar points of view. The quality of the candidate came first, beyond nationality and even (within reason) beyond cost. 'I've tried to do this all through my career, ask, "What's in the best interest of the players?"' says McDermott. 'And we've got super-talented, serial-winner players. If we could match that and find somebody who when they came in had the "wow factor" . . .

'And somebody who could help us do something – I was born in 1967 – that I've never seen in my lifetime. That was our ambition: trying to meet the ambition of the players.'

McDermott used his extensive network to take advice from friends in the club game who had overseen major managerial appointments. He delved into the FA's own annals, finding 'in the dungeons and archives' analysis of candidates going back to 2014.

Bullingham hired two external data companies who built a profile of what successful international managers looked like and then tailored it to mesh with England's player base. The top 50 coaches in the world were matched against the criteria and a shortlist emerged. 'I joked with the team afterwards, because it came up with a list you and I could have come up with in the pub in ten minutes,' Bullingham says.

'But actually it was incredibly valuable to see the relative strengths and weaknesses and there are some amazing things you can do with data, like looking at which coaches are good at developing players, which are good in knockout tournaments and so on.

'Playing style was important; tactical flexibility was important. Being a proven winner was important – and a proven winner relative to the resources they had. It's a bit like xG for managers. With the budget and players available, did they over- or underperform? It's looking at the details and seeing if they added value.'

As mentioned previously, three distinct categories emerged from this process. There were coaches with high potential who were still developing their careers, 'elite' coaches already achieving top results and demonstrating top-level qualities, and finally the 'super-elite' – those at the pinnacle of their trade who had won big, managed big (in terms of players and clubs) and were recognised as being among the very best in the world.

Then came a crucial piece of filtering. Excluded were coaches who had not worked at the top of the English game and demonstrated a knack with English players. This left five 'super-elite' candidates, the best of the best in terms of fitting the FA's needs. Bullingham and McDermott started with them.

This led – though the FA have never confirmed this – to the sounding out of Pep Guardiola and approaches to other targets, with the FA recognising they had to be personal, patient and discreet. A normal recruitment process would involve multiple candidates, a series of interviews, a series of presentations and then board meetings to choose the best one.

'But with the top five (coaches) in the world, we felt it should be more of a "rifle shot approach", where we were going really specific and speaking to them. And, putting it crudely, you're selling to them as much as they're selling to you,' Bullingham says.

'The overwhelming criteria was I wanted someone we could put in front of the players and they would say "thank you, you've given us a chance to win."'

The last of the five the FA reached out to was Thomas Tuchel who, initially, proved hard to even get on the phone. Eventually he took a call from McDermott. The conversation was supposed to be of the brief, 'are you interested?' sort, but they talked for well over an hour.

Once Tuchel is in he is all in, say those who know the German best, and when McDermott travelled to Munich for face-to-face discussions, he was met with a whirlwind. 'There was a connection straight away. He loved football. He loved English football. He asked me a million questions about the Euros and about the players,' McDermott says.

'He'd had an incredible experience at Chelsea. A bit like when you speak to Mauricio [Pochettino – whom McDermott worked with at Tottenham], he just loved the Premier League, feels there's something magnetic about it.

'Thomas is almost Latin in the way he speaks. There's a warmth and tactileness. He comes alive when he's speaking about the team, the players, the games. I'm not sure [managing England] was something he was thinking of before our initial call, but he was certainly hooked.'

Wind back. Actually, McDermott met two whirlwinds. His day in Munich ended with dinner with Tuchel, but began with a one-to-one with Anthony Barry.

'I knew of Anthony,' McDermott says. 'He made a really big impression on his UEFA Pro Licence course. I presented on it and he did an incredible [thesis] around set plays – throw-ins. I remember Guy Whittingham [the FA's Pro Licence and Alumni lead] talking about him.

'When we sat down, just me and him, again what came through was passion. I just love the fact he's gone abroad, done his apprenticeship in the lower leagues as a player and is very humble about that, but then has also been at Chelsea and Bayern Munich and worked with Ireland, Belgium and Portugal.'

Indeed, Barry's CV gives him a range of reference points unique in the English game. As a player, he was in the same Everton youth team as Wayne Rooney and was at clubs in every one of the top six divisions of English football, including Yeovil Town, Chester City, Accrington Stanley and Wrexham.

He began coaching with youth players at 'Stanley' and then Wigan, where by 31 he was assisting first-team manager Paul Cook and working with Reece James and Dan Burn. He gave talks in prisons and schools to hone his presentation skills and was brought to Chelsea by Frank Lampard, who was in the same cohort when Barry aced his Pro Licence course.

Helping Barry – a pin-sharp Scouser – get top marks was his verbal skills. At one point the students (who also included Michael Carrick and Kolo Touré) were lectured in the art of communicating under pressure by a professional hostage negotiator, who then posed a scenario where the coaches had to keep an imaginary hostage alive by talking to the captor.

Barry, calm and empathetic, was a revelation in the role play. In the evening, Steve McClaren, a course observer, said to the group: 'Anthony Barry. Wow.'

McDermott describes Barry as 'an excellent field coach, an excellent deliverer. It's a little like with Steve Holland and Gareth, there's a real yin and yang to him and Thomas.

'Anthony is excellent at questioning and excellent at being a devil's advocate or an agitator at times. Yet if he thinks we should go left but we decide we're going right, he's right behind it. A really good team player. He challenges Thomas and challenges the group. A really bright football thinker, just obsessed with football, obsessed with coaching.'

To get Barry as part of the Tuchel package was a considerable bonus. None of the candidates identified in the 'super-elite' bracket were English, though several in the tiers below were and the FA talked to at least three English candidates, partly with an eye on the future. If their time wasn't now, these could be England managers further down the line.

However, hiring Barry alongside Tuchel would allow the FA to get an outstanding young English coach into their system, one who would be working directly with the England team. Why was nationality not decisive when it came to the top job? 'Just because of the depth of the talent pool,' Bullingham says.

'We were starting with the priority we wanted to have someone to help us win. In our role you would love to be sitting in a room analysing a talent pool where there are between five and ten English managers you felt could win tournaments. We didn't feel that. We thought it was a relatively small talent pool and we wanted to go beyond it.'

Bullingham's first encounter with Tuchel and Barry was in an unusual location. McDermott's trip to Munich left him eager to bring the chief executive back out to Germany to see the pair, but they were desperate to stay under the radar. So, a meeting was organised at a German airport, where the FA hired a private room and McDermott and Bullingham flew there on separate flights – just in case they were recognised.

The meeting? 'I think it's safe to say Thomas blew us away. He had a PowerPoint presentation about how to put a second star on the shirt and it was so well thought through, right down to what the next eighteen months would look like in terms of days at St George's Park and how he would get the best out of players, how he would link with players, how he was going to maintain relationships, what he felt was important going into the World Cup,' Bullingham says.

'It was the type of presentation you might expect on a third or fourth meeting – and still be impressed by – but this was the first proper meeting. And it wasn't just the presentation and slides, it was the passion and eloquence with which he was delivering it. It was brilliant.'

McDermott wasn't at all surprised, but 'I was pleased Mark wasn't disappointed. In that more formal environment where you're presenting, Thomas excelled just as much as in the more informal, conversational environment.

'I sometimes think you've got to be bilingual (in any top football role). You've got to speak the language of the training ground, but then there's also the executive level, especially with the England job. And Thomas is very articulate, whatever the setting.'

* * *

As the dust settled on Senegal, a reasonable question to ask was: where is the real Thomas Tuchel? Where did that guy go? Where was the dazzling tactician who won the Champions League, the gifted man-manager who had been rousing players ever since burying that Mainz pin badge on a mountain, the 'super-elite' candidate who blew the FA away?

The newspaper analysis did not spare the German. '[Tuchel] already looks bored and there are glaring signs that another dalliance with an expensive foreign coach is doomed to disappointment,' wrote one of the shrewdest football commentators on Fleet Street, the *Mirror*'s Andy Dunn. The *Telegraph* opined: 'Tuchel's England were meant to be fun but the joy has gone,' and one of your authors, in *The Times*, wrote an interrogation headlined 'Forget gimmicks, it's time for Tommy Tactics to do his job.'

On the airwaves the reaction was just as harsh. A caller to talkSPORT, Dan from Leeds, caught the mood of certain supporters. 'I'm sorry but bring in Eddie Howe,' he fumed, adding that England 1 Senegal 3 had just one saving grace: taking place on a Tuesday, at least it had not made him miss *Coronation Street*.

At the City Ground, Tuchel's parting message had been: 'The World Cup is not next week.' He did not panic. He used the three months before England's next games well. He threw himself into a whirl of reviewing and problem-solving with his closest staff.

There is analyst James Melbourne, goalkeeping coach Hilário, the French performance expert Nico Mayer – and of course Barry. In a sit-down with regular England writers a few months later, the number two painted a vivid picture of the intensity his boss brings to the evaluation process.

Tuchel's WhatsApps, he smiled, can arrive any time, early in the morning, late at night. 'His mind never switches off. For both of us, there's always another clip, another training session, another game. Enough is never enough. He's obsessed with building teams and building players. That's why we're so aligned. The messages can come at any hour and I have to be honest, I can answer at any hour as well,' he revealed.

Barry had actually arrived for the interview at St George's Park looking a little frazzled. Later, he explained he had come straight from an informal catch-up with his boss, where the idea was that they would have a coffee and chew over a few tactical thoughts. How long had the meeting lasted? 'Five or six hours.' As happens regularly, talking football, the pair had got carried away.

That summer, he and Tuchel had looked at their first two camps – especially the June one – from every angle. Their biggest takeaway was that they had tried to do too much. They were still getting used to what McDermott calls 'the cadence of international football', where coaches are with their players only periodically and have to find ways to influence them within short time frames, without overloading them.

Tuchel and Barry reflected that having called up 35 players for their first two camps, and stretched those camps to last a combined 20 days, they should slim selection and the length of get-togethers down. They also reflected on group dynamics having felt there had been a lack of chemistry in their squad for the June games. And a lack of hierarchy.

Players, they felt, need a sense of who the leaders are, which are 'in charge of the shirt' and which are challenging across the specific positions.

In future, squads would be smaller and pecking orders clearer. There would be a focus on making every moment in camp sharp, and shorter get-togethers might help with that.

Another vital takeaway from the brainstorming involved tactics and playing principles. Against Andorra in Barcelona and Latvia and Albania at Wembley, England had been asked to break down opponents who were well drilled, physically competitive and content to sit in low blocks.

Senegal, while much more ambitious, were also highly organised and athletic. The view of Tuchel and Barry was that England's challenge typified issues increasingly faced in elite football in general. Tuchel described his side as 'frozen' against the Senegalese and 'stuck' versus Andorra away.

'The game evolves,' said Barry. 'In the middle area of the pitch we really feel the game has become stuck, particularly in the Premier League. Everybody is so good now. They have so much information. They know how to set up. Mid-blocks, deep blocks.

'We are really trying to focus on how to accelerate the game across those 24 metres in the middle, those four cuts of grass [split by the halfway line]. [Football] changes. Last year it moved. It was really the 12 metres, the two cuts of grass [just outside the opposition penalty area] . . . we felt if we dominated there all the acceleration would come.'

On 28 June, Tuchel and Barry were at the Tehelné pole stadium in Bratislava to watch Carsley's Under-21s win a second successive European Championship, defeating Germany in the final. They were excited by the talent of the Young Lions, especially Elliot Anderson, whose performances as a number six – a position introduced to him by Carsley – were a revelation. Anderson could be one of the keys to unlock the 'stuck middle'.

The Nottingham Forest starlet was one of two new call-ups included in Tuchel's first squad of 2025/26, for the September qualifiers versus Andorra at Villa Park and Serbia in Belgrade. The other was Djed Spence, rewarded for a buccaneering previous season with Tottenham. Left out were some big names: Kyle Walker, Phil Foden, Jack Grealish and Trent Alexander-Arnold. Injuries absented Jude Bellingham, Bukayo Saka and Cole Palmer.

The selection caused surprise, but Tuchel was beginning to implement learnings from his first two camps. He reduced the sizes of both his 'long list' (those players contacted in advance by the FA to ask them to be available for duty) and his final squad. Now the latter contained only 24 players and the way the names were divided out on FIFA's website gave a clue to his thinking.

Four full-backs, four centre-backs, six midfielders, seven attackers. In other words, two players for each outfield position in a 4-3-3 plus one 'wildcard' – who Tuchel indicated was Eberechi Eze.

His first four matches had taught Tuchel a reality of England management. Outside tournaments, where the diet is generally qualifiers against smaller nations and friendly fixtures, it is hard for players to feel the sense of jeopardy experienced in so many big matches for their clubs. He felt the solution was to create jeopardy himself and the way to achieve it was competition for places.

Throughout his England there would be one player 'in charge of the shirt' and one on their shoulder, challenging for the place. There would be clarity and a sense of competitive urgency. Those not in the squad would know the two players in front of them and be able to observe what they needed to do to get in.

'I understand international football better now,' said Tuchel at his squad announcement. 'We will work from Tuesday on exactly the [playing patterns] we want to see. And the players need to drop their club hats, the way they play with their clubs, and buy into these ideas and from there we go.'

He reflected on the Club World Cup in the USA, which he and Barry attended in July, saying 'it was unbelievably hot and very hostile conditions to train and to play', but that there was no need to get hung up, yet, on the dynamics England might face at the following summer's World Cup. 'First we need to qualify.' This was a further effort to focus his players.

The other topic he had to address, inevitably, was 'repulsive-gate'. Were things okay with him and Jude?

'I used this word unintentionally, just to make it very clear. There was no message, no hidden agenda. I fully understand it's my responsibility that I created these headlines. I'm sorry for the upset,' he said. 'I thought I might have a little bit more credit with you guys [the media], that I do all this in my second language. I did it on the morning after a loss and not a lot of sleep.'

Observers noted a different edge to England's training at St George's Park before the home fixture with Andorra. Tuchel and Barry were encouraged. But when the Andorrans proved stubborn once more, restricting the score to 2-0 despite England's 83 per cent possession and 46 touches in the opposition box, the knives came back out. The BBC asked: 'Have turgid England regressed under Tuchel?' and Roy Keane, scoffing at the 'sideways, backwards passes', suggested England had 'fallen into old ways'.

It was not how everyone saw it. The *Sunday Times* saw signs of progress – 'quicker passing, better pressing, penetration from wide' – and Tuchel talked about progress too. 'If you look in detail at our match in Barcelona against Andorra we got stuck around the middle circle. Now we pushed them further back. We were five minutes longer in the last third of the field, so we're on it,' he said.

He particularly loved Anderson's performance on debut: 'Just a very, very good football player. He has physicality, loves passing, very mobile. A pleasure to see.'

And so to Serbia. England would be playing at the Rajko Mitić Stadium in Belgrade, where entry to the pitch is via a 73-metre concrete tunnel, daubed with red and white graffiti, drawn by Red Star Belgrade ultras, a swirl of hellish imagery and pairs of eyes staring down on players. A slogan reads: 'The best were created here, the biggest fall here.'

'Afraid of nothing,' Tuchel said.

When Bullingham and McDermott were scrutinising candidates, they perceived one of Tuchel's greatest attractions to be his record in crunch games and his approach was to project certainty, to assert England's toughest qualifier would 'bring out the best' in his team.

He knew saying this was staking his credibility on the game in such a way that it was a gamble, but felt it important to back up in public what he was saying to players privately. On matchday minus one, before the players left St George's Park to fly to Serbia, he gathered them and showed data from the Andorra home match.

'The numbers are there. The meterage on the pitch is different. You are going to take off,' he told them. 'The only thing you are missing is the threat of playing against a good opponent. I'll see the best from you then.'

His line-up was forthright: Ezri Konsa and Marc Guéhi as centre-backs with their ability to play a high line, Noni Madueke and Anthony Gordon – starting his first World Cup qualifier – as flying wingers. The attack-mindedness of Reece James and Tino Livramento behind them. And, in central midfield, young Anderson entrusted to partner Declan Rice again.

In the match programme, Dragan Stojković, Serbia's coach, recalled playing for Yugoslavia against a classic England side featuring Bryan Robson, Gary Lineker, Peter Beardsley and John Barnes. This was 1987, Bobby Robson was in charge, and Yugoslavia were destroyed. 'It was a hurricane,' Stojković said. 'You couldn't tell where the thunder was coming from, where the lightning would strike.'

And here came the storm. Here came the deluge. Here, from the fog of critics' doubts, came something classic from England again. Here came Thomas Tuchel's England at long last.

They were sensational. Harry Kane then Noni Madueke scored in a two-minute blitz, Madueke's showcasing how to rip through the middle – before it gets stuck – with lightning-bolt football. A quick ball from Anderson, an improvised flick from Morgan Rogers, a surge into the box and nerveless finish from Madueke. Konsa added a third just after half-time, Guéhi a fourth in the 75th minute and Marcus Rashford rolled home a penalty at the end. It was England's best performance since beating Italy in a Euro 2024 qualifier in March 2023 and their biggest victory over significant opposition since, well, when?

Tuchel purred about 'perfect teamwork' and, as he stood chatting to reporters outside the conquered arena, on a balmy Belgrade night, allowed himself to reminisce about being a teenager in Krumbach, playing football in the garden with his collar up, pretending to be Chris Waddle and of his love of Paul Gascoigne. He was clutching Pete Davies' seminal book about Bobby Robson's squad at Italia, *All Played Out*.

You sensed a romantic who had been waiting to fall in love with the England job and just experienced the moment.

***

When Tuchel started back in January 2025, McDermott helped him adjust to the job. 'That effervescent, warm character we experienced in interviews came into the building. You can just tell he loves players. I know there were questions of "why not earlier?" but for me the January start was really important. November to March [the normal pause in the international calendar] can be hard work when you're used to being with players all the time.

'Starting in January brought an excitement about March rather than a pining for March and Thomas loved going around the clubs, getting to know different people,' McDermott says.

'I went with him to Tottenham. I introduced him to Pat Jennings and he told Pat that he used to be him in the garden and his brother was Ray Clemence. Pat still talks about that now.

'Then he met Ossie Ardiles. He said, "1978, you were number one." I was with him meeting Kenny Dalglish and people like that. There's still the child in there that gets excited.'

From the moment he walked into St George's Park, Tuchel's employers observed him enthusing staff, working with intensity and – this particularly impressed them – putting great energy into forging connections with players. They were satisfied by his first half-season, despite the disappointment of Senegal. But it was when 2025/26 began that they really felt he came into his own – a view Tuchel shares.

Serbia was 'fantastic', says Bullingham. 'It was always the match that was going to decide qualification and the way we played, the way he set the team up – it was just a brilliant brand of football and so decisive.'

For McDermott, it was not a relief, it was 'that's what I've been seeing'. 'What you've seen in training, you're not surprised. But it's brilliant. That's now going from the training ground on to the pitch and the players are in their element.'

Tuchel's squad for the October matches away to Latvia and at home to Wales was a doubling down. A big doubling down.

He named the same group he took to Serbia, including Ruben Loftus-Cheek, who was drafted in for the Belgrade trip after Adam Wharton suffered a knock, with the only changes those enforced by injuries – Bukayo Saka coming in for Madueke and Jarell Quansah for Livramento.

This meant omitting Bellingham, who was unavailable in September because of an operation but now back playing for Real Madrid. Inevitably, some read it as proof Tuchel really did have a problem with the star.

When reporters asked this question he was robust, rebuking one who suggested that to win World Cups, teams need their best players on the pitch: 'Do you have proof? Do you have proof of that?' He explained the selection – which also involved leaving out Foden and Grealish – 'it is not against Phil, not against Jack, not against Jude.

'Even if you can turn around and say it is, it is not. It's for the guys who were in the camp and performed to that level. Why should I change this?

'After the Serbia match, I went into the dressing room and I told them what I told you. Imagine then I have a phone call and leave four players out, and say, "Now I pick A, B, C and D, and not you" – what would you think as a player? "Didn't you tell me that was exactly how you wanted it, and now I'm out?" I think as a player you would. For credibility, as a coach, you need to walk the talk.'

Nonetheless, it was hard not to cast the mind back to another thing Tuchel said as he gushed in Belgrade about the performance he had seen. 'There was no attitude after a mistake, there was no frustration, there was no waving, there was no eyeballing, there were no bad words. It was just a team ready to work and put 90 minutes' effort in.'

You then thought about what he told talkSPORT before saying his mother found Bellingham repulsive. '[Jude] brings an edge which we welcome and is needed if we want to achieve big things.

'It needs to be channelled towards the opponent and towards our goal, not to intimidate teammates or be over-aggressive towards teammates and officials, but always towards the solution, towards winning.'

But in Riga, England won 5-0 again, playing yet more fast-paced, incisive, collective football. And in the match with Wales, a Wembley friendly, Tuchel's side went 3-0 up inside 20 minutes before easing to victory by that score. Wales were a good side but chased shadows. After, McDermott chatted to Ben Davies, one of his former players at Spurs. 'Ben just thought we were relentless in the style and the running. And Ben's been around the block,' McDermott says.

'Craig Bellamy [Wales's manager] said that as well. Craig rang me and just said, "we were hit by a whirlwind there."'

For the final games of the year, at home against Serbia and away to Albania, Bellingham and Foden were back in the squad. Tuchel was all smiles. 'A no-brainer,' he said of the recalls and even joked, 'My mum is out of the picture now.' But the lines had been drawn. The way forward for both players 'is make sure you keep this thing going and make sure you accelerate the thing because we have something going here. We are building something, we are super-excited to have you back, but the message is, contribute to it.'

Barry's sit-down with reporters was two days before the squad announcement. He outlined just how much importance the England coaching team place on behaviour – which Tuchel once told his assistant 'is what brings [tactics] to life – behaviours are the building blocks that make the difference for the top teams.'

Barry revealed, 'We're trying to build Team England. It's all about connection. International football is about connection. Connection to each other, the mission and the game model. If you create a brotherhood that can connect to the nation, then you have a chance.'

For them, the blend beats the big names when creating a team. He and Tuchel 'have a 360-degree profiling of all the players, psychological, technical, tactical, physical, and we don't view them as just individual players but how they interact with each other; how will this player psychologically affect this player psychologically; tactically, how can he play with him tactically?'

They did the same profiling at Bayern Munich. 'What is the best XI? Does that mean the most skilful XI, the players with the biggest profile? I'm not sure,' Barry said. 'If you build a band and then you put 11 lead singers on the stage and throw them one mic, will they produce top music? I'm pretty sure it won't happen. You need drummers, you need guitars, you need backing singers.'

The affection Tuchel has expressed for Bellingham publicly is real. He sees him, essentially, as a genuine, whole-hearted kid from Birmingham blessed with an extraordinary competitive spirit. Someone who wants to succeed so badly he can find it hard not to show it when he feels things are not right. A Bruno Fernandes type. Harness those, guide those, and they will give you everything. But they cannot express themselves to the detriment of the group.

That the team comes first was re-emphasised in Tuchel's next team sheet. For the final home qualifier against Serbia, Bellingham and Foden still found themselves on the bench as he stuck with Morgan Rogers at number ten. Rogers, as throughout qualifying, performed excellently in his selfless, diligent, play-it-simple way, and when

Bellingham replaced him in the 65th minute, he had a lot to do to show Tuchel he should be back in the team.

But he did it. Having worked hard and showed glimpses of his enormous talent, in the 90th minute, Bellingham went to the edge of his own box, collected possession, shifted away from an opponent and drove forward with purpose and audacity before releasing Foden with a terrific diagonal pass.

Foden, playing in the new position Tuchel earmarked for him, false nine, flashed forward and fed Eberechi Eze with a perfectly judged pass and Eze, with a stroke of his right boot, arced a divine shot into Predrag Rajković's top corner. Wembley's last goal of the year was its best.

England followed up that 2-0 victory by winning by the same score to pass another test of character in the lively Air Albania Stadium, Tirana. Kane scored his 77th and 78th England goals and Nico O'Reilly, with his athleticism, nervelessness and sheer ability – born from his academy background as a midfielder – wowed at left-back in only his second international.

But there was a Bellingham backlash. Starting for the first time since June, he had powered around the pitch, contributing in defence and attack, clearly hungry to reassert his primacy. However, he was visibly annoyed to be replaced by Rogers in the 84th minute. It was not a big reaction – but enough to prompt questions of Tuchel in the post-match press conference. He said he would 'review' Bellingham's reaction and 'behaviour is key'.

The following day, the back-page headline of the *Daily Mail* was 'Leave Jude at home' and their chief football writer argued that a 'wonderful, generational talent' was also an 'ego warrior' who in the name of team unity should not be considered for the World Cup.

The England coaching team reject that view. As well as liking

Bellingham personally, they understand his youth, winner's intensity, and that after his remarkable start at Real Madrid he suffered a period complicated by injuries and family issues. There is player-of-the-tournament potential in him.

As the finals approached, they were asking the same simple question about all the players: 'Do they help us win the World Cup?' If the answer is yes – and yes in terms of the blend on and off the pitch – that player would be included in Tuchel's final squad of 26.

* * *

The Radio Bar in Stuttgart was a little too cool for 'YMCA', but Tuchel is an open-minded sort and seemed amused by the experience of a World Cup draw like no other. Rio Ferdinand presented, Andrea Bocelli, Lauryn Hill and Robbie Williams sang, and Donald Trump received the new cobbled-together FIFA Peace Prize from his unctuous friend Gianni Infantino. The Village People closed the show – with a suitably out-of-whack performance where, inadvertently or otherwise, they rushed on to the stage with the backing track already blaring 'Young man!' halfway through the intro to their most famous song.

At the ceremony, at the Kennedy Center in Washington DC, England were placed in Group L with Croatia, Ghana and Panama. At least the pillage people weren't there – Iceland.

Group L would be the last to begin, giving England an opening match against Croatia six days into the tournament on 17 June, in Arlington, Texas. Then Ghana in Foxborough on 23 June and Panama at the MetLife Stadium, New Jersey, on 27 June. 'Difficult group, difficult opener,' Tuchel said. 'No one can be underestimated.'

Reviewing his first year as head coach, he was excited by

England's prospects, though. A 'brotherhood' had been built within the squad, he and Barry believed. They felt they had hit upon the right rhythm for camps with their mantra of 'quicker, dirtier, more intense' training and a challenge to players joining up of 'when you're on, you're on.'

A hierarchy had indeed emerged, with Kane and Rice cemented as the main leaders and clear competition for every playing spot. A little indicator that the right mentality was there had come in the squad's determination to complete qualifying without a drop in standards and thereby make European history as the first country to finish with maximum wins and zero goals conceded, in a qualifying campaign spanning eight matches or more.

The players came up with the target themselves; Tuchel did not need to set it for them. 'That was probably a Jordan Pickford one, and the defence,' McDermott says with a chuckle. 'But then what was really pleasing was in Albania, Dean [Henderson] played and made a really good save. So he's now part of the success as well; he's part of the clean sheet [record].

'I think what we're seeing built is a real unit. Thomas is very tactile; he will involve the players, have conversations with the players and Ant is very good at it as well.

'They have a senior leadership group. A group of top, top pros, including some younger guys. So we've got a really good group of players who have won, and who are coming into their elements really.'

Tuchel had set a hare running at his November squad announcement by declaring he was open to extending his tenure beyond the World Cup. Once again, the FA were able to keep talks private and the outcome was contract extensions for him and his staff.

Announced on the day of the draw for the 2026/27 Nations League – effectively the start of the next international cycle – 'Team

Tuchel' would remain in place until the end of Euro 2028, a 'home' tournament, with the semi-finals and finals to be played at Wembley.

Inevitably, critics suggested the FA were in danger of repeating their mistake with Fabio Capello, who was rewarded with an expensive new deal on the eve of the 2010 World Cup only to fail. But Capello was never nearly as invested in England, and his push for an extension was opportunistic – whereas Tuchel did not seek improved terms and was willing to ignore firm interest from Manchester United to stay.

'Because of the impact Thomas had, we had a conversation around when would be appropriate [to talk to him about extending] and decided that would be after qualification,' says Bullingham. 'And it was just a very easy conversation to have.

'He was loving the job. We were really enjoying having him. The benefits were, with regards to the World Cup, the team and everyone around the team would have full clarity on the fact he was continuing. There would be no distractions. There would be no one asking about anything. I think otherwise every press conference would be full of those questions.

'From a timing point of view you always look at these things before [a tournament] – because it's too late afterwards. I know some people said we should have waited, but the reality is no one, on any fixed-term contract, waits to the end of that contract before they start thinking about their future.

'We always think about things well beforehand and renewed Gareth a couple of times before tournaments and we'd done the same with Sarina Wiegman [who was handed a new deal in the run-up to the 2025 Women's European Championship – which she won as England coach].'

And if the FA had told Tuchel to wait until his contract expired before talks, what would that have said? 'That "we don't really trust you". Someone said to me, "why don't you wait and if he wins the World Cup then re-sign him?", and I said, "do you not think if he wins the World Cup his value will be significantly higher?" And he might have a few other offers . . .' Bullingham suggests.

The 'golden opportunity' of Euro 2028 was part of the FA's thinking. 'I remember talking to Gareth about this: when you have a home tournament it's an amazing experience. Both the pressure and opportunity are immense because you feel a whole country behind you. So you want to have someone who has worked with the players, who has the record, to give yourself the best chance of winning,' Bullingham says.

Turning Tuchel from short- to long-term hire should have additional benefits when it comes to player development. Having introduced/promoted a clutch of younger talents, most notably Rogers, Anderson, Madueke, Livramento and O'Reilly, there was faith the German would continue fulfilling one of the wider briefs of any national boss – husbanding that country's future resources well. 'When Thomas goes to visit the Under-21s, it's got a different meaning now, hasn't it?' Bullingham says.

McDermott's football life has centred on development. On his phone he keeps juxtaposed images of the great basketball coach John Wooden and one of his protégés, the NBA great, Kareem Abdul-Jabbar. The first image is of Wooden giving Abdul-Jabbar some tough coaching love in the player's debut professional year. The second, almost four decades later, is Abdul-Jabbar tenderly helping a tiny, frail Wooden – who was 97 – across a basketball court. It is a poignant encapsulation of the magic of the teacher/student relationship.

The technical director is also confident Tuchel will guard England's future well. The German has said when he retires from front-line management, he already knows his dream job. Three guesses. Nope? An Under-15s coach. He started with a Stuttgart academy team, after all.

'I've worked with a number of head coaches and when you see him work and see the passion he brings to the training ground, you can tell he has worked with young players,' McDermott says. 'And if we go for a walk around Spurs [England habitually practise at Spurs' training ground before Wembley matches] or if he's coming to a press conference there, he'll start looking at the Under-9s or Under-10s and go over and watch them. And then he sort of gets into the session and he'll be saying, "Brilliant, brilliant."'

Tomorrow, and tomorrow, and tomorrow. And yet, for Harry Kane and Declan Rice, for Bukayo Saka and Jordan Pickford, for Jude Bellingham, Marc Guéhi, Morgan Rogers and the rest – tomorrow is now.

For England, tomorrow is now.

For an incredible generation of English footballers who have come so near yet so far, for their success-starved, 60-years-of-hurting supporters – it feels time.

For Tuchel himself, for his hopeful employers, the 2026 World Cup is a chance to do something eternal. Shouldn't England have seized one of those before now?

Barry has a memorable way of describing Tuchel's impact when he arrived in English football at Chelsea – where Barry was on the staff. 'He floated in, he didn't walk. I'd never seen anything like him in terms of personality, methodology and way of working.

'He was almost like a UFO.'

And now to shoot for that second star.

ACKNOWLEDGEMENTS

JONATHAN NORTHCROFT

I did not expect, as a Scotsman, to write a book unpacking and celebrating a transformation of the England football team. To do so takes some inspiring, and some reshaping of what the England team represents – and it is possible that only Gareth Southgate could have pulled it off. Thanks to him for making England so palatable that they are (almost) enjoyable for even tartan eyes to watch.

Thanks to Rob, for all the years of friendship, conversations and sharing of ideas on the road – and for prodding me to do this when the idea of completing an England book at such a busy time seemed mad. Thanks to David Luxton and Rebecca Winfield at David Luxton Associates too, and to Joe Hallsworth and the team at Blink. This is our first dance and I'm blown away by your energy, professionalism, fresh thinking and ideas.

Thanks to David Walsh, the best around – but more importantly, the most humble of legends. A friend and inspiration.

Thanks to Greg Demetriou and Andy Walker for all the conversations, insights, help and trust shown down the years. Likewise to Joanna Manning-Cooper.

Thanks to that understated but vital operator, Robert Sullivan, and to Martin Glenn – not just for the contribution to this book but for saving my local club (Leicester) back in the day. The friendship, chats and interview for this book from Adrian Bevington are hugely valued too. And also, the help and kindness when covering England always received from Jo Plummer, Anna Bush and back in the day, Mark Whittle and Jo Budd.

Thanks to Henry Winter for putting up with me in Doha. Thanks, Lulu's supermarkets. Thanks, Michael Church for the chicken shawarma. And Martin Samuel, Matt Lawton, Matt Dickinson, Ian Hawkey – decades spent at the tops of their games, whose talents have helped shape my understanding of England and beyond. Without the incredible backing from my editors at *The Sunday Times* and *The Times*, Nick Randall, James Restall, Tom Clarke, Joe Hare, David Bates, Matt Tench, Alex Butler and Nick Greenslade, I couldn't have done this. And nobody can do anything at the paper, on Sport, without Lucy Dupuis.

Thank you, Jesse Lingard, for the chat down the line from Seoul. Thanks, Wayne Rooney and Paul Stretford, the columns have been a career highlight. David Moyes – the same applies over an even longer period and working with you at tournaments has been such a pleasure right from the first in 2010. Every time we talk, I come away understanding the game better.

Thank you, Rob Sloman, Ben Lyttleton, Rachel Richardson, Holger Quest, Raphael Honigstein, James Ellis. Also, Jason Burt, Sam Wallace, Dave Hytner, Simon Mullock, Steve Bates, Paul Hetherington, Mike McGrath, John Cross, Ian Ladyman, Dom King, Jacob Steinberg, Paul Hayward, Ollie Holt, Oliver Kay, Charlie Wyett, Dan King, Alyson Rudd, Owen Slot, James Gheerbrant and the many other great operators (and pals) I get to knock about with on the England beat.

And a major thanks to Steve Cooper – your insights, your time, your explanations and your enthusiasm for the project were so enriching.

Finally, to Jan: who relegates Harry Kane to a distant second in terms of 'finest things to come out of Walthamstow'. None of it is possible without your love and support. And to Cora and Ishbel. It's okay for you to support England . . . as your second team. And to Mum, Mat and Dad – the dearest Englishman of them all.

ROB DRAPER

Like Gareth Southgate, pretty much my first memory of England is running home from school to catch that Bryan Robson goal in 1982. It's a journey you embark on with the innocence of a child, never imagining quite how many blows you will take over the years. As a reporter, you detach from it emotionally but, of course, you never can totally. From the Amazonian jungle to the southern tip of Africa, I've typed words in haste trying to make sense of it all. In Gelsenkirchen, Cape Town, São Paulo and Doha, each time you analyse an exit, you feel a little like you've taken a punch to the solar plexus. England runs deep, even if we don't always quite know why or what it means.

All of what Jonathan says goes for me too. Especially all the journalists he mentions who make the job the pleasure it is. The Sundays crew in Russia 2018 was an elite team! To that list I would add Sami Mokbel, Joe Bernstein, Nick Harris, Cara Sloman, Mike Richards, Ian Herbert and Kathryn Batte from Team Mail. And Jonathan's friendship and support has got me through many a tournament. Though never take his advice on how to walk home through Rio de Janeiro in the early hours of the morning.

Huge thanks too to Kelly Hogarth and Raheem Sterling for your help. (We took it down to the wire but we got there!). To Harry Kane and Rachel Richardson for ensuring we got time amidst the oompah bands in Kirchweidach. To Gary Neville, for all the insights over the years and your support. To Dan Ashworth, Duncan Watmore, Jonny Zneimer, Nick and Rebecca Levett, who all gave up time to speak. Their insights helped to shape this story. They helped us piece bits of the jigsaw together but any mistakes are ours. To Clive Ellington, whom I spoke to before the Euro 2020 final and who is a genuinely inspirational man. To Martin Fairn at Gazing, the first to open my eyes to Red2Blue. Six years on, he's still coaching me!

Dele will never properly know the moment he gave my family. But thank you nonetheless.

To Dad, Mum would be really proud now! To Chris, with whom I ran home to watch that Bryan Robson goal in 1982, who still has that England shirt (well done, Eliana!) and who got us the tickets for the Euro 96 semi. As Gareth says, you remember where you were and who you were with when you watch England. In the early years, it was you.

And to Helen, Oliver and Anna. Too many tournaments away, too much time hiding in my office. But it's you that makes it meaningful.

BIBLIOGRAPHY

BOOKS

Dyer, Kieron with Oliver Holt, *Old Too Soon, Smart Too Late* (London: Headline, 2019).

Eastwood, Owen, *Belonging: The Ancient Code of Togetherness* (London: Quercus 2021).

Hayward, Paul, *England Football: The Biography* (London: Simon & Schuster, 2022).

Honigstein, Raphael, *Das Reboot: How German Football Reinvented Itself and Conquered the World* (Yellow Jersey, 2015).

Keegan, Kevin, *Against the World: Playing for England* (London: Sidgwick & Jackson, 1979).

Lyttleton, Ben, *Edge: Leadership Secrets from Football's Top Thinkers* (London: HarperCollins, 2017).

Lyttleton, Ben, *Twelve Yards: The Art & Psychology of the Perfect Penalty* (London: Penguin 2015).

McManus, John, *Inside Qatar* (London: Icon, 2022).

Meuren, Daniel and Schächter, Tobias, *Thomas Tuchel: Rulebreaker* (London: Biteback Publishing, 2021).

Palacios-Huerta, Ignacio, *Beautiful Game Theory: How Soccer Can Help Economics* (Princeton University Press, 2014).

Perrin, William G., *British Flags* (1922).

Southgate, Gareth and Woodman, Andy, *Woody & Nord: A Football Friendship* (London: Penguin, 2004).

Southgate, Gareth, *Anything is Possible* (London: Century, 2020).

Southgate, Gareth, *Dear England: Lessons in Leadership* (London: Century, 2025).

Williams, Ben, *Commando Mindset: Find Your Motivation, Realize Your Potential* (London: Penguin UK, 2020).

ARTICLES

Burt, Jason, 'How mistakes of Euro final forced Gareth Southgate to rebuild', *Daily Telegraph*, 16 November 2022.

Gerrard, Steven, 'Weight of history has led to culture of fear and that must change', *Daily Telegraph*, 29 June 2016.

Interview with Thomas Tuchel, *ZEITmagazin MANN*, 5 September 2017.

Kay, Oliver, 'England "control freak" Capello and chaos at the 2010 World Cup', *The Athletic*, 1 June 2020.

Office of the Director of National Intelligence, 'Assessing the Saudi Government's Role in the Killing of Jamal Khashoggi', 11 February 2021.

Palacios-Huerta, Ignacio, 'The Beautiful Dataset', London School of Economics.

Rooney, Wayne, 'Wayne Rooney: Sven's fight with Fergie and angry Hodgson – my World Cups never ran smoothly', *The Times*, 19 November 2022.

UK Parliament, 'Former Football Association executives urge reform of FA governance', committees.parliament.uk, 12 December 2016.

Wallace, Sam, 'St George's Park, for all its ambitions, may end up as a patron of failure', *The Independent*, 7 November 2011.

Walsh, David, 'Gareth Southgate: The making of a modern manager', *The Sunday Times*, 1 July 2018.

Winter, Henry, 'Dave Reddin: We needed a new culture – not 'blood on the shirt' again', *The Times*, 17 July 2019.

PODCASTS / YOUTUBE VIDEOS

The Coaches' Voice, 'The Bus Stop', Allan Russell, 2021.

The Diary of a CEO Podcast, 'Episode 214', with Jesse Lingard.

The High Performance Podcast with Jake Humphrey and Prof Damian Hughes, 2 June 2021.

The Lockdown Tactics, 'Episode 5: Danny Rose', May 2020.

The Players' Tribune, 'It Was All a Dream', Raheem Sterling, 22 June 2018.

The Players' Tribune, 'Dear England', Gareth Southgate, June 2021.

Training Ground Guru, 'Southgate takes England on Royal Marines Boot Camp', 6 June 2017.

YouTube, Birmingham City, 'The Rise of Jude Bellingham'.

YouTube, Thomas Tuchel Rulebreaker Lecture, 2012.

TV DOCUMENTARIES / INTERVIEWS

Bobby Robson: More Than a Manager, written by Gabriel Clarke, directors: Gabriel Clarke and Torquil Jones.

The Long Walk: The History of the Penalty Shoot-Out, FIFA+, director Rob Sloman, released November 2022.

Forces Net, '"We've hugged and shed a tear": Gareth Southgate praises Royal Marine's impact on England footballers.'

Forces TV, *How this Royal Marine Inspired England To World Cup Semi-Finals*.

ITV, Mark Bullingham interview with Gabriel Clarke, 25 November 2022.

Sky Sports, *Sir Trevor Brooking – 'The Future Game'*.

Sky Sports Football, Rob Green on *Monday Night Football.*

Talk TV, *Piers Morgan Uncensored*, 'Hassan Al-Thawadi interview'.

OTHER MEDIA

'An Open Letter to all MPs in Parliament', Marcus Rashford, 15 June 2020.

LinkedIn, 'The hidden art of strategic planning for major tournaments: World Cup 2018', essay, Dave Reddin.

LinkedIn, 'Dislocation of Expectation', Ben Williams, 24 June 2017.

Radio 4, *Today*, edited by Raheem Sterling, 29 December 2021.

Speech at FWA Gareth Southgate Tribute Evening, Ben Williams, 20 January 2019.

Speech at FWA Tribute Dinner, Wayne Rooney, January 2017.

TED Talk, 'Beautiful Game Theory, Beautiful Economics', Ignacio Palacios-Huerta.

The Baroness Casey Review, 'An independent review of events surrounding the UEFA Euro 2020 Final at Wembley'.

Written Statement, *UK Covid-19 Inquiry*, Lee Cain.